Made in America and the Hidden Stories of The Sopranos

Second Edition

Steve Else

 A catalogue record for this book is available from the National Library of Australia

Second Edition

Copyright © Steve Else, 2024

All rights reserved. Without limiting the rights under copyright reserved above, no part of this publication may be reproduced, stored in or introduced into a database and retrieval system or transmitted in any form or any means (electronic, mechanical, photocopying, recording or otherwise) without the prior written permission of both the owner of copyright and the above publishers.

Publisher:
Inspiring Publishers
P.O. Box 159, Calwell, ACT Australia 2905
Email: inspiringpublisher.com
http://www.inspiringpublishers.com

National Library of Australia Prepublication Data Service

Author: Steve Else

Title: **Made in America and the Hidden Stories of The Sopranos**

ISBN: 978-1-923250-43-7 (pbk)

To Mom
and
Rachel

About the Author

Steve Else holds a Ph.D. in the philosophy of religion from the University of Birmingham. He has taught in universities and schools in both England and Australia, where he now resides.

Twitter / X: @steveelsewrites
YouTube: @steveelse4090
Email: steveelsewrites@outlook.com

Table of Contents

Introduction: The Ground Floor 1

Part One: All That You Dream 19

    Chapter One: I Can't Go There 21

    Chapter Two: This Thing of Ours 41

    Chapter Three: I am a Nice Dream 55

    Chapter Four: Maybe You Need More Medication 69

    Chapter Five: So Much Tragedy in Your Life 85

    Chapter Six: Oh Yeah? 93

Part Two: Satanic Black Magic 103

    Chapter Seven: Focus on the Good Times 105

    Chapter Eight: A Beautiful, Innocent Creature 123

    Chapter Nine: I'm Not Most Guys 131

    Chapter Ten: Beware! Children Playing Under Leaves 139

    Chapter Eleven: The Governor of Maryland 153

    Chapter Twelve: You're A Natural 165

Part Three: Going Home **175**

    Chapter Thirteen: On Entering This Diner Please Check
                                   in Your Weapon 177

    Chapter Fourteen: Holsten's...195

    Chapter Fifteen: Weather - Cold, Sunny 219

    Chapter Sixteen: It's Done... 239

Part Four: Living in a Dream **247**

    Chapter Seventeen: We Don't Talk Like That Here............. 251

    Chapter Eighteen: In the Czech Republic Too
                              We Love Pork.. 269

    Chapter Nineteen: No Hay Banda 277

Conclusion: Everything Comes to an End...................... 299

Acknowledgements... 313

Bibliography... 315

And I say this only by way of characterizing those rash, dangerous times and certainly not in order to direct the reader's sympathy to my inconsequential person, which deserves only a place in the background of these memoirs.

Serenus Zeitblom,
from Chapter XXXIV of *Doctor Faustus*
by Thomas Mann

Introduction
The Ground Floor

In debates over the greatest television drama ever, *The Sopranos* always performs well. Depending on who is asking and answering the question, its company in the higher echelons of the results often includes the likes of *The Wire, Six Feet Under, Brideshead Revisited, Breaking Bad, M*A*S*H* and *The Singing Detective*.[1] There is inevitably a bias towards productions from English-speaking and economically advanced countries, the USA and UK in particular. The criteria for inclusion and positioning often remain unspoken, as if what 'best' means is obvious and universally agreed upon. Those who wish to preserve artistic standards and high culture are probably horrified at the thought of anyone privileging *Lost*, but would disagree amongst themselves over the brutal realism of *Oz*.

There is usually a bias towards more recent productions, so it will be interesting to see how *Succession* fares in the future. There is certainly an argument for choosing shows that impressed with particular seasons, such as the first of *True Detective*. Science-fiction for no good reason usually fares relatively poorly, which

---

[1] Compare the lists compiled in 2010 for *The Guardian*, in 2022 for *Rolling Stone* and 2023 for *Time Out*.

affects the perception of contenders such as the reimagined *Battlestar Galactica*, or old favourites such as *Star Trek* and *Doctor Who*. *The Twilight Zone* has done extremely well, despite its lack of a recurring cast and narrative development between episodes.

There are a number of reasons often drawn upon to explain why *The Sopranos* is esteemed so highly. A wonderful cast of actors was assembled, with a mix of the experienced, such as Nancy Marchand and Dominic Chianese, and those who had yet to make their names, like James Gandolfini and Edie Falco. However, it would be very difficult to argue that in this *The Sopranos* stands above, say, *The Wire*. The producers and directors were drawn from the best in the business, and during and after the show went on to more achievements. Some of them also contributed to the writing: as well as the creator David Chase, who had worked on highly regarded dramas such as *Northern Exposure* and *I'll Fly Away*, the team included Terence Winter, who went on to become the creator and showrunner of *Boardwalk Empire*, and Matthew Weiner, who in the same capacities gave us *Mad Men*. But, here too, *The Sopranos* does not appear to out on its own in front of these, or the likes of *Six Feet Under*.

One of those numerous strengths which is the focus of this book is the depth of its storytelling. *The Sopranos* enthrals fans of the Mafia tale and those who enjoy a story well told no matter what the genre. It covers topics that are the staples of television drama like family, sexuality, wealth and crime, but also investigates philosophical ones, such as the meaning of existence and the nature of the afterlife. It is here where, perhaps, it nudges ahead of its rivals. Crucially, this also includes stories that are only implicit in the narrative: these are no more than hinted at in the flow of events on the surface, and serve as a reward for repeated watching. To see that they are present is enough of a challenge, but going further delivers rare insights into the meaning of the show; not going this extra mile equates to accepting a less than comprehensive understanding. It is these stories that will receive detailed analysis here. It is the lack of recognition of the role played by hidden stories throughout *The Sopranos* that explains why the finale is still misunderstood to this day. Made in America, the twenty-first episode of the sixth season (6.21), follows a logic used in the show since the first season. There is nothing new in it that should befuddle a viewer who has been paying attention to the form and content of the previous storylines.

Made in America is from start to finish a dream of the central character Tony Soprano, which he has after falling asleep in the safehouse at the end of the previous episode The Blue Comet (6.20). This is without doubt a landmark statement: no published author before now has even considered the possibility that it is a dream, and therefore none has argued why this is not so. As I show throughout, no authors, including well-known ones, do anything but proceed on the assumption that the episode is a standard narrative in the waking world of the characters, like the vast majority of the others. This turns out to be a calamitous error in terms of the understanding of the show and the final fate of key characters. It is the final dream of a number of his and other characters that are presented during the run of the show, and what it contains and how it is shown is very much in keeping with all of those that came before. It is constructed of the gamut of emotions, imagination running wild, recent and older experiences, prejudices, false assumptions, misinterpretations, family members, friends and enemies. It is not the first time that a dream has not been explicitly acknowledged as such, but never before has one taken up the entirety of an episode. Previous dreams in the show will be explained with reference to the light they shed on Made in America.

Although it is possible that the narratives commonly referred to as dreams are not always precisely that, they will be described in that way in most cases. There is an argument for the use of concepts such as hallucinations or near-death experiences for some of them. Chase, with regard to those in Join the Club (6.2) and Mayham (6.3), stated: 'I, frankly, would not call those dreams', elaborating later: 'alternate universes... That's what I consider them, as an artist. Something spiritual was happening'.[2] Dream or state of deceptive consciousness are the preferred terms here for simplicity, and because these narratives have much more in common artistically than any differences.

Not all of the hidden stories in *The Sopranos* are dreams: some take place instead in the waking world of the characters, but fly below the surface of conventional viewing. An example for clarification comes in the episode Mergers and Acquisitions (4.8). It is possibly the least significant of them all and does not intrude upon the plot in any way; but it is humorous and fleshes out a little a character, Pasquale 'Patsy' Parisi, who plays more of a background role in Tony's crew, as well as showing how the writers construct and hide the stories which are the focus of this book.

It is Patsy's twin brother, Phillip 'Spoons' Parisi, who first appears in the show. He is the acting capo (captain) of the

---

[2]Alan Sepinwall *The Revolution Will Be Televised*, p. 37.

crew run by Corrado 'Junior' Soprano, Tony's uncle, who was arrested a few months previously. In Guy Walks into a Psychiatrist's Office... (2.1), he is sent to pick up Gigi Cestone, then a soldier in Junior's crew, from the airport, even though just before Spoons arrives, we see Gigi being dropped off there by Paulie 'Walnuts' Gualtieri. They converse during the drive home, and the subjects of Tony trying to kill his mother and seeing a psychiatric therapist are brought up by Spoons. It turns out that this is the real reason why he has been sent on a fool's errand: Tony is unimpressed with his gossiping, and so at the end of the journey he is executed by Gigi.

A season later, in Mr. Ruggerio's Neighbourhood (3.1), Patsy is still struggling to come to terms with the death of his brother. The crew are at Satriales, the pork store that is owned and frequented by them, and the day is doubly difficult for Patsy because it is the birthday of he and Spoons. Tony, the man who ordered the hit, tries to distract him, probably more for himself than Patsy, and Gigi, the man who pulled the trigger, is sitting across from him. He later reports to Tony that Patsy has been drinking heavily lately and thinks he knows who killed Spoons. During FBI surveillance of Tony's home, they spot Patsy in the backyard with a gun, which he aims at Tony and Gigi inside, but changes his mind. Apparently very drunk, he urinates in the swimming pool instead, and it is obvious that he believes that one or both of them killed Spoons. Neither of them are aware of his presence, but later, when Tony returns to Satriales, Patsy is there by himself. He forces him to say that he has put his grief about his brother behind him, but there is a double meaning to the conversation, and both know what the other is really saying and leaving unsaid.

In Mergers and Acquisitions, the hidden detail concerning Patsy is set up at a meal the crew are having with their mistresses. The woman with him, who is older than the other women, says 'I'll have what I always have', to which he replies 'chicken mario? Fifteen years of chicken mario. Can't you try the veal chop or something for once?' She stands her ground: 'what are you giving me a hard time for? I like the chicken.' The expression on Tony's face is of someone forced to sit through a domestic dispute, and possibly not for the first time. It continues with Patsy saying 'maybe I'll have a steak', to which she responds 'you don't need a steak!' The final comment is his: 'I know I don't need a steak!'. Not long afterwards, Tony is in a session with his therapist Jennifer Melfi. They are discussing his marital infidelities, and he tells her: 'business associate of mine's got two full families. One up here, one down in Sea Girt. And the second wife busts his balls identical to the first.' She comments that it 'sounds like a complicated arrangement'.

There is no explicit link between these two scenes beyond the presence of Tony, but close attention provides one: Patsy is the man he works with who has two families. The woman at the meal with him is unusual in two ways: she is older than the other mistresses, and she and Patsy having been eating at that restaurant for fifteen years. The others that appear throughout the show are at the younger end of the scale and do not stay around for long. They are there to provide casual fun to complement what is offered by the wives, which does not involve arguing with the men as she does with Patsy: let the men pay, laugh at their jokes, and satisfy them sexually. She should not be 'busting his balls', but neither Patsy nor anyone else questions it; their relationship is more like that of a married couple than a short-term sexual liaison. She is clearly the 'number two wife' who is second in the pecking order and restricted to socialising with the other mistresses. The other wife is Donna, who, in The Weight (4.4), attends the housewarming party held by Furio Giunta, a member of Tony's crew, with the other wives, children and friends of the men. She is the mother of Patrick and Jason, the two sons of Patsy who appear, and it is she who celebrates the engagement of the former to Meadow, Tony's daughter, in the dream that is Made in America.

The surreptitious inclusion of this and other stories adds a level of mystery and intrigue beyond the consistent emphasis on ambiguity and uncertainty. The attention of the viewer is held fast by the realisation that, as in real life, Nobody Knows Anything (the title of the eleventh episode of the first season). The central task of this book is to show the role played by these stories in the overall narrative of *The Sopranos*, and in particular the final episode; as such, it is the first full-length analysis of Made in America that has been put forward, which is surprising given that it was broadcast in 2007. Evidence will be presented that demonstrates that the only consistent and accurate way to interpret it is as a dream of Tony, and this will be used to illuminate the hidden stories from elsewhere in the show; in this way, the finale will be understood properly and seen as not at all unique.

To be precise, this book is not about the meaning of Made in America, but its nature. What is being done here is a prerequisite to discussing the meaning of the episode; anyone investigating that must first determine what type of narrative is being presented. Meaning and nature are two different concepts, but how one is understood can affect the other. In *The Sopranos*, different types of narrative are employed; to have any chance of developing a comprehensive understanding requires knowing which is being utilised. This point will be expanded upon in Chapter One.

In dreams every aspect is the product of the person who is asleep. Whoever speaks or acts, and however they do it, is done according to the perspective and experiences of the author of the dream, and the same is true for the setting. As Sigmund Freud put it in his landmark study *The Interpretation of Dreams* in 1899: 'every dream deals with the dreamer himself. Dreams are completely egoistic. Whenever my own ego does not appear in the content of the dream, but only some extraneous person, I may safely assume that my own ego lies concealed, by identification, behind this other person.'[3] Whoever appears to be speaking in Made in America, it is only Tony who truly does; in the finale everything is him. He is the conductor, orchestra and audience; whatever is said or done by his family, friends or enemies, is in truth through his own agency and understanding of that person. The setting of a scene is limited to his experience and memory of that place.

It must be remembered in studying the dreams that are presented in the show that the entity that produces them, the mind, is fantastically complex. This was a given when Freud began the practice of psychoanalysis in the 1890s, and over a century of research since then has shown it to be even more so. Dreams share in this complexity, and therefore it is wrong to expect to be able to interpret them in a straightforward or simplistic way. Chase has been open about being a psychoanalytic patient

---

[3]From pp. 434-435.

short-term sexual liaison. She is clearly the 'number two wife' who is second in the pecking order and restricted to socialising with the other mistresses. The other wife is Donna, who, in The Weight (4.4), attends the housewarming party held by Furio Giunta, a member of Tony's crew, with the other wives, children and friends of the men. She is the mother of Patrick and Jason, the two sons of Patsy who appear, and it is she who celebrates the engagement of the former to Meadow, Tony's daughter, in the dream that is Made in America.

The surreptitious inclusion of this and other stories adds a level of mystery and intrigue beyond the consistent emphasis on ambiguity and uncertainty. The attention of the viewer is held fast by the realisation that, as in real life, Nobody Knows Anything (the title of the eleventh episode of the first season). The central task of this book is to show the role played by these stories in the overall narrative of *The Sopranos*, and in particular the final episode; as such, it is the first full-length analysis of Made in America that has been put forward, which is surprising given that it was broadcast in 2007. Evidence will be presented that demonstrates that the only consistent and accurate way to interpret it is as a dream of Tony, and this will be used to illuminate the hidden stories from elsewhere in the show; in this way, the finale will be understood properly and seen as not at all unique.

To be precise, this book is not about the meaning of Made in America, but its nature. What is being done here is a prerequisite to discussing the meaning of the episode; anyone investigating that must first determine what type of narrative is being presented. Meaning and nature are two different concepts, but how one is understood can affect the other. In *The Sopranos*, different types of narrative are employed; to have any chance of developing a comprehensive understanding requires knowing which is being utilised. This point will be expanded upon in Chapter One.

In dreams every aspect is the product of the person who is asleep. Whoever speaks or acts, and however they do it, is done according to the perspective and experiences of the author of the dream, and the same is true for the setting. As Sigmund Freud put it in his landmark study *The Interpretation of Dreams* in 1899: 'every dream deals with the dreamer himself. Dreams are completely egoistic. Whenever my own ego does not appear in the content of the dream, but only some extraneous person, I may safely assume that my own ego lies concealed, by identification, behind this other person.'[3] Whoever appears to be speaking in Made in America, it is only Tony who truly does; in the finale everything is him. He is the conductor, orchestra and audience; whatever is said or done by his family, friends or enemies, is in truth through his own agency and understanding of that person. The setting of a scene is limited to his experience and memory of that place.

It must be remembered in studying the dreams that are presented in the show that the entity that produces them, the mind, is fantastically complex. This was a given when Freud began the practice of psychoanalysis in the 1890s, and over a century of research since then has shown it to be even more so. Dreams share in this complexity, and therefore it is wrong to expect to be able to interpret them in a straightforward or simplistic way. Chase has been open about being a psychoanalytic patient

---

[3] From pp. 434-435.

himself, and writes about the practice, and dreams, from a highly informed standpoint[4]. This is to be borne in mind at those times when the explanation of the mechanisms and symbols involved in Made in America, and other episodes, seems obscure or tortuous. Those readers that have taken the time to reflect on their own dreams will have developed an understanding of this already.

For the purposes of my argument a detailed overview of the study of the characteristics of dreams is not required, only an understanding of how Chase uses them in *The Sopranos*. In my analysis of Made in America, I will elucidate the language and grammar of altered states of consciousness established throughout the show. References to appropriate sources from other authorities will be used to illuminate this, particularly Freud, the father of the practice which is central to the show. It will not be pretended that his research has not been superceded or falsified in the past century; it will be used only to clarify what Chase is trying to achieve. The focus will only be upon the less controversial of Freud's ideas, those which have stood the test of time and accord with the experiences of most people, as opposed to, for example, the Oedipus Complex, although that is alluded to in the dream in Meadowlands (1.4), when Livia Soprano, Tony's mother, appears in the guise of Jennifer, a woman he is sexually attracted to; and in his realisation, in Amour Fou (3.12), that he has been seeking out women who remind him of Livia. The use of Freud will show that there is precedent for how dreams are presented in *The Sopranos*, and will add to the strength of my

---

[4] 'Mark Lawson talks to David Chase', in Janet McCabe and Kim Akass (ed.) *Quality TV: Contemporary American Television and Beyond*, p. 187.

argument that they equate to the best interpretation of Made in America.

The nature of my argument will make it seem to some like I am seeing things that are not there, or twisting those that are to suit a particular agenda. However, how I will interpret Made in America and other episodes is standard practice for understanding the work of filmmakers that Chase admires and is influenced by, the likes of David Lynch, Stanley Kubrick, Luis Buñuel, and Ingmar Bergman, who speak to the audience through a panoply of subtle signs and symbols that is not the norm in mainstream cinema. Those who feel that my argument is deficient in these ways are likely to not be familiar with the work of such artists and are advised to make themselves so. I have not invented a private language in order to construct the argument but, rather, am treading a well-worn path.

There is no single term or phrase that is used universally to identify this type of filmmaking, but those that are include expressionist, formalist, avant-garde, experimental and surrealist; this is partly because no two filmmakers, or auteurs as they are also known, in this area work or communicate in exactly the same way, even though there are similarities. Their aim is not to represent external reality, and the beings and things which constitute it, exactly as they look to an observer. The focus is subjectivity, the inner life of the mind, the activity of thoughts and emotions; because of the difficulty of representing such matters the language is metaphorical, utilising symbols and signs to hint at the subject matter. It is, as Little Carmine Lupertazzi might say, 'very allegorical'.

Chapter Nineteen deals in depth with a film that stands in this lineage, so here that will be complemented by a brief elaboration of *Persona*, an influential film by Bergman from 1966. The narrative concerns a young nurse, Alma, who is assigned to care for Elisabet, an actress who no longer talks or moves. They relocate from the hospital to a seaside cottage, where Alma tells Elisabet secrets about herself, and later comes to believe that her patient is studying her for an unknown reason. Their relationship becomes tense, although Elisabet begins to talk; Alma has sex with the husband of Elisabet, who calls her by that name. The fact that Elisabet hates her son, and tried to induce an abortion when carrying him, is revealed, but the confession is spoken by Alma. The film ends with her desperately denying that she is Elisabet, and, as she leaves the cottage, a crew are filming.

There has been a huge amount of debate about how to interpret *Persona*. That it ends with Elisabet being filmed, and begins with a boy in hospital watching images on a projector screen which may include Alma, suggests that the story of the two women may be a fiction within a fiction, perhaps representing the psychological condition of the boy; or that the viewer should at least question what they believe they are being told about their relationship. Importantly, this would mean that, although cameras and screens are seen, they are not objectively part of the narrative, not 'really there', but are to be taken as signs or symbols of the need to watch in a different way. Themes that are commonly highlighted in analyses of the film include motherhood, the role of the unconscious, and identity; relevant to the last of these are the times when one face is superimposed on to another, and the resemblance of Alma to Elisabet, which may indicate that they are not two separate women, but different aspects of one. In this case, as with the cameras and screens, one or both of them should not be taken to be truly existing, but representations of something else.

This type of storytelling is not only visible in cinema and television. Before these media were developed it had been common in literature, and still is. An example that is helpful for the reader to study is the short story *A Country Doctor* by Franz Kafka, published in 1918. At face value it concerns an aged doctor, the narrator, who must visit an ill boy in a village miles away. It is the depths of winter and his horse has died because of the cold, but a unknown young man appears suddenly from his pigsty with two horses, and the doctor departs, even though the mysterious arrival makes it clear that he is interested sexually in Rose, the servant girl, even though she is very much against it: '"no!", shrieked Rose, fleeing into the house...I heard the key turn in the lock'; as the doctor leaves he recounts: 'I could just hear the door of my house splitting and bursting as the groom charged at it.'[5] In the blink of an eye, the doctor is at his destination, even though it is miles away. His patient does not appear to be ill, but implores the doctor to let him die, and, after a blood-soaked towel is spotted in the hands of his sister, a second examination reveals that he is dying because of a wound infested with worms. The family and village elders strip the doctor naked and place him on the bed with the boy; the story ends with him climbing out of the bedroom window and attempting to return home to Rose, but the going is very slow, and he is racked with regret: 'betrayed! A false alarm on the night bell once answered – it cannot be made good, not ever.'[6]

---

[5] Kafka *The Complete Short Stories*, p. 236.
[6] *Ibid.*, p. 241.

A Country Doctor has been subjected to a great deal of analysis in the century since it was published. As with *Persona*, it is not my intention here to recommend a particular reading, only to suggest ways in which it might be interpreted that will simultaneously shed light on Made in America. Sexual violence towards Rose is strongly hinted at, but the alleged perpetrator, the groom, appears out of nowhere with the solution to the doctor's problem, and his horses are hardly affected by the cold which killed another. The confusion which characterises the rest of the story, and the regret on which it ends, leaves room for the conclusion that the groom does not actually exist, that he serves as a symbol of the sexual urges of the doctor, who is the true rapist; from this point of view, the pigsty represents the slavish submission to base desires. He deals with the anguish which this deed causes him by a consoling fantasy of doing something noble: trekking miles through a winter blizzard to treat a suffering child, who, along with his family, also may not objectively exist. There is much more that could be, and has been, said about this fascinating story, but the possibility that it is not to be taken literally, that much of the narrative, not just the surreal events, are metaphors for the emotional turbulence of the narrator, is highly instructive for understanding the psychoanalytic themes of Made in America.

Studying works of art in this tradition is usually a challenging process, which involves not just examining clues in a different way, but also making do with far less direction as to what constitutes a clue than usual. An apparently simple scene in which little happens, such as a character sitting in a room by themselves staring into a fireplace, can be full to the brim with significance. Many people do not enjoy art which asks so much of them, and there is nothing wrong with that; but those wishing to understand *The Sopranos* must have at least a working knowledge of how information and meaning are conveyed in such stories. Anyone who reads the rest of this book and feels that inappropriate questions are being asked, that I am 'over-reaching', as Agent Dwight Harris of the FBI put it, is lacking key conceptual tools relating to the type of filmmakers that inspire Chase and his writers.

Part One of this book is concerned broadly with dreams in the show, and begins, as it must, by addressing the prevailing views of the finale offered by commentators. Despite the fact that we are now in a time when most people have the opportunity to express and publish their opinions through one medium or another, it is extremely hard to find anyone to whom it has even occurred that Made in America is anything but a standard narrative. This is as true of the minority who have had the opportunity to discuss *The Sopranos* with members of the cast and crew, as it is of the rest of us. In the first chapter, as a propaedeutic to the explanation of my reading, suggestions are made about weaknesses in those of previous commentators, which may go some way to accounting for their missing the myriad clues to the finale being not what it appears.

Chapter Two deals with a very exclusive sub-set of commentators, those who were involved in the production of the show. Chase has given many interviews during and since the initial run, and these are, not surprisingly, popular sources for those wishing to uncover the secrets. One would expect him to provide valuable evidence in this regard, but there are reasons to suspect that this might not be so. The same question is asked of contributions by Michael Imperioli, who has become the most high-profile member of the cast when it comes to providing insight and interacting with fans.

Evidence that suggests that Made in America is a dream, one that Tony has after he falls asleep in the safehouse at the end of The Blue Comet, is outlined in Chapter Three, and it turns out that there is plenty of it. Attention then turns to earlier episodes, including one in the first season, and the prequel film *The Many Saints of Newark*, to show that the finale is not the first or last time that deceptive consciousness masquerades as standard narrative. None of the other three that are examined are dreams, in the strict sense as occurring while a subject is asleep, but are caused by factors such as substance abuse and boredom.

In Part Two, what is potentially the strongest evidence for the theory that Made in America is a dream is considered, namely, the change in the behaviour and attitudes of certain characters. Despite the widespread failure of commentators and viewers to grasp this, it is shown to be in the most part both radical, in the sense of a significant departure from how they have appeared previously, and yet lacking sufficient or any obvious explanation for why it is so. It is discovered that plausible reasons do in fact exist, but they are ones that are carefully hidden in the narrative, so much so that, as with the change, they have been completely overlooked. This argument is then augmented by the presentation of two hidden stories from earlier seasons which, although not stemming from dreams or states of deceptive consciousness, relate to unexplained behavioural changes.

The remaining chapters of Part Two address the characteristic of dreams to include elements which are ludicrous or impossible; if Made in America is a dream, then it should be expected that this will be true of it. Such things are usually jarring and difficult to overlook, and the discovery of them will not only go a long way towards confirming the thesis of this book, but will also raise serious questions about the accuracy of commentaries and how closely many viewers are paying attention. Two more hidden stories from previous episodes are then uncovered. These do not relate to things which cannot happen, as the pool from which these can be drawn is small, but to aspects of the narrative which do not sit easily with what surrounds them.

Season Six of *The Sopranos* heralds a turn towards an even more pessimistic tone than is discernible in what came before. Many conclude that the cut to black at the end of Made in America signals the end of the life of the central character, and, in line with this, Part Three is concerned with the theme of death, which recurs throughout the episode from the beginning and intensifies as the end approaches. This is relatively uncontroversial when compared to other parts of my argument, but there are still numerous errors that must be corrected and omissions highlighted, the most important of which being the way in which Tony dies. A definitive answer to this question is offered, one which is unsurprising and stares the viewer in the face, but has still been completely overlooked. This is complemented by an examination of the death of a character who remains in narrative obscurity until the prequel film, but whose life and absence has an impact from the beginning.

One more task is necessary to complete the argument that Made in America is an unacknowledged dream: to compare its features to other dramatic presentations of this phenomenon. If it is a dream, then there will be strong similarities with those of Tony and other characters which are depicted in other episodes, and one does not have to be a diehard fan to know that there are plenty of these to choose from. The focus then moves to studying the work of a filmmaker who has had a profound influence on Chase, namely, Lynch. His groundbreaking film *Mulholland Drive* is one of a number of his works which make use of dreams and other varieties of altered consciousness, and as it was released in 2001, during the original broadcast of *The Sopranos*, it is very possible that this may have been opportune from the point of view of inspiring the showrunner of a television program which placed the study of the mind at the forefront of its concerns. Can Made in America be viewed as being a part of the artistic lineage of *Mulholland Drive*?

I conclude by reflecting on the premise for the book, the fact that commentators and viewers of *The Sopranos* have overlooked key parts of the narrative. Despite the huge amount that has been written and spoken about the finale, its unique status has flown under the radar. A false positive, a part of an episode that some believe is a deceptive state of consciousness masquerading as a standard story, is discussed. Finally, two possible explanations for the failure in commentary are suggested: one relating to a suspected agenda of Chase, and the other a judgement on the value of dreams as devices in fiction.

Part One

All That You Dream

Chapter One:
I Can't Go There

The rationale for this book is the revelation of the existence of stories, hidden just below the surface of the main narrative of *The Sopranos*, and to demonstrate their relevance to it. To this end, a literature review is required to investigate and justify this bold claim, as it passes implicit judgement on various recognised writers, and many more who will be unknown to most readers, covering endless pages of print and online material.

Only seven days after the broadcast of Made in America, an article, entitled 'There is no answer - deal with it. Tony Soprano is dead. Long live Tony Soprano', was published by the *Toronto Star*.[7] The author, Rob Salem, describes it as 'deliberately ambiguous', i.e., no interpretation or analysis of it is correct or better than any other: 'I would suggest that all ideas are equally possible, and therefore all equally "true" - I think Chase's ambiguity is a gift to the Sopranophile. Pick your own ending. You can have your cannoli and eat it too.' This is not the last time that such an opinion has been aired, although Salem also contradicts himself: 'The truth is, no one knows what the truth is, except for series creator David Chase, and he's not talking.' What is it: is there a

---
[7]Entertainment, p. 4.

true reading of Made in America, or is none better or worse than another? Is there a truth or not? Perhaps one could be generous and view this as a failure of expression, as opposed to a logical inconsistency at the heart of the argument; as evidence for the pressures of modern journalism and the requirement to publish anything, as long as there is something for the reader to spend their money on.

Seven years later, Alex Suskind occupies the same position with respect to Made in America, opining that 'people still can't come to terms with its lack of finality'; he, however, extends its reach: 'anything Sopranos-related...means whatever you want it to mean'. This grandiose theory is not automatically incorrect, although it requires much more support than can be given in a short article,[8] be it a philosophical argument resulting in a theory of meaning, or evidence from other episodes.

Perhaps the best-known source of secondary literature is Alan Sepinwall. Unlike most commentators, his output began during the initial broadcast of the show, while he was the television columnist at *The Star-Ledger* in Newark, New Jersey, a newspaper which appears in the show itself numerous times, such as at the end of The Legend of Tennessee Moltisanti (1.8), when Christoper 'Chris' Moltisanti steals multiple copies of an edition which does him the honour of mentioning him directly. More recently in 2018, Sepinwall joined *Rolling Stone* as chief television critic.

The position Sepinwall takes on the final scene of Made in America is one of complete subjectivity: each viewer is free to interpret it in whichever way they choose. This means that there

---

[8] 'David Chase can't escape "The Sopranos" finale'. *The Daily Beast*.

is no definitive answer available, or even possible, to the question of whether Tony dies at the end, which, he admits, is 'puzzling and infuriating', describing Chase as 'a singer who turned his back to the audience'.[9] But what does this mean exactly? Is it that viewers can literally and consciously choose whatever theory takes their fancy at that point, even if they change it later? But reasoning requires evidence, not whim. Or is it that viewers will base their conclusions on their own perspectives, none of which is better or more privileged than another? But this cannot be true, either, as it means that someone who is watching something for the first time is as justified in their response as someone who has studied it repeatedly over a long period. This is relativism, and means that there is no reason for anyone to trust the chief television critic of *Rolling Stone* on such matters, more than someone who has only just purchased their first television set.

Sepinwall probably means the latter of these two options, that the flexibility in interpretation comes from judgement, rather than free choice or volition; but this lack of precision in expressing his ideas is a weakness when it comes to the analysis of something as challenging as *The Sopranos*. His position, that someone can take from Made in America whatever feels right to them, misses a key analytical step. Many published commentators and viewers are able to spot parallels, references and ongoing themes in a show, but one frequent characteristic of those productions that have the term 'art' applied to them is the existence of even deeper and more carefully hidden elements.

In my experience of studying television, film, literature and philosophy, the intention of the author is highly unlikely to

---

[9] Matt Zoller Seitz and Alan Sepinwall *The Sopranos Sessions*, p. 305.

be simply to provide the viewer with a blank canvas for their own interpretation; in fact, I cannot think of a single example. Granted, a central theme in literature and philosophy over the past century and a half has been what is variously called subjectivism or perspectivism. But authors who promote this, the likes of Friedrich Nietzsche and Virginia Woolf, are not saying that one perspective is as good as any other, if for no other reason than the logical paradox that ensues. If one states that all perspectives are equally valid, then one is saying that that statement is not simply a perspective but a truth, i.e., it is true that all perspectives are equally valid; but this means that one is saying that it is a better account of how things are than others. To counter that, one may say that the statement, that all perspectives are equally valid, is itself only a perspective, but that means that the contrary position, that all perspectives are not equally valid, is of equal merit. The logical mess one finds oneself in here is why relativism has a bad name, even amongst those who are believed to be proponents of it.

Artists, and their mediocre counterparts also, have something to say about the nature of reality beyond the variety of perspectives upon it, and that is their primary intention. Before a commentator concludes that the intention of an artist is laissez-faire relativism, 'believe what you want about what I have put upon your plate', they need to exhaust their analysis and be very sure that they have not overlooked anything. Chase himself does not hold with relativism: 'it's true nobody knows anything, but some people know less than others'.[10] Sepinwall makes statements about what is being conveyed through the final

---

[10] Lawson op. cit., p. 218.

episode, such as the materialism of modern American culture,[11] which means that he does believe that some perspectives are better than others.

There is no doubt that Sepinwall is a very successful journalist. His name is recognised by fans of *The Sopranos* partly because of his connections, which allow him to get interviews with the likes of Chase, and, to a lesser extent, his knowledge of the history of television. It is when he steps outside of these fields, however, and into artistic analysis that weaknesses become apparent. His summaries of episodes and narrative themes are well suited to readers of newspapers and magazines, and appropriate to the vast majority of television shows. But *The Sopranos* is something quite different: it aims for and achieves the standards of high art, and is the brainchild of a writer who is a devotee of the work of visionary filmmakers. Sepinwall is aware of the influence on Chase of filmmakers such as Lynch and Jean-Luc Godard,[12] but this does not inform his reading of Made in America, despite suggesting that the two black men who enter Holsten's, the diner where the final scene takes place, call to mind those who try to kill Tony in Isabella (1.12). He could not be more wrong when he describes the final scene as 'shot and edited unlike anything else in the history of this show'.[13]

Sepinwall is very confident that he understands the message of the show, but then undercuts this, apparently without realising it, by admitting that 'the show zigged when we expected a zag', criticising those who 'expected a familiar narrative'.[14] Similarly,

---

[11] *The Revolution Will Be Televised*, p. 34.
[12] *The Sopranos Sessions*, pp. 101-102 and 329.
[13] *Ibid.*, p. 314.
[14] *The Revolution Will Be Televised*, p. 41.

'the idea that Tony dies flies too much in the face of everything the show had previously done in terms of narrative and theme. Narratively, this was never a show that cheated, or tried to trick its audience'.[15] Sepinwall has never spotted any of the hidden stories that are revealed in this book, nor does he appear open to the basic possibility that they might be there.

The next commentary to consider is *The Sopranos: Definitive Explanation of 'The END'*, by someone with the username MasterofSopranos. This is a blog that was first published in 2008 and added to over the intervening years. I have been unable to discover anything about him (based on the username I will assume male gender) relevant to the blog, such as professional experience or qualifications, but, judged on the merits of the arguments offered, this is someone who has a deep knowledge of the show and appropriate skills in critical analysis. This is confirmed by the positive feedback listed on Page 1, from impressive sources such as the *New York Times* and Pulitzer Prize winner Michiko Kakutani.

His position is the popular one that Tony is murdered at the end of the final scene by the mysterious figure who is credited as Man in Members Only Jacket. Unlike most viewers, though, he provides a huge amount of evidence to support this claim including, but not limited to, the behaviour of that individual; where Tony is looking at any given time; the internal layout of Holsten's; events and symbolism from other episodes, particularly in Season Six, such as Members Only jackets being worn by Eugene as he executes Teddy Spirodakis in Members Only (6.1), and Ray-Ray D'Abaldo as he participates in the attack

---

[15]*Ibid.*, p. 40.

on Silvio 'Sil' Dante in The Blue Comet;[16] and also comments made by Chase before and after broadcast of the finale. Much use is made, as one has come to expect in discussions of the finale, of the words of Robert 'Bobby' Baccalieri, Jr., from Soprano Home Movies (6.13), about death: 'you probably don't even hear it when it happens, right?'. There is a tenacity to the argument that is lacking from Sepinwall; if I am ever the victim of a shooting in a public place, I would like MasterofSopranos on the investigation team.

He constructs a convincing argument that 'for Chase to truly complete his vision' Tony's execution had to be witnessed by his family.[17] His fear of losing his family, which manifested at the beginning of the show as sadness at the ducks leaving his swimming pool; his deleterious effect on his family and those of others; his intense experiences while in a coma; these and other elements are woven together, to highlight the tale of a man who repeatedly fails to take redemption opportunities, and eventually finds himself backed into a corner with no further options. MasterofSopranos is right in a sense: Tony's family, along with friends and other acquaintances, are there with him as he dies, but the truth is not as straightforward as it looks.

At times, MasterofSopranos is agonisingly close to discovering that Made in America is an unacknowledged dream. He states that the building in the mural is a reference to the afterlife; points out that certain, supposedly unfamiliar, patrons in Holsten's, namely, the woman who enters with long curly hair, the scoutmaster, and

---

[16]Page 4.
[17]*Op. cit.*, Page 3, Note from the Author.

the Man in Members Only Jacket, resemble characters who Tony knows well, although he is not always correct in their identities, and believes that Chase 'randomly' shows many of the diners;[18] he also does the same with AJ's new therapist, although that is noted more widely. Why, then, does he not ask why this highly unusual state of affairs is so? It has never occurred before in the show outside of dreams, and would give anyone to whom it happened pause. The fact that the finale, and the final scene in Holsten's in particular, is much more symbolic than the vast majority of the other episodes must be commented upon. He states that Chase uses point of view techniques to put the viewer inside Tony's head,[19] but does not consider the possibility that the whole of the episode takes place there. Similarly, he also misses inconsistencies, both within the finale and with earlier episodes (including with the final scene of the previous one), and the other absurd and impossible elements of Made in America, which are a characteristic of the dreams previously depicted in the show and the psychological phenomenon generally. One way in which this manifests is through unrealistic changes in the character and behaviour of key figures, and although the change in, for example, Anthony 'AJ' Soprano, Jr., Tony's son, is noted, its scale and lack of realism is not.

A major way in which the analysis offered by MasterofSopranos goes off track is in the insistence that Tony is relaxed and calm throughout the final scene. 'There are multiple shots of Tony smiling and his expressions are of happiness, *not* paranoia'.[20] To a certain extent that is true, apart from the wary glances at the Man

---

[18] *Ibid.*, Page 3, Part III and Page 5, shot 9.
[19] *Ibid.*, Page 4, Part VIII.
[20] *Ibid.*, Page 1, Part I, Section A.

in Members Only Jacket, but happiness is over-egging it; relief is a more appropriate term. The error can be seen most precisely when MasterofSopranos comments on Meadow struggling to park: 'Chase (at least partially) does this to increase the tension and anxiety of the scene for the viewer';[21] rather, it is the state of Tony's consciousness, fearful and desperate, that leads to him dreaming that his daughter is having trouble coming to rescue him. In making this point MasterofSopranos draws on Chase,[22] but, as will be shown later, that is not as sensible as it sounds. He is also wrong in imputing to Chase a lack of interest in the identity of the person who kills Tony: he 'failed to offer anything concrete as to who was behind it. Therefore I do not believe the issue is that important to him and should not be to us.'[23] The episode does in fact strongly hint at who it is who causes the death of Tony.

The overwhelming paranoia and nagging anxiety that eats away at Tony does much more than putting an appropriate expression on his face; it underlies and creates from scratch the whole scene, and what precedes it in the episode. To see it, one must not just look at the scene, but beyond it. The very bricks and mortar are paranoia and his doomed attempts to conquer it. This requires on the part of a commentator a precise understanding of the mechanisms at work in dreams as portrayed in *The Sopranos*, one of which is described by Freud thus: 'my theory is not based on a consideration of the manifest content of dreams but refers to the thoughts which are shown by the work of interpretation to lie

---

[21] *Ibid.*, Page 5, Final Scene Shot By Shot, #65 through #75.
[22] James Greenberg 'This Magic Moment'.
[23] *Op. cit.*, Page 4, Part VIII.

behind dreams. We must make a contrast between the *manifest* and the *latent* content of dreams.'[24] As in so many other contexts, how someone appears in a dream, the manifest content, may not reflect the true tone at work, the latent content, in their role; they may look relaxed or even ecstatically happy, but other features of the dream may tell a very different story. Freud concluded that the latent content 'is of far greater significance' than the manifest.[25] Whatever is seen on screen during dream sequences is accompanied by much more that is left unpresented.

Although the focus of the blog is an explanation of what happens when the screen cuts to black, extensive reference is made to the rest of the episode, and previous ones going all the way back to the Pilot (1.1). This means that MasterofSopranos cannot be excused for not seeing that Made in America as a whole is a dream, or for missing the other hidden stories. As the blog was published in 2008, it means that his conclusion has remained largely unchanged for approximately sixteen years, with no evidence that it has been fundamentally reevaluated at any point, despite the amount of secondary material that has been published since then, and the release of *The Many Saints of Newark* in 2021.

Another commentary to consider is the *Sopranos Autopsy* website by Ron Bernard. It consists of his analyses of every episode of the show, although the promised one on *The Many Saints of Newark* has still not appeared. Bernard has read widely in secondary literature and the humanities more generally, an intellectual background which allows him to connect with the

---

[24]*Op. cit.*, p. 215.
[25]*Ibid.*, p. 247.

mindsets of Chase and the other writers. His position with regard to Made in America is alluded to in the first paragraph of the analysis of the episode: '"Definitive" interpretations often feel like an attempt to "get the last word in," like an effort to end the discussion rather than invite discussion. They close doors rather than open them...I would never describe my take as definitive. Or even *correct.*' In the next, he states that he wants to protect 'the ambiguity and wonderful mystery that David Chase has worked into his series', something that is particularly true of the finale, and to do this he later claims that he is not trying to give an account of what Chase was thinking;[26] this last point is an odd one to make, given the length and content of the article on the finale.

Ambiguity and mystery are popular words amongst supporters of postmodernism, and this is how the finale ends for Bernard, openly and without definite structure. The answers that viewers naturally want about what happened to Tony and the rest of his family are withheld, and to see and accept this is to adopt the appropriate stance. Those who refuse to do this he labels as 'truthers' and portrays them as impolite and small-minded: 'I've been insulted and mocked by the truthers for even suggesting that there are multiple ways of reading the final scene.' Such people, in his eyes, ignore evidence to the contrary of their position, but when asked by myself what arguments he had against my view that Made in America is a dream, he replied: 'I don't like to make an argument against a particular theory'.[27] But how, then, is the discussion he wants to promote to proceed,

---

[26] *Ibid.*, You, Me and the Tree.
[27] *Ibid.*, Responses.

and what logical form can it take? Perhaps he has received poor treatment, and if so he is right to complain, but not by referring to them as 's***birds' and 'f***ing fascists'[28], comments which only serve to cheapen his own argument. He confesses to his own take being 'rooted in very personal emotions' to do with the death of two friends, and while he deserves every sympathy for his loss, one cannot ignore the lack of balance in his reasoning that it may have caused.

I have read and taught many of the thinkers who are taken to be representative of postmodernism, the likes of Nietzsche, the later Ludwig Wittgenstein and Richard Rorty, and share Bernard's admiration for the ambiguity so often propounded in *The Sopranos*, the readiness of Chase and his team of writers to not give definite answers. However, there are certain inconsistencies and errors in reasoning in Bernard's analysis which must be highlighted, not least because they stand in the way of him properly understanding the finale and the other hidden stories.

The first is that he is guilty of one of the common excesses of postmodern thought, which is paying insufficient attention to that little thing called reality. Postmodern thinkers are correct that, because of the limited and perspectival nature of knowledge, getting in touch with and describing reality are by no means easy tasks; but it is still there. Two people may stand in the middle of a busy road at dusk and argue about whether the car speeding towards them is a Ford or a Volkswagen, but whatever it is, they had better move out of the way. Relating this to Made in America, it is of course true that viewers differ greatly about the meaning, but the question can and should still be asked about what sort

---

[28] *Ibid.*, Everyone Has Their Own Reasons.

of reality it is presenting. Bernard writes: 'True-believers will find the face of Jesus on a piece of toast, while the rest of us see only the random markings of radiant heat…We all see what we want to see, but only truthers and fundamentalists insist that everyone must see what they see.'[29] This is correct to an extent, but what all agree on is that they are confronted with a piece of toast, something which can be described and investigated. A similar error is made by Bernard when he confuses fact and value by assuming that Tony's statement, 'I'm a good guy, basically' (from The Second Coming (6.19)), is of the sort that is not dependent in any way on evaluation.[30]

Bernard equating the holding of a theory to be true, and providing evidence in support, with fundamentalism is an error common amongst defenders of postmodern positions. It is what philosophers describe as a category mistake, the confusing of one type of statement or concept with another. Fundamentalism is a claim about metaphysical or religious truth, usually involving corollaries such as the literal truth of a text such as the Bible or Qur'an, and the falsity of religions other than the one followed by the person or group making the claim. But believing a theory about a work of art to be correct, and giving reasons in support, is not in any way fundamentalist, even if someone else finds the reasons to be wholly unconvincing. It is telling that Bernard draws upon the review of Made in America by Emily VanDerWerff / St. James to support his category mistake, in that she reports having had a fundamentalist upbringing.[31] Such people are often

---

[29] *Ibid.*
[30] *Ibid.*, The Death of the Author.
[31] 'The Sopranos: "Made in America"', *AV Club*.

highly sensitive to the strongly-held convictions of others, but those who arrogantly dismiss the views of others about a work of art are not fundamentalist – just arrogant. More category mistakes that Bernard makes are his confusion of ambiguity and inherent meaninglessness,[32] and not realising that there might be a difference between meaninglessness and inherent meaninglessness.[33]

A second weakness is his overlooking the absurd elements of Made in America, of which there are many. Bernard misses things like the unrealistic changes in the personality and behaviour of various characters, the medical recovery of another that beggars belief, inconsistencies in the plot, and a comment from Carmela Soprano, Tony's wife, that deserves a place in *Fawlty Towers*. If he had remembered the decisive influence of the work of Lynch on Chase, these might have been corrected; in a very real sense the episode is a mess, and deliberately so, but Bernard is insistent on fitting it into a rational framework, his postmodern sensibilities notwithstanding. He spots the association between advertisements seen by Benny Fazio and Walden Belfiore in Oyster Bay, and in the next scene AJ and his girlfriend Rhiannon Flammer listening to Bob Dylan's 'It's Alright Ma, I'm Only Bleeding' (1965), in which advertising is mentioned, but does not connect it to the other associations in the episode or ask why there are so many.[34] Association is a common function of the mind in both its waking and sleeping states, particularly with things that cause strong emotions in us.

---

[32] *Ibid.*, The Death of the Author.
[33] *Ibid.*, 'Home', But Is It Art?
[34] *Ibid.*, 'Made in America'.

Of the three commentators discussed here, if I were to recommend one to someone new to appreciation of *The Sopranos*, it would be Bernard, although the others are worth reading also. He understands the type of art that Chase wishes to produce, and the influences at work upon him: the output of Lynch, Bergman, and so on, and the unusual ways in which they pass on information to the audience. He also makes a great effort to avoid a narrow focus on the final scene in his analysis of Made in America; many commentators focus on one aspect and think they have solved it, whilst ignoring or taking as read what comes before.

However, all three of the commentators have no, or barely any, understanding of the role played by hidden stories on multiple occasions throughout the show. Even though some of the hidden stories are more integral to the overall narrative than others, seeing all is required to avoid gaps in one's comprehension; and in some cases, these gaps are better described as chasms. Most viewers of *The Sopranos*, like other television shows or films, do not consult commentators in order to help them understand what is going on, something that is obvious from contributions to discussions on social media; but the minority that do are more likely to have read one or more of these three than any others; apart, perhaps, from those who were involved in the production of the show and who are covered in the next chapter. This goes a long way to explaining why the existence of the hidden stories, including that which constitutes the final episode, is not recognised by fans. Commentators, including but not restricted to Sepinwall, MasterofSopranos and Bernard, do not just lack the right answers, they have not even realised that the questions exist. They would be advised to bear in mind a distinction between meaning, authorial intention, and the nature of the narrative.

Meaning is what a subject takes from what they are viewing, which can be alternatively expressed as the relationship between the subject and the object of perception. What is the message of what is being viewed, or its purpose? What can be learned from it? Are any reactions more appropriate than others? Meaning is at least as diverse as the number of combinations of possible subjects and objects of viewing, but even more so, because factors such as the context of the subject, their level of understanding in relevant areas, and their state of mind also impact upon the meaning that is generated. Different people will derive different meanings from the same episode of *The Sopranos*, but each will find that the meaning they take may vary, depending on whether they watch it for entertainment or academic study, are feeling happy or sad, and so on. Meaning is subjective in that it is highly dependent on the nature and state of the viewer, and if this is not grasped then someone is likely to make a comment along the lines of 'Chase has never been willing to explain the meaning of that final scene.'[35]

Authorial intention is what the creator is intending to communicate or achieve through their work. This is on similar ground to meaning, but the crucial difference is that what a creator intends to say may not be what the audience hears; the message may not be received accurately. The intention may be only about what is explicitly in the work, or it could be lying below the surface, needing to be teased out. It could, of course, be nothing more than the creator producing something which is

---

[35] Sepinwall *The Revolution Will Be Televised*, p. 38.

enjoyed by others, and for which they will part with their money; as all artists have to pay the bills this is probably an element in the creation of most works, apart from those by artists who are independently wealthy. In his analysis of Made in America, Bernard discusses Roland Barthes' famous essay from 1967, 'The Death of the Author', which argues that the role of the creator in determining the meaning of a work has been overstated; but this familiarity with such ideas does not insulate Bernard from a lack of clarity when applying them.

The nature of the narrative refers to the type of story that is being told. Consider all of the different ones that have been employed within *The Sopranos* alone: regular narratives depicting daily life, memories, flashbacks, dreams, nightmares, visions, drug trips and near-death experiences. To know which of these is being utilised by an author is extremely important, because to treat a memory as an account of events happening in the present, or a nightmare as a report of waking reality, will cause significant problems for an interpretation of an episode or segment. The sheer variety of readings of Kubrick's 1980 film *The Shining* is illustrative in this regard.

These concepts are central to television criticism. Understanding the distinction between meaning, authorial intention and the nature of the narrative properly, and using the terminology precisely, would improve the contributions provided by commentators on *The Sopranos*. Sepinwall demonstrates some awareness of this when he distinguishes between the meaning of the final scene in Holsten's and the events: 'we know what the scene *means*, but we don't know what *happened*'[36];

---

[36]*The Sopranos Sessions*, p. 320.

but he is wrong in expressing confidence about the meaning, as there are many meanings, not just one. Bernard, with respect to the piece by Chase published by the Director's Guild of America in 2015[37], writes that he 'gave a fairly thorough explanation of some of his shooting, editing and staging decisions for the final scene. But he didn't go too much into what it all *means*'[38]; in so doing, he confuses authorial intention and meaning. The same mistake is made by Andrew Greeley: 'What did the series mean? It meant that there was no meaning at all. Like all stories, *The Sopranos* had no meaning because life has no meaning.'[39] This, in addition, is another example of the confusion of meaning and inherent meaning.

Practically nothing will be said about the first of these concepts in this book. This is because, as the definition makes clear, the scope of meaning is effectively endless, limited only by the number and condition of conscious beings who are able to watch the program and draw meaning from it. There will be similarities between the meanings elicited by different people, because there are all sorts of similarities between those people, but it is not in this area that the critical mistakes in the interpretation of *The Sopranos* have been and continue to be made. The personal take of this author is not required to correct these.

The clarity and consistency that is being called for here may sound like pedantry or philosophical quibbling to some, but that is not so. These concepts are regularly employed by commentators, as they were by those involved in the production

---

[37]Greenberg, *op. cit.*
[38]*Op. cit.*, 'Made in America'.
[39]'An Ending With No Meaning', *Chicago Sun Times*.

of the show; no language, everyday or abstract, can function if words are not used in the same way over and over. Granted, there is a common tendency to use some of these concepts interchangeably, particularly meaning and intention, but at the level of discourse that these commentators are participating in, that inconsistency is not permissible.

The false assumption about Made in America that is shared by all of these commentators, and virtually all of the others too, published or not, is about the type of narrative that it is. Not once do any of them ask this question, but to fail to verify what type of story is being depicted is to open oneself up to fundamental error, and this indeed is what has happened. Most episodes are regular narratives, so assuming that will in most cases not cause a problem, but on certain occasions it will. It would not be an understatement to describe the occurrence of that here as potentially the most significant mistake ever made in television criticism.

Chapter Two:
This Thing of Ours

It is perfectly understandable that, when trying to understand *The Sopranos* in more depth, people turn to those who were involved in its production; in fact, it would be strange if they did not. Who else would know better the intricacies of the show than those who wrote, directed, acted, and so on? The most obvious one to start with would be Chase: he is the creator and showrunner, wrote or co-wrote a number of the episodes and oversaw the writing of the rest, directed the first and last episodes, and chose the cast and crew. He has been much in demand for interviews since the show became popular, and has obliged with a number over the years, despite apparent reticence.

However, it turns out that Chase is not as reliable a source as many believe him to be. It is undeniable that he knows the show better than anyone else, given that he created and developed it, but it is this very fact that means he has good reasons to not be as forthcoming with interviewers as one would hope. What follows is evidence that, not only is Chase at times obscure in his answers, but that he even goes so far as deliberately giving the wrong answer.

First, Chase states explicitly that he wants to preserve the mystery of what he has created. In response to being asked by Brett Martin whether Tony died, he says: 'I'm not saying anything. And I'm not trying to be coy. It's just that I think that to explain it would diminish it.'[40] He clarifies this elsewhere, asking of creators who do demystify their work: 'Why are you explaining it? Why didn't you just write the explanation first and send it out as a flier?'[41] It is difficult to not sympathise entirely with this position. The television shows, films, and books that I have enjoyed the most are generally those which require ongoing reflection about what they are saying; they keep calling to the viewer to return again and again. Imagine the effect on our enjoyment, and the reputations, of the likes of *Twin Peaks* or *Doctor Faustus*, both multi-layered and highly complex works, if Lynch and Thomas Mann had revealed everything about them.

The Sopranos would not be half the program it is if Chase had explained it in depth beforehand or even afterwards. As if one could not guess, he declares: 'I like mystery. I like allusion. A lot of times, I prefer that to knowing what happened.'[42] Here the influence on him of filmmakers with the same values comes through: the likes of Buñuel ('one of my inspirations'[43]), Federico Fellini and Roman Polanski; French films of the genre specifically;[44] the theme of openendedness found in many European films[45];

---

[40]'"Sopranos" creator on "pissed" fans'. *Entertainment Weekly*.
[41]Sepinwall *op. cit.*, p. 34.
[42]*Ibid.*, p. 32.
[43]Seitz and Sepinwall *op. cit.*, p. 380.
[44]*Ibid.*, p. 386.
[45]Michael Imperioli and Steven Schirripa, *Woke Up This Morning*, pp. 102-103.

and also the television series *The Twilight Zone*, something he shares with Weiner and Winter.⁴⁶

Bearing all of that in mind, there are times when Chase goes beyond preserving the mystery and makes statements which are problematic or even untrue. In 2007, he explained why he named the finale as he did: 'it was about the extreme amount of comfort Americans have, especially people with money. And specifically, it was about the war in Iraq - it was made in America, and as you saw in the show, Tony and Carmela just didn't want their son to go, and they could afford to see that their son didn't go'.⁴⁷ This sounds plausible given how things look in the finale, but it omits key factors, including the clue to the alternative title that is hiding in plain sight (see Chapter Three), and the unusual nature of the episode, which will be shown to be an unacknowledged dream, and therefore means that the viewer must understand what they see in a different way. It should also be borne in mind that Made in America is no more concerned with the high living standards and wealth of people in the USA than other episodes are.

It is also contradicted by an explanation Chase gave years later in the final *Talking Sopranos* podcast: the phrase 'Made in America' came from a person in Marketing at HBO and was suggested for the promotion of the whole of the final season, 'and when it came time to name that episode I figured just call it that'.⁴⁸ Are we really expected to believe that Chase could not think up an appropriate title for the finale, and was satisfied with an unused promotional slogan? There is no way that he would be

---

⁴⁶*Ibid.*, p. 447.
⁴⁷Interview for GQ, December 2007, quoted by Bernard *op. cit.*, 'Made in America'.
⁴⁸10.18.

that lazy, and it is a pity that Imperioli and Steven Schirripa did not realise, too, and challenge him on this.

Chase also obscures as much as he reveals in the following comment about the family conversation in Holsten's: 'what they're talking about is how good those onion rings are. For me, food is always central to a feeling of family and to a feeling of security and happiness.'[49] Tony's desire to be with his family is undoubtedly a factor at work here, and his relationship with food is important throughout the show. But there is a powerful and timely reason why he should not have ordered onion rings, and if he did, why Carmela would not have failed to comment on his decision; it goes back to the traumatic events at the beginning of Season Six. It is not an accident that Chase neglects to mention it, because it is one of many clues to the nature of the unusual narrative being presented.

There is a similar feel to his remark about why the final scene ended up as it did: 'you go on instinct...As an artist, are you supposed to know every reason for every brush stroke? Do you have to know the reason behind every little, tiny thing? It's not a science; it's an art. It comes from your emotions,...from your subconscious.'[50] It is true that we all find it impossible to explain fully why we make the decisions about complex issues that we do, but the final scene was obviously meticulously planned by Chase for very specific reasons. What these are will be returned to repeatedly throughout the course of this book.

There is a plethora of evidence to demonstrate that Chase was firmly in control of as many aspects of the production of

---

[49] Greenberg, op. cit.
[50] Sepinwall op. cit., p. 39.

The Sopranos as he could be. According to Schirripa, he did not allow actors to change dialogue once it was in the script;[51] this prioritising of the writing is confirmed by Imperioli[52] and many other sources. Robin Green, writer of a number of episodes, states that Chase had the 'final edit' on everything.[53] Jason Minter, Chase's assistant during a period of the show, reports that he would make edits even to the cut of an episode which had been approved by the director: 'David did things like that constantly. He knew exactly what he wanted';[54] this is confirmed by director Jack Bender.[55] This authority was exercised from the beginning of the creative process; Imperioli recounts a time when a board full of ideas from the writing team, representative of hours of work, was completely wiped by Chase without consultation;[56] and director Alan Taylor remembers tone meetings, where directors confer with writers before shooting, as tough, 'like a graduate seminar', and, according to him, fellow director Tim Van Patten likened it to 'defending your life'.[57] Chase does not deny any of this: 'the direction of the show was up to me...The showrunner decides the architecture.'[58] That this can be a very productive working arrangement is not questioned here, and it would be pointless to do so, given the success of the show; it is highlighted only in order to raise doubts about certain comments by Chase.

---

[51] Imperioli and Schirripa *op. cit.*, p. 65.
[52] *Ibid.*, pp. 241 and 256.
[53] *Ibid.*, p. 309.
[54] *Ibid.*, pp. 209-10.
[55] *Ibid.*, p. 397.
[56] *Ibid.*, p. 259.
[57] *Ibid.*, p. 404.
[58] Seitz and Sepinwall, *op. cit*, pp. 362-363.

In a 2005 interview, Mark Lawson asks him about eggs: 'There's apparently an obsession with the theme of eggs in *The Sopranos*. Very bad to eat an omelette or step over cracked eggs...because you will normally die...Is any of this conscious?' His first response is: 'no, it's...coincidence'[59], to which is added: 'no, it's completely unconscious. It's surprising to me because mostly people eat Italian food on the show, and there aren't a lot of big egg dishes. So I don't know what that's about.'[60] Sixteen years later, in the final *Talking Sopranos* podcast and in response to the same question, this time from Schirripa, he answers only with a puzzled expression and a joke about taking acid.[61]

There is no way that these are, on either occasion, the best answers that Chase could give. The repeated use of eggs to foreshadow injury, death or an event of similar unpleasantness is manifest, and includes, but is not limited to, Carmine Lupertazzi, Snr. having a stroke whilst eating egg salad in Two Tony's (5.1); Tony stepping in broken eggs just before he decides to execute his cousin, Anthony 'Tony B' Blundetto, in All Due Respect (5.13); Adriana La Cerva offering to prepare eggs for her fiancé Chris before admitting that she is an FBI informant, a disclosure that leads to her murder by Sil in Long Term Parking (5.12); and Ralph 'Ralphie' Cifaretto making the same offer to Tony, before their argument over Pie-O-My ends in his death in Whoever Did This (4.9).

The symbolism of eggs is common knowledge amongst commentators. For Seitz and Sepinwall, they are 'frequently a

---

[59]Lawson, *op. cit.*, p. 215.
[60]Ibid., p. 216.
[61]25.05.

harbinger of death',[62] and numerous examples are provided to back this up.[63] Ilene Landress, executive producer, recalls that 'nobody was conscious in the writer's room about that', although she admits that there is an association of some kind.[64] One other comment is worth noting, and it is from none other than Chase himself in a 2017 interview: when asked whether 'the egg thing' was something he was aware of, he replied 'absolutely!'.[65]

Lawson also asks Chase about the recurring use of 3 o'clock, and here, too, the response is surprising: 'it's deliberate in the case of Paulie Walnuts...We don't use it for any particular reason...it's not intentional in any of the other characters' lives.' He then goes on to state 'I don't believe so' to the possibility that there may be any 'deliberate symbolism' utilised by the writing team.[66] But this is simply not true, and in Chapter Thirteen it will be shown how the number three appears often during Made in America, as an indication that something terminal is happening to a major character.

There are other examples of Chase being less than honest. 'I've never watched the series. I've watched a couple of episodes, parts of episodes'[67]. The only way in which this could be true is in the sense that he may not have watched one episode after another, all the way through, as viewers do; in which case, one wonders why he bothered saying something so obvious.

---

[62]*Op. cit.*, p. 176, footnote 38.
[63]*Ibid.*, p. 311; they do the same for occurrences of the number seven.
[64]Imperioli and Schirripa, *op. cit.*, p. 354.
[65]Seitz and Sepinwall, *op. cit.*, p. 341.
[66]*Ibid.*
[67]Natalia Marcos '"The Sopranos" creator David Chase: "I've never watched the series. I've watched a couple of episodes"', *El Pais*.

Otherwise, this contradicts what we know of his working practices and personality; there is no doubt that he will have watched each episode multiple times, both as a whole and scene by scene. Elsewhere he is more credible: 'I've never seen the whole show since it went off the air'.[68]

Another comment that contradicts what we know about his scrupulous attention to detail: when asked by Schirripa why Tony is carrying, of all things, a canned ham, as he returns with his family to their home after the conclusion of the war in Made in America, Chase replies: 'I don't know that I thought it through that much'.[69] There is, it turns out, a very good reason why Tony is carrying a canned ham, and it will be explained in Chapter Ten.

One more, on Meadow's parking troubles as the finale reaches its climax: 'I don't know why. I didn't write that because I had some plans where it's supposed to mean *this*. I just thought this will be interesting film...It didn't mean anything'.[70] This is a less than satisfactory answer, because the focus on the repeated failure to park is a device used to heighten the tension for the viewer, and to keep from Tony the person who he considers to be his guardian angel.

In no way is it being suggested that Chase should be blamed for being less than fulsome in his answers to such questions. One cannot expect a writer, or any artist, to spend years creating a complex and deep opus, and then to explain it all at the first opportunity, in the same way that someone would not cook a meal and then throw it in the bin uneaten. To enjoy such works

---

[68] Imperioli and Schirripa, *op. cit.*, p. 105.
[69] *Talking Sopranos* 91, 39.55.
[70] Imperioli and Schirripa, *op. cit.*, p. 103.

of art is to consume them, to investigate them, to peel away one layer at a time. It would probably be better, though, if he were to respond along the lines of 'I'm not going to answer that question', whenever he feels that answering would compromise the integrity of the show. At times, he makes it harder for us to understand his work, which is hardly easy, anyway; one can understand if he does not want to make it easier, but there is no need to do the opposite.

Before anyone concludes that there is no point to hearing what Chase has to say about his show, it should be stated that he can be very enlightening; his memory, even in recent live interviews, is excellent. Take the following comment on the ending: 'the only thing I would say definitively about it is, whatever happened, Tony put himself there. It was the world as he saw it. He was responsible for where he ended up – wherever that is.'[71] As will be demonstrated, this is unambiguously correct, and one wonders whether 'the world as he saw it' is a subtle reference to dreams. On the same topic: when asked about the cut to black, Chase said that it is to do with the 1849 poem *A Dream Within A Dream* by Edgar Allan Poe, which asks 'is *all* that we see or seem, but a dream within a dream?'.[72] Earlier in the interview from which that is taken, it is stated that the poem is concerned with the transitoriness of existence, a theme which is also present in Made in America, but the evidence presented in this book strongly suggests that this interviewer also misses a subtle clue about the narrative. This is ironic, as Chase claims

---

[71] 2012 interview with *Men's Journal*, quoted by MasterofSopranos, *op. cit.*, Page 2, Shot 113.
[72] Martha Nochimson 'Did Tony die at the end of The Sopranos?', *Vox*.

that she falsely reported him as confirming that Tony is still alive after the cut to black.[73]

Like all of us, Chase is a fallible human, and, probably because of the number of interviews he is required to participate in, he also provides information, more than he intended, through slips of the tongue. When asked about how far ahead he planned the final scene in Holsten's, he replies: 'I think I had that death scene around two years before the end', after which Matt Zoller Seitz remarks: 'you realise, of course, that you just referred to that as a death scene'; a pause, Chase utters an expletive, and laughter all around ensues.[74] It is noticeable that he does not make any attempt to repair the damage, such as 'oh, I meant what many take to be the death scene.'

Chase should be defended from the tendency of some to attribute questionable motives and personality traits to him on the basis of this evasiveness: 'he can seem brooding at times, and his clever sense of irony and sardonic wit can lead some fans to think he's trying to mindf*** us. We've all seen his "I'm-smarter-than-you" smirk'.[75] The photo that is provided as proof shows nothing of the sort, only an introvert who does not relish being the object of public scrutiny, and is probably tired of having their photo taken.

Another source of information from inside the production of the show comes from Imperioli and Schirripa, who are much more visible figures than Chase. As well as playing central characters, Chris and Bobby respectively, they host the *Talking Sopranos*

---

[73]Seitz and Sepinwall, *op. cit.*, p. 325.
[74]*Ibid.*, p. 389.
[75]Bernard, *op. cit.*, 'Made in America'.

podcast and take it on the road to venues around America and abroad. The podcast focuses on each episode in turn and the prequel movie *The Many Saints of Newark*, in most cases with contributions from members of the cast and crew. Imperioli and Schirripa also co-authored *Woke Up This Morning: The Definitive Oral History of The Sopranos*, which is partly based on the podcast.

In an interview with Steven Van Zandt, Schirripa stated that, with regard to the question of whether Tony is alive at the end of Made in America, there is 'no wrong or right answer'[76], a position taken, as has been noted, by other commentators. Elsewhere, he suggests that Tony survives, while it is Imperioli who argues that no definitive answer is possible: 'when you come to the last sentence of the book, the book is over. There's no wondering what happens after the book is done.'[77] He, too, also leans at times towards an optimistic interpretation of the ending.[78]

Both always treat Made in America as if it is a regular narrative, and the only suggestion that it could be anything else comes in the form of a brief mention of the argument of my 2018 YouTube video, which is referenced on *Sopranos Autopsy*.[79] However, a faint inkling that something might not be right with the story is sometimes evident. Schirripa, of Carmela, Meadow and AJ staying in the safehouse, says that 'it doesn't seem like they're that hidden',[80] and registers surprise that Meadow would go into New York after the incident with Salvatore 'Coco' Cogliano in

---

[76]*Talking Sopranos* 89, 16.47.
[77]Imperioli and Schirripa, op. cit., p. 479.
[78]*Talking Sopranos* 91, 28.55 and 52.41.
[79]*Ibid.*, 58.04; 'Made in America'.
[80]*Ibid.*, 1.06.17.

The Second Coming.[81] For his part, Imperioli says that Agent Harris has become a 'weird version' of Tony,[82] and also sees as bizarre the lack of reaction by Carmela to hearing of AJ's plan to join the army.[83] Nevertheless, they do not spot anything untoward in the behaviour of certain other key characters, particularly in how it might contradict what has been seen of them before.

While much can be learned from the reminiscences and interviews of Imperioli and Schirripa, particularly about the personalities and working habits of members of the cast and crew, from the point of view of the thesis of this book, their value is limited by the lack of sustained and deep analysis of the storylines. This may be because they have an ongoing friendship and working relationship with Chase, who has been interviewed by them on more than one occasion on the podcast. To initiate discussions about hidden aspects of the narrative that Chase himself does not want to disclose would be counterproductive, on both personal and professional grounds.

Another reason is that Imperioli was part of the writing team. He wrote four episodes: From Where to Eternity (2.9), The Telltale Moozadell (3.9), Everybody Hurts (4.6) and Marco Polo (5.8); and co-wrote Christopher (4.3). He therefore has more of a personal interest than Schirripa in preserving the mystery of the narrative and, like Chase, cannot be blamed for that. But one of those episodes – Marco Polo – also happens to be one which contains one of the hidden stories. When told by one of the fans about his interest in the subject of the parentage of a major character

---
[81] *Ibid.*, 1.08.05.
[82] *Ibid.*, 1.24.24.
[83] *Ibid.*, 1.45.47.

which might be solved in that episode, Imperioli responds with only a discreet smile,[84] but clearly one of someone who knows the answer, which he should as he wrote it. See Chapter Eleven for the answer to the question.

Deficiencies, most of them unintended and others possibly deliberate, on the part of commentators on *The Sopranos* and those involved in the production of it, have been outlined in this and the previous chapter. It is now time to shine a light squarely on what has remained hidden because of these failings.

---

[84]*Talking Sopranos* 90, 32.13.

Chapter Three
I am a Nice Dream

The intention of Chase for Made in America, and it is no coincidence that he is also the sole director and writer for the first time since the opening episode of Season One, is to ensure that the life of Tony ends in a way that is consonant with how he lived it. Dying before waking up from a dream is a very fitting resolution, given what we have been told about his personality and behaviour. He has repeatedly failed to take opportunities presented to him, not only through his therapy with Jennifer, to look himself square in the mind and take responsibility for the man he has made of himself. Furthermore, dying in a safehouse, where he is hiding in fear for his life, is his being literally cut off from his wife and children in a manner that feels very appropriate, as he has been progressively cut off from them emotionally because of the cumulative weight of the decisions he has made, as a husband and as a father. As the Boss of a Mafia family, he has failed to inspire loyalty and trust in his subordinates and business partners, even going so far as to take the lives of some who arguably did not deserve it, in performance terms, if not moral. He has barely anyone left to defend him and his interests against the Lupertazzi Family. He is, however, doing his best, as he has habitually done, to shield his mind from these uncomfortable truths, a response which has achieved nothing but miring him in peril.

Many fascinating puzzles and quandaries have been put before the viewer since the beginning of *The Sopranos*. What is represented here is one more of these, but of a multi-layered nature, something quite different as befits the finale of such a ground-breaking show. Not only does one have to work past the deluge of tricks and obfuscations to see that it is there, a task that virtually all have failed in, but it then has to be solved. This book succeeds in both of those tasks. As will be explained more fully in Chapter Fifteen, something else that Tony is diverting his and our attention from is the precariousness of his physical health, which perhaps more than any other aspect of his life has suffered from a lack of attention over the years.

There are recurring subtle hints in Made in America that we are watching a dream and the first is the episode title. All of the previous eighty-five episodes, and the subsequent film *The Many Saints of Newark*, have titles that relate to them specifically in some way.

Kennedy and Heidi (6.18) primarily refers to the two teenage girls in the car that is involved in the accident after which Tony murders Chris. The name of the former, the passenger, is an instance of a theme in the final season of murdered leaders: at the wake Tony compares Chris' widow Kelli to Jackie Kennedy, and in other episodes the names and images of Abraham Lincoln and Julius Caesar appear. The name of the latter, the driver, has stumped commentators searching for a secondary meaning. None have noted that there is a deity in China of the same name, and the common mission of gods to oversee decisions about the life and death of mortals is relevant: although Heidi is not responsible for the accident, she does refuse to return to the scene, which gives Tony the opportunity to murder Chris. Chinese religious thought is usually of a monist nature, avoiding sharp dichotomies such as that between good and evil, which fits with the morally ambiguous world of the show.

He is Risen (3.8) is a phrase used by Aaron Arkaway, the narcoleptic boyfriend of Janice Soprano, sister of Tony, when asking Jackie Aprile, Jr. if he has heard about 'the good news', the resurrection of Jesus Christ. It also refers implicitly to the arcs of two characters. Ralphie is promoted to the rank of capo, which is good news for him, but not Tony, who detests him but feels he has no choice but to use him to fill the vacancy left by the reliable earner Gigi, who has a fatal heart attack on the toilet. Jackie, Jr. also improves his standing in the eyes of Meadow. His initial attempts to consummate their relationship are frustrated, but after crashing his car whilst under the influence of alcohol she asks if she can spend the night with him. Her words, 'I want to go with you', imply that she wants more than just a place to sleep.

Boca (1.9) is a reference to Boca Raton, Florida, where Junior has been taking his girlfriend Bobbi Sanfillipo for a number of years. In addition, travelling to Boca Raton requires travelling south from New Jersey, and Boca means 'mouth' in Spanish, which taken together allude both to the oral sex Junior performs on Bobbi, and the mistake she makes of ignoring his warnings not to talk about it to anyone else. After jokes by Tony and Carmela make him realise what she has done, their relationship quickly 'goes south', i.e., deteriorates, and ends with Junior firing her from her job and, in another reference to oral sex, shoving pie in her face. The mouth of Meadow also brings disaster to the life of

Don Hauser, her school football coach, after she tells Tony that he is in a sexual relationship with Ally, a girl on the team.

Unlike these and all the rest, the title Made in America is not specific to the episode. 'Made' is a Mafia term, to be made is to be initiated, but that happens to no one. The phrase 'Made in America' is not heard or seen. Comments are made by various characters, such as AJ, about national and international issues affecting the USA, but there are no more than in many other episodes.

It is therefore a highly unusual title, although this has not been noted by any other commentator. The unconvincing explanation offered by Chase was dismissed in the previous chapter. The title does, however, connect to the episode in an oblique way, because it is an anagram of a phrase which describes the unusual nature of the events that transpire: 'I am a nice dream.' This too has not been spotted by anyone else. It is very cleverly hidden behind the Mafia reference in 'made'. If the writer of the episode, Chase, had just used a standard anagram that had no relevance to even the genre as a whole, such as 'American Media', or a nonsensical one like 'Aim a Crane Dime', it would have been much more likely to be discovered. The Mafia reference has the effect of convincing the viewer that they need delve no further to understand the meaning.

I Am a Nice Dream, the true title of the finale, unlike Made in America, does say something about the episode. It tells us that the nature of the narrative is not that which has been widely taken for granted, and that Chase is using a story-telling technique that he has made great use of before. The previous dreams are mostly those of Tony, but also Jennifer, Chris and Carmela. The title suggests that, like in those dreams, the viewer will be privy to the deepest fantasies and fears of the subject, witness unlikely or surreal events, and meet again those who have died, and indeed this is what happens. This final dream differs from all that have been shown before in that it takes up the entirety of an episode. It is also different from most depictions of states of altered consciousness in that it is explicitly unacknowledged. Usually, it is made clear that someone is dreaming after the fact when we see them waking up, as with Carmela in Cold Stones (6.11), by them beginning the scene in bed, as Tony does in The Test Dream (5.11), or through the occurrence of implausible events, such as the appearance of someone who has died, as Carmine, Sr. does in the same scene.

It is fitting that Chase should have employed an anagram to conceal the true nature of a dream in the final episode of a show that has placed so much emphasis on the practice of psychoanalysis. Freud was convinced that the sleeping mind uses all sorts of tricks to hide the true meaning of dreams from subjects, which he grouped under the term 'distortion', including, similar to anagrams, the technique of word associations. In one example, a female patient 'saw her... fifteen-year-old daughter lying dead "in a case". Although her initial instinct was to interpret it as wish fulfilment, through analysis she remembered that 'at a party the evening before there had been some talk about the English word "box," and the various ways in which it could be translated into German', one of which is 'Büchse', which could also be 'used as a vulgar term for the female genitals.' She recalled that her pregnancy had not been a happy one, and wished that her unborn child might die; 'in a fit of rage after a violent scene with her husband, she had beaten with her fists on her body so as to hit the child inside it.' The dream did therefore qualify as the fulfilment of a wish, but one from fifteen years before.[85] A far more tortuous example from one of his own dreams begins with a fictional place name of Hearsing, which he believes to be made from parts of the names of real places near to Vienna, takes in its similarity to the English word hearsay, the name of a friend, a poem about a dwarf from a German humour and satire magazine, and the name of a port in the Netherlands, and concludes that he had been dreaming about ereutophobia, the fear of blushing![86]

The accuracy of the interpretations of the dreams in these examples is not the point here, nor whether Chase agrees with them; what is salient is how they help him to tell stories. In the hiding of 'I am a nice dream' within the anagram 'Made in America' he is giving yet another nod to a body of work that has been a recurring narrative device in the show. An illustrative use of distortion in the form of word association occurs prior to this in the first part of the dream in Calling All Cars (4.11), with different meanings of 'in the driving seat', which is then elucidated in the subsequent therapy session.

The initials of the given title, MIA, are also a common abbreviation for the phrase 'missing in action', used to refer to those involved in a war whose current whereabouts are unknown, suggesting that they are dead, seriously injured, captured by the enemy or have deserted. Tony is involved in a Mafia war at the beginning of Made in America, and by the end he will be permanently missing in action. There is only so much that can

---

[85]*Op. cit.*, pp. 237-38.
[86]*Ibid.*, p. 406.

be achieved with the rearrangement of a set of letters, so this connection is possibly no more than a happy coincidence.

The clues to the true nature of what the viewer is watching in Made in America begin immediately. Tony awakes in daylight, from what looks to have been a deep slumber. This is hardly likely to have been the case as he is in fear for his life, because the war with the New York Mafia Family, headed by Philip 'Phil' Leotardo, is going very badly. The previous episode, The Blue Comet, ended with him drifting off to sleep. Taken together, using the language of dreams developed in the show up to this point, these are a strong indication that he has not woken up as the viewer is led to believe. This is not the first time that dreams begin with Tony apparently waking up in bed: this also occurs in The Test Dream and Join the Club, but none of the commentators discussed earlier make this connection.

What is also not at all obvious, even for those watching this immediately after The Blue Comet, is that things have changed since we left Tony at the end of it, lying in the dark and staring at the door, and it is not just the time. The bed is no longer simply a mattress and pillows: the mattress is covered with a sheet and Tony by a blanket. In addition, he is dressed differently as, when he fell asleep, he was all in black, in a leather jacket, trousers and shoes, but he wakes in grey pyjamas. As well as the discontinuity, the change of colour away from one which is redolent of death is telling: throughout this dream his mind struggles to console him with optimistic images. On the bedside table there is a radio and a bottle of beer. The camera angle does not show the table as he enters the room, and, coupled with the dark, this means that it is impossible to tell whether they were there or not, but waking up to beer and classic rock on the radio smacks of wish-fulfilment, given what we know of him.

An alternative explanation for the change in the sleeping arrangements is that more time has passed than is being suggested. This is supported by Tony commenting later that he has not eaten a green vegetable for a while, and Phil losing patience with Butch 'Butchie' DeConcini over his failure to locate their target. But this does not rule out Tony dreaming that days, even weeks, have passed. Unnatural skips forward in time are a common feature of dreams, and the first of a number in this episode happens very soon. It should also be noted that many of the aspects of the narrative that will be presented as evidence for it being a dream can be interpreted in different ways, although there are some that cannot; my argument rests greatly on the sheer number of them, i.e., on a quantitative foundation.

The creation of a false reality that is more pleasant than the true one we are faced with is a common tactic of the dreaming mind. This is true of all of us, not just those hiding in fear for their life. Freud wrote that dreams 'are not meaningless, they are not absurd; they do not imply that one portion of our store of ideas is asleep while another portion is beginning to wake. On the contrary, they are psychical phenomena of complete validity - fulfilments of wishes'.[87] As will be demonstrated in the remainder of this chapter and some of those that follow, there are other elements of this dream in Made in America that amount to wish fulfilment, and the same is true of previous dreams and other deceptive perceptions of reality in the show, some qualifying as hidden stories, some not.

---

[87] *Ibid.*, p. 200.

Beer lingers in the consciousness of the dreamer through association, as the next scene begins abruptly with Tony sitting with Paulie at night in a van emblazoned with the product name Steinholz Beverage. This is the first skip forward in time, from the morning of the first scene. While they are waiting for Agent Harris, the song Denise by Randy and the Rainbows is played on the radio. The following lyrics are heard: 'you're my dream and I'm in heaven every time I look at you. When you smile it's like a dream'.[88] The name of the wife of Chase is Denise, and this, in conjunction with the appearance of his daughter Michele DeCesare as Hunter Scangarelo later in the episode, is likely to convince commentators that this is the explanation for the inclusion of the song.

The house that Carmela and their children Meadow and AJ are staying in is reminiscent of Whitecaps, the house on the Jersey Shore that the final episode of the fourth season (4.13) takes its title from. They would have purchased it, had Tony's ex-girlfriend Irina Peltsin not informed his wife that he had recently had sex with her cousin Svetlana Kirilenko. The two houses used for filming are not far away from each other, in Long Branch and Sea Bright. This is more wish-fulfilment: his sleeping mind is rewriting painful family history. There is also a dose of over-protective anxiety at work, in that there is probably no need for them to be worrying about their safety from deliberate attacks. As Tony said to Carmela in the previous episode: 'families don't get touched, you know that'.

The next clues are provided in the following two scenes. The first takes place at the post-funeral gathering for the

---

[88]Lyrics by Neil Levenson.

murdered Bobby. Patrick, boyfriend of Meadow, turns the table conversation to the 2006 movie *Dreamgirls*. AJ angrily interrupts saying 'you people are f***ed! You're living in a dream!'. Soon after, he says that joining the army and killing Al-Qaeda terrorists would be more noble than watching 'these jack-off fantasies on TV' about how the American army is beating them easily. That is what the viewer is doing, watching a fantasy, but one created by a dreaming mind.

The following scene takes us back to the safehouse where Tony and his crew are still holed up. An episode of *The Twilight Zone* is being watched on the television and its haunting music is heard. The choice of *The Twilight Zone* of all possible programs by Chase is significant: with its memorable stories depicting bizarre variations on reality, it points to the fact that for the viewer of Made in America things are not as they usually are. It is also worth noting that the episode is called The Bard and tells the story of Julius Moomer, 'a streetcar conductor with delusions of authorship' according to the closing narration of Rod Serling, who uses black magic to conjure up William Shakespeare. This reference to magic, albeit one for which we must go beyond Made in America to fully appreciate, is another suggestion that reality has been altered in some way.[89]

Magic realism is an artistic device whereby the line between fantasy and reality is blurred for the purpose of better depicting the everyday world. Events which are untrue or impossible are woven into the narrative as if they are truly occurring, but

---

[89] For more on the debt that Chase owes to this program, see his article in *Variety*: 'The Sopranos' Creator David Chase on "The Twilight Zone": "It Made a Mammoth Impression".'

are to be interpreted only metaphorically. In literature it is associated with the work of Gabriel Garcia Marquez and Jorge Luis Borges, and Lynch, a major influence on Chase, has used it extensively, for example, in *Twin Peaks* and *Lost Highway*. Strictly speaking, nothing in Made in America qualifies as magic realism, because we are watching a dream where it is common for things to happen that are not possible in the waking world. It is straightforward realism.

Indeed, in addition to this television, screens and images of one sort or another appear incredibly often in Made in America. There are the screens used by the FBI to monitor the funeral of Bobby; the television being watched by Harris when he hears of the execution of Phil; that in the family home watched by AJ and Rhiannon; the security monitors in the backroom of the Bada Bing!, the stripclub owned by Sil, on which Neil Mink stares at the semi-naked dancers; this cuts immediately to the monitor in Sil's hospital room, where is also located a television, on which Tony watches a clip from the 2006 film *Little Miss Sunshine*; and the screen of the jukebox in Holsten's. To these should be added the photo of Domenica shown by her mother Janice to Junior; that of Chris that the cat is fascinated by; and the photo of Phil used by Paul 'Little Paulie' Germani. There are the mirrored walls in the Bada Bing!; the mirror in the facility where Junior is staying, in which certain people are framed perfectly; the glass entrance door to Holsten's, which Tony keeps an eye on; the reflections of the two black men in the glass counter; and the reflections of the façade of Holsten's in the windows in the wall behind Meadow as she tries to park. Images of one sort or another include the painting of Vesuvius erupting; the FBI recording the conversation between Tony and George Paglieri;

the emblem of the Lone Wolves film production company on glass; and the images which fill the far wall at Holsten's. Finally, there are the discussions of *Dreamgirls*; and of the screenplay *Anti-Virus*, which Little Carmine hopes to turn into a film.

All of these are framing devices, common in film, television and literature, used for the purpose of advising the viewer to question the veracity of what they are seeing. They are utilised by Bergman in *Persona* for this very reason. On one level, it is known that what is being seen is not true because it is a television program, but even the usual practice of suspending one's disbelief may not be enough. The more screens, images and references to false realities that are presented, the greater the likelihood that the story is unreliable, even by the standards of televised fiction.

When Patrizio 'Uncle Pat' Blundetto visits Tony in the back room at the Bada Bing!, to warn him that Janice is trying to get her hands on Junior's money, there is another dream-themed song playing: I Dreamed I Dream by Sonic Youth from 1982. It is very hard to recognise as it is muffled, most likely because it is playing in the main area of the club.[90] This is an unusual song to be playing in a strip club, which adds to the feeling that something is not quite right in the episode.

The final clues of this type are provided in the last scene. As Tony enters the diner, Little Feat are heard singing 'all, all that you dream', a line from the song All That You Dream from 1975.[91] When he is examining the jukebox selections two songs

---

[90]This is pointed out by Cinematography Appreciation in a comment on my YouTube video 'The Sopranos "Made in America": Tony's Final Dream'.
[91]Lyrics by Paul Barrère and Bill Payne.

mention magic in their titles: This Magic Moment by Jay and the Americans from 1968, and Magic Man (Live) by Heart from 1975.

There is one more reference to dreams and it is the most carefully hidden of them all. On the left side of the mural is a football player who is identified as 'Michael Shea, Class of 1977'. There was no significant player by this name at either the NFL or College levels, or who played in the Newark area, at that time. There was, however, a porn movie released in 1977 called *The Secret Dreams of Mona Q*. Tony was approximately eighteen at the time, by which point his sexual urges would have been at full throttle. There is a Michael Shea among the cast who is credited as 'Forest Pixie'. This does not make him one of the main stars, so why of all of them does his name appear on the mural? It is another example of the random association common in dreams. Tony as a football fan would remember that the New York Jets played at that point at Shea Stadium, in the Queens borough of New York City; and in the previous episode he met Eric Mangini, the then Head Coach of the Jets, in Vesuvio's, the restaurant owned by Artie and Charmaine Bucco. The image of the football player on the mural therefore bears the imprint of Tony's adolescent sexuality, in addition to his love of the sport. The latter was in evidence many times throughout the show; and in *The Many Saints of Newark,* in both 1967 and 1972, there are posters on his bedroom walls of football players in similar poses to those of the figures in the mural. As an interesting aside, in a reference to the psychological condition which plagues him in his later life, in 1967 there is also a poster of Alfred E. Neuman, the fictional character from *Mad* magazine, and his catchphrase 'what, me worry?'.

The choice of onion rings to begin the meal also points to something not being quite right. Tony informed his crew, in Mr. & Mrs. John Sacrimoni Request... (6.5), that his digestive system could no longer tolerate onions, after the trauma experienced by his body because of his shooting by Junior in Members Only.[92] No subsequent information is provided pertinent to his overcoming this, so if the final scene is in the waking world, why did he do this and why did Carmela or AJ not say anything? This question will be analysed further in Chapters Fourteen and Fifteen.

Close attention to Made in America reveals repeated suggestions that the viewer is being presented with the subconscious mind of Tony, as it struggles to process what is happening to him. It shows that the nature of the narrative is not what it has been widely assumed to be. This episode, as an explicitly unacknowledged dream, is the type of story-telling technique that should be expected from a writer so committed to ambiguity as Chase is. It is, however, not the first time that he has used it in *The Sopranos*, and for that we need to go all the way back to the first season.

---

[92]None of the commentators discussed earlier remember this when analysing the scene in Holsten's, which amounts to a serious oversight.

Chapter Four
Maybe You Need More Medication

Isabella is the penultimate episode of the first season and it begins with Tony not in good shape. At the Bada Bing!, Chris reports that he just visited him and that 'he looked tired'; Sil suggests that he has hypoglycaemia and is not impressed with the counter that Tony might have depression, even though Chris provides supporting evidence that 'he is sleeping all the time' and 'not taking care of himself'.

The next scene, indeed, begins with Tony in bed, pretending to be asleep and being uncommunicative with Carmela. She thinks he should contact Jennifer and might need more medication, and, despite his negative response, her comment does sink in as will be seen. He tells her that he is taking lithium and Prozac as directed by his therapist, and bottles of both, labelled as prescribed by her, are visible in the bathroom cabinet. He suggests that he is feeling bad because of the disappearance of Salvatore 'Big Pussy' Bonpensiero, but what is left unsaid is that he is wondering whether his old friend has become an informant for the FBI.

As soon as Carmela leaves, Tony goes to the window and sees a beautiful young woman, who later introduces herself as Isabella, hanging out washing in the garden of his neighbours Bruce and Jeannie Cusamano. What only becomes clear later in the episode is that she is a figment of his imagination. This means that he is experiencing hallucinations, but although he is displaying symptoms of depression, waking dreams such as these are associated with the severe clinical form, often called psychotic depression, that can require hospitalisation.[93]

Another explanation is put before the viewer after Isabella walks away and Tony goes to the bathroom for his bottles of lithium and Prozac. It is impossible to be certain, but the manner in which he empties one of them into his hand suggests that he is not paying attention to directions for proper use, as does his sitting in the shower with a befuddled expression and the camera angle rotating in a way that implies that his view of reality is askew. Hallucinations are possible side-effects of controlled use of both lithium and Prozac when prescribed for medical purposes, as are his fever and sweating, and even more so if taken improperly or in combination. What he experiences is consistent with a serious and potentially fatal condition known as serotonin syndrome.[94] This knowledge should be a warning to be ready to question the veracity of other things seen in the episode.

As Tony first sees Isabella, the song Tiny Tears by Tindersticks from 1995 begins. It opens with 'you've been lying in bed for a week now',[95] but, rather than depression per se, its subject

---

[93] Information provided by the National Health Service of the United Kingdom.
[94] Charles H. Brown 'Drug-induced serotonin syndrome'.
[95] Lyrics by Tindersticks.

is a broken relationship between a man and a woman and the poor communication between them. It can be interpreted as an indication of the state of Tony and Carmela's marriage, particularly 'you were too busy looking into your affairs to see those tiny tears in her eyes'. He has numerous affairs before and after this, but, at this point specifically, he is failing in his duties as a husband by losing himself in hallucinations of a beautiful woman who does not even exist.

As Tony is walking towards Isabella to introduce himself, he steps through an arch that seems out of place in a number of ways: the colour and style, where it is positioned, and the flowers that decorate it. The later discussion with Bruce reveals that, although there is an arch in the garden, it looks quite different, just a simple brown wooden construction, so it plays the role in Tony's hallucination of a gateway to an alluring encounter. In addition, there is no break in the fence which separates their properties, through which Tony apparently walks towards the new resident next door, and he in fact leans on the section which had disappeared when talking to Bruce.

At his next meeting with Isabella, he takes her to lunch, but the restaurant does not look like anything that one would find in or near to Newark. It is as if they have been transported to Italy, to which the conversation soon turns, as she somehow guesses correctly that his family are from the Avellino area, and then tells a story that is relevant to the stonemasonry trade of his grandfather. This supernatural knowledge is subtly emphasized by the choice of music that scores this scene, Milonga del Angel as performed by Al di Meola in 1996.[96] Milonga can be translated

---

[96] It was originally composed by Ástor Piazzolla in 1965.

as dance or music, but also colloquially as lie or falsehood. This angel sitting before Tony is not being truthful about her origins. The white curtains, billowing in the breeze, call to mind the same effect on the canopy when he first saw her in the garden of the Cusamano residence. The next scene interrupts the lunch, as Meadow shouts to him to come down to eat, and the switch is so pronounced it is as if Tony is being woken suddenly from a dream that he is having upstairs in his bedroom at home.

Another subtle clue that there is something not quite right about Isabella is that, on careful inspection, it can be seen that she does not speak to or interact with anyone else, not even during the lunch in public with Tony. She is also not referred to by anyone else, except Jennifer, and only then after he has realised that she was a hallucination.

Tony has a vision of Isabella nursing a baby, inside the type of stone house that his grandfather may well have lived in and built many of. She calls him Antonio. As Jennifer helps him to see by the end of the episode, although Isabella is beautiful, for a change this does not explain his interest in her. His mind is looking to fill the emotional gap left in his life by the woman who raised him. The point is emphasized by the dinner with Livia, his mother, which follows, in which she comments on his bad breath, shows no sympathy for his suffering, and mentions a woman from Pennsylvania who shot her children and set fire to their house. At the same time, she is aware of and encouraging the murder of the son with whose own children and wife she is eating, and later in the episode her own take on infanticide narrowly misses being realized.

The next time we see Isabella, she is again in the Cusamano garden struggling with the canopy. Tony is staring at her, but

Carmela sees what he is doing and is unsurprisingly angry, saying that she should emasculate him. This might sound like independent confirmation that Isabella is not a figment of his imagination, but, later on, after Bruce tells him that there was no Italian dental student staying at his house, Tony checks with Carmela and she denies that the conversation took place. With hindsight we can now understand why, when she opens the curtains in the bedroom, just before Tony stumbles to the window and sees Isabella for the first time, she makes no reference to there being anyone she does not recognize in her neighbours' garden.

After the imaginary conversation with Carmela, Tony visits Montclair. The area where the newsstand and the Donuts shop next door are situated is hardly rundown, but the yard behind the latter is not inviting, so it should be a surprise, if one is paying attention, to find him walking out of it, still with a dazed expression, through a door marked Montclair Physicians' Suites, and shortly afterwards finding him in an appointment with Jennifer. This is another clue that his hallucinations are continuing, but not in a way that will later receive explicit confirmation. We see the exterior of her offices at other times, such as in Meadowlands, when Sil visits a dentist on the same corridor, and we also know, from Employee of the Month (3.4), that when she leaves work she walks down a stairwell into an underground carpark. The supposed entrance in the rundown yard is not consistent with these at all. At a wake earlier, Michael 'Mikey' Palmice tells Junior that their hit on Tony will take place at a newsstand he uses by a medical centre, but it is not specified that this is where he has his appointments with Jennifer.

The therapy session looks at first glance identical to the many others that occur throughout the show. It takes place in her office, and they sit in their usual positions. However, there are three things that should give the viewer pause.

The first is how Tony is dressed: this is the only time that he has made no effort towards his appearance before meeting with Jennifer. For every other session bar none, no matter how bad he is feeling, he is always clean shaven and respectably dressed, at least in smart trousers and a short-sleeved shirt, often in a suit with or without a tie. Here he is dressed barely casually, his shirt unbuttoned so that his vest is visible, and he has not shaved. The obvious rejoinder to this is his current state of mental health, and that it should be no surprise that he has not paid close attention to his appearance, given that this is possibly the worst we get to see him during *The Sopranos* as a whole, with the exceptions of when he is incapacitated by food poisoning at the end of the second season, and in the aftermath of his shooting by Junior at the start of the sixth season. This is a fair point, but it should be remembered that both of those are also the occasion of potent dreams, and, furthermore, his condition here does point towards a more significant issue with the veracity of the session.

The second thing to note is how Tony refers to Isabella as a 'beautiful piece of cooz'. Although his language and behaviour in the presence of Jennifer are sometimes not of the highest standard, such as when he threatens her after she is critical of Livia in the following episode, I Dream of Jeannie Cusamano (1.13), or when she rejects his amorous advances in Two Tonys, it is most unusual to hear him talk about a woman this way in front of her. Perhaps this, too, could be explained by his current condition.

Nevertheless, the final aspect of note about the session is by far the most striking, and it relates to the fact that, of all the therapists who appear in the show, perhaps Elliot Kupferberg aside, who Jennifer is treated by, she is arguably the most professional. There are certainly question-marks over the practice of Wendi Kobler who Meadow visits in No Show (4.2), and Sandy Shaw who treats Janice in Christopher. Jennifer is not immune to error, but she makes an effort to avoid it, and apologises if it happens. She does have feelings for Tony of a sexual nature, and is in some sense personally dependent on treating him, but all that is in another league entirely from what she does here. She sees Tony looking dazed and dishevelled, hears him saying that he feels nothing, empty and dead: `like f***ing King Midas in reverse here, everything I touch turns to s***...I'm nothing'; and talking of shooting himself, and yet her response is to `push the Prozac to sixty milligrams'. What he is reporting are known and dangerous side-effects of Prozac use or overuse, and the last thing that she should be doing is increasing his dosage.[97] This is a serious lack of professional judgement, with potentially long-term and even fatal consequences, and not what we see from her at all other times.

This is the most powerful evidence that, fortunately for our view of Jennifer and her professional reputation, what we are seeing is not real. The final touch is added immediately afterwards, when we find that Tony has purchased the Prozac from an archaic establishment. It is a chemist that has been operating since 1907, and has in the window strange looking

---

[97]Sarah Boseley `Happy drug Prozac can bring on impulse to suicide, study says', *The Guardian*.

concoctions of different colours in bottles and vials of varying size and shape. There are handwritten 'open' and 'push' signs on the door and, overall, it does not look like the sort of place that anyone in their right minds would trust to provide them with medical services. Such businesses are still referred to as chemists in some countries, such as the UK, but in the USA they are known as pharmacies. Lo and behold, he then meets Isabella on the street outside the shop. This short scene strongly suggests that he is not only using his medication incorrectly, but also procuring it from disreputable sources.

When Tony calls Jennifer, after discovering that he had hallucinated Isabella and the conversation with Carmela, she tells him to 'discontinue the lithium'; his reply that he 'already flushed it' sounds laudable, but still demonstrates that he is making his own decisions about his treatment, as opposed to letting himself be directed by a qualified professional. This poor judgement is still evident three seasons later when, in The Strong, Silent Type (4.10), after the death of his horse Pie-O-My, he doubles his intake of Prozac without consulting her. To anyone who has not been paying attention, the direction by Jennifer would sound like she is admitting that the earlier experiment with increased medication was a failure, but that was Prozac, not lithium. Either she is such a poor doctor that she cannot even keep track of which drugs she is giving to her patients, or, more likely, she never told him to take more Prozac, and the lithium she is referring to is what she directed him to take a while ago, before this period of intense depression began. This prescription of lithium by her is not seen directly, but is suggested early in the episode: as already noted, he tells Carmela that he is taking it as directed by Jennifer, and a container with the official sticker is seen in his bathroom cabinet. Both of these, however, could be hallucinations.

After he survives the attempt on his life ordered by Junior, he is taken by Carmela to meet Jennifer, not in her office as usual, but in her car in an undisclosed location. She is wearing casual clothes, and it is clear that the meeting is at his request, because he is intent on knowing whether she has told anyone that he is her patient. He makes references to what he believes to be his previous meeting with her, that survival gave his system 'a kick-start', the same phrase that she used to explain the increased Prozac she was prescribing; he refers to saying he wanted to kill himself, and he mentions Isabella and his dream of her with the baby. However, although Jennifer helps him to understand that Isabella is a mother-replacement, she does not respond to any of the references with familiarity. She is new to this conversation, because the earlier part took place only in the imagination of the man she is treating.

As Tony is having an ongoing hallucination of a beautiful Italian woman who cares for and listens to him, it is no surprise that another beautiful woman of Italian heritage who treats him in a similar way, albeit in a professional capacity, should appear. He talks more to Jennifer about things that are very personal to him than anyone else, his wife, friends and lovers included. Her importance in his life is shown in a number of ways, such as appearing in other of his dreams, including more than once in Funhouse (2.13), and her ending of her treatment of him occurring in the penultimate episode The Blue Comet, not long before he dies. He also allows her to say critical and challenging things to him repeatedly, such as 'you've caused much suffering yourself, haven't you?' in The Strong, Silent Type. When she refuses his romantic overtures in Two Tonys, she explains why: she tells him that she could not 'sit silent' over his lifestyle, does not like his values, including the way he treats women and others generally, and remarks that he is 'not truthful'. In response, he shouts 'f*** you!' in her face, and 'you're a f***ing c***' as he storms out; others who have hurt his feelings in this way have been on the receiving end of much more injurious treatment.

As can be seen now, this hallucinatory appointment that Tony imagines with Jennifer is cleverly delivered, not least because it is sandwiched in the middle of another hallucination that our attention is focused on. The presentation at that particular point in the episode lulls us into thinking that it is really happening. After all, if Tony is experiencing symptoms of depression and other psychological difficulties, who else would he turn to? By this point in the show, it is a given that Jennifer's psychiatric skills will be called upon, as she has already helped him to make progress with what ails him, by prescribing suitable medication and highlighting the destructive impact of Livia on his life. This assumption, on the part of the viewer that the writers have created, is utilized for a narrative sleight of hand trick that, even to this day, is missed by those who have watched the show multiple times or even written about it. Given that it is explicitly stated that Tony's perception is affected by over-use of his prescription medication, the viewer should be wary of taking anything they see in Isabella as reality, not just the titular character herself. Taking seriously Chase's influence, by filmmakers such as Lynch, Kubrick and Bergman, means always being open-minded about the nature of the narrative that is being depicted. Here a scene that purports to be a standard narrative of objective events turns out to be, not a dream like Made in America, but a drug-induced deceptive state of consciousness, and hence a different kind of hidden story.

The hallucination in Isabella is also part of the pattern visible in Made in America, in that it conforms to the Freudian distinction between the manifest and latent contents of dreams. From the point of view of the former, it appears to be nothing but a pleasurable experience for Tony, containing his developing relationship with a beautiful young woman. However, peer below the surface, and one sees the emotional pain that conjures up this hallucination: the fear that he has been betrayed by his best friend, and the long-term dysfunctional behaviour of Livia.

Isabella plays the role of the beautiful assistant of the magician. The writer uses her to hold our attention while the main trick is performed, namely, to temporarily obscure the fact that she is a figment of Tony's imagination, but also to hide a second more subtle trick that the writer does not announce or reveal to the audience. In this respect, Isabella serves a similar function to the sentient robot Ava in the 2014 film *Ex Machina*, written and directed by Alex Garland. The premise is that computer programmer Caleb Smith is given the opportunity to visit the home of Nathan Bateman, a reclusive billionaire, who tells him that he wants him to spend time with his creation Ava, to help him to decide whether it is truly conscious and capable of thought. It soon becomes clear that things are not as straightforward as he has been led to believe. *Ex Machina* is a fascinating and complex film, and it turns out that Ava is not the only robot, although this is not explicitly revealed.

Caleb is initially under the impression that Nathan wishes him to apply what has come to be known as the Turing Test (Alan Turing, from whom it takes its name, began by referring to it as the imitation game).⁹⁸ This takes the form of a human observing a conversation between another human and a computer, whilst being unaware which is which; this requirement, however, rules out Caleb as he knows that Ava is a robot, and therefore cannot operate as an independent third party. By the strict definition of the Turing Test it is not possible for it to be run in the context *Ex Machina* takes place in, but there is a not too dissimilar challenge facing the audience, and to pass it requires spotting a number of subtle clues.

Caleb always wears blue, until he makes a startling discovery, after which he opts for darker shades. His earliest memory involves the colour blue, and the name of the company that supposedly he works for, and Nathan owns, is Blue Book. He has no brothers or sisters and both of his parents are dead. Nathan asks many questions of Caleb, and is more interested in his emotional reactions to Ava than his rational conclusions: 'I want to have a beer and a conversation with you, not a seminar…Answer me this: how do you feel about her? Nothing analytical, just…how do you feel?' During his interview sessions with Ava, Caleb is sitting in the smaller area as if he is the primary object of scrutiny. One of the central themes of the film is anthropomorphism, the tendency of people to ascribe human characteristics to non-human phenomena; this is not something that computers are usually prone to. In treating Ava as a person rather than a robot, as a she rather than an it, he succumbs to this mistake. This is why Nathan quizzes Caleb about his response to the painting *5, 1948* by Jackson Pollock: a consciousness bordering on the human may be able to find order among the chaos. Along similar lines,

---

⁹⁸See his 1950 article 'Computing Machinery and Intelligence'.

on a hike with Nathan, Caleb stares at a glacier intently, and, if the viewer does the same, the head of a giant snake appears in the ice dominating the screen.

The decisive clue to there being something unusual about Caleb is what he does to investigate his own nature: he uses a razor blade to cut deeply into his arm. Blood runs and he pokes the wound with his fingers, but shows no sign that he is feeling pain. This is the shocking discovery, though it is not explicitly confirmed: Caleb realises that, like Ava, he is an artificial intelligence, but one composed of flesh and blood, one who thinks and reacts much more like humans do.

This is not the end of the challenge for the audience, however. There is one more artificial human left to be revealed, and this occurs, again only implicitly, after Ava escapes from its confinement. Nathan overpowers her, but is stabbed in the back by another robot Kyoko. The blade is pushed into the hilt at or near to his spine, but he remains standing and manages to hit Kyoko hard. Ava then pulls out the blade and pushes it fully into his chest; again he remains upright, and staggers a significant way down the corridor before collapsing. Blood is visible from both wounds, but it does not spurt out from the pressure of the heart pumping, as would be expected, but leaks out, as if from a container of still liquid. His reaction is more akin to extreme shock than pain. The words he speaks are those of an artificial being who has realised that he is not human after all: 'okay... f***ing unreal'.

In *Ex Machina* there are two artificial intelligences masquerading as humans: Caleb and Nathan, and both draw on the distraction caused by Ava to hide from the audience and themselves. The true role of Ava for the viewer is alluded to earlier, and described in a conversation where Caleb asks: 'did you give her sexuality as a diversion tactic?...Like a stage musician with a hot assistant?' Nathan replies: 'A hot robot who clouds your ability to judge your AI?' In addition to those already outlined, Garland makes use of other traditional cinematic techniques to communicate to the audience on levels below that of the main events and dialogue. One to watch out for is reflection in mirrors and glass walls, which invites the question: is the person who we think they are? The compound in which Caleb meets Nathan has many reflective surfaces, as does the Blue Book office at the beginning of the film.

Ex Machina uses much of the same cinematic language of signs and symbols that is used for the hidden stories in *The Sopranos*. It can be discerned in the lack of explicit confirmation of the hallucinatory nature of the appointment with Jennifer in Isabella, and in the revealing of the bigamy of Patsy in Mergers and Acquisitions. But whereas the latter is only an amusing titbit about a character who is rarely in the foreground, the former is more significant. It is one more insight into the mind of the central character and his misuse of drugs, and, in that way, it is reflective of something integral to the plot, not just of this episode but *The Sopranos* in its entirety, because Tony has a habit, destructive both to himself and others, of overindulging in all sorts of pleasures, from food and alcohol to women and gambling.

As another of the hidden stories embedded within *The Sopranos*, it is therefore vital to understanding the finale correctly. Even though the appointment with Jennifer is a drug-fuelled waking hallucination that takes place in the yard behind the Donuts shop or in the nearby streets, rather than a product of Tony's sleep, the link is profound. The fact that there has been no recognition of this goes some of the way to explaining why Made in America is misunderstood to this day. The nearest that previous commentators have got is when Imperioli and Schirripa look a little confused when agreeing that Tony must take a 'back doorway' to Jennifer's office from the yard behind the Donuts shop, without comprehending the ridiculousness of it.[99]

---

[99] *Talking Sopranos* 12, 36.59.

Chapter Five
So Much Tragedy in Your Life

The habit of Chase of secreting hidden stories in the narrative of *The Sopranos* can also be discerned through close attention to the most recent addition, the 2021 prequel film *The Many Saints of Newark*. It focuses on the life of Richard 'Dickie' Moltisanti, father of Chris and something approaching a surrogate father to the young Tony. He is one of the most successful members of what is at that time called the DiMeo crime family.

The Many Saints of Newark is a story from beyond the grave told by Chris, who is murdered by Tony decades after the time of the events depicted. This supernatural perspective is reinforced when, in 1972, at a family meal, the teenage Tony laments that the toddler Chris always cries when he is around him, and an old female relative tells him that babies can know all sorts of things from 'the other side' that they bring with them at birth. The dead narrator trope is one that has been used many times in literature, and in other films, such as *American Beauty* (1999), *Casino* (1995), whose director Martin Scorsese has had a great influence on Chase, and *Sunset Boulevard* (1950), a personal favourite of Lynch, another filmmaker admired by Chase.

At the beginning of the film Dickie takes young Tony to greet his father, Aldo 'Hollywood Dick' Moltisanti, on his return from Italy with a young bride called Giuseppina. She is a dark-haired beauty, and, as Tony stares at her, it is easy to see the moment as the beginning of his life-long fascination and troubles with others of her ilk. Aldo, it is quickly discovered, is belligerent, coarse and hot-tempered. At the Confirmation party for Janice, he shows the priest a photo of his new wife in a bikini. At Satriales, he tells the rest of the crew a story about two members of the Rat Pack, Frank Sinatra and Dean Martin, feeding laxatives to a donkey and releasing it into a party to see it 'kicking and shitting over everybody', after which he laughs loudly and obnoxiously.

Aldo seduced Giuseppina with romance and dreams of a better life in the USA, but once there he becomes unloving and cruel. He is dismissive of her first steps in learning English. He yells at her for leaving her douchebag in the shower, drags her out of bed and then kicks her down the stairs. Dickie later confronts him about this, and it is learned through the argument that he did the same to his first wife, Lena, Dickie's mother (and also the sister of Hugh DeAngelis, the father of Carmela); he also beat Dickie regularly when he was a child. Things turn physical after he calls the women he married 'sluts', and the end result is Dickie killing him.

At the wake for his father Dickie is very troubled. He says to Junior, who has Giovanni 'Johnny Boy' Soprano as a brother (as well as Ercole, who never appears on screen), that he is alone now; Junior invites him to think of him as his brother from that point on, although the way that the film ends strongly suggests that there is not a great deal of authenticity to these words. Dickie's suffering is important to bear in mind in what follows, as it has already been noted, with respect to Tony in both Made in America and Isabella, that powerful emotions of this sort are used by Chase and the other writers to act as fertile ground for altered and deceptive states of consciousness. This is the latent content of dreams, that which lies hidden beneath and generates what is seen, although in *The Interpretation of Dreams* Freud focuses exclusively on those that occur during sleep.

Shortly afterwards, Dickie seeks out another member of his family: Salvatore 'Sal' Moltisanti, Aldo's twin brother. He has not been mentioned previously in the film and is in prison because, according to him, he murdered a fellow mobster. Dickie introduces himself, which suggests that they have never met before, or they have but it was some time ago. Sal has a different personality to Aldo, which may or may not be due to the experience of being incarcerated. He is thoughtful, insightful and listens carefully. When Dickie says he very much wants a son Sal warns him of the danger of wanting things too much, referencing Buddhism for this advice, interest in which had by this point, 1967, grown as part of the cultural developments in the USA. He listens to jazz and asks Dickie to bring him a copy of Miles Davis' 1957 album *Birth of the Cool*; Aldo preferred opera, which was heard in his car during his fight with Dickie. Sal does not converse with the other inmates: 'I mostly read all day.' In short, he is an unusual prisoner and mobster, and might end up being the type of father to Dickie that Aldo was not.

Unfortunately, in being just what Dickie needs Sal may be too good to be true. Careful attention to the way in which he is portrayed raises awkward questions. The first is: why does he not interact with any other character? Apart from Dickie this man is an island, and even he, according to his own testimony, was not allowed to visit him because Aldo forbade it, a statement which turns out to be true in a different sense to that in which it is first taken. In the three scenes he appears none of the other prisoners or guards demonstrate any awareness of his existence. Nor does anyone else from his family or crew visit or even mention him. Dickie does not discuss him with others, and, given that he finds the visits meaningful, one would expect him to mention them to his wife or mistress. The only other character in *The Sopranos* who is like this is Isabella who, as we know, is a figment of the imagination of Tony.

Another question relates to the need to explain how the insightfulness of Sal borders on telepathy. During their initial meeting, he seems to know that the account given by Dickie of the death of Aldo is false. In that which follows the murder by Dickie of his mistress Giuseppina following an argument, Sal asks him if he celebrated Christmas with his wife or mistress, and states that when he did it with his mistress there were always arguments. One instance of such unjustified knowledge claims would be odd, but two definitely requires further investigation.

The answer to both of these questions is that Sal exists only in the mind of his nephew. Here again the nature of the narrative presented to the viewer is not what it appears to be. It looks like a standard account of everyday events in a fictional world, but there is an extra layer of pretence that has been added. Reality did not provide Dickie with a meaningful role-model so he conjured up his own. Sal is Aldo 2.0, wiser and more helpful. He listens to him, offers him advice, and is even in tune with new trends in philosophy and music. This more open-minded and hipper version of Aldo is a replacement ordered by Dickie for the father he murdered. Sal first appears shortly after this highly traumatic event, and the third of his three visitations follows immediately upon another, the discovery that Giuseppina has betrayed Dickie by having an affair with Harold McBrayer, a rival and black gangster, and her murder which occurs as a consequence. After the first of these events, he tells Junior that he feels extremely lonely and this must intensify after the loss of another loved one, even though he murders them both himself.

In addition to this trauma, Dickie is subject to two other risk factors for hallucinations.[100] While driving during the outbreak of the Newark Riots, something is thrown at him by one of the rioters and he receives a wound to the head. He also drinks alcohol excessively, although this is more apparent later on in the film, and is probably no greater an intake than that of many of his peers. One of these in isolation increases one's chances of experiencing hallucinations, but all three so much the more. In the case of Tony, the risk factors which lead to him conjuring up Isabella are mental illness (anxiety), his misuse of prescription drugs (Prozac and lithium), trauma, or at least the fear of it (the disappearance of Big Pussy) and his dysfunctional relationship with Livia.

For whatever reason, Sal is the only person that Dickie is comfortable bearing his soul to. His comment that he wants to 'do a good deed' shows that he cannot admit to a lover or friend that he feels guilt over the way he lives. During their final meeting, Sal voices Dickie's questions about why bad things happen to good people, i.e., himself, before he does. Sal suggests Dickie

---

[100]https://my.clevelandclinic.org/health/symptoms/23350-hallucinations.

stay out of Tony's life, but there is no obvious reason why he would say that as there is no evidence that he has ever met him. Why show this concern for Tony? Because it is what is troubling Dickie, and his emotional turmoil is the foundation of all of the meetings with Sal. There is a shakiness to the camera that is easy to miss during this scene, representing this lack of balance inside Dickie.

One more piece of evidence that Sal does not truly exist is his vanishing act which brings down the curtain on the second meeting. As part of his drive to be a good person, Dickie tells him that he is coaching a baseball team of blind children; despite the reaction of Sal, Beep baseball became popular around the time the film is set and is now played globally. What appears at first to be a memory of Dickie begins, but as it unfolds it soon takes on the characteristics of a false reality: the events happen in slow motion, the children and parents chant his name, one of the mothers calls him 'a saint', and the accompanying music has an ethereal quality. There is nothing else in the film to suggest that Dickie actually devotes time to handicapped sport. When the sequence ends Sal is nowhere to be seen: either Dickie entered a one-off fugue state so deep that Sal could leave without him noticing or, more likely, one dream displaced another. Perhaps Sal disappears because Dickie fears that the other mobsters would ridicule him if they heard of his interest in Beep baseball; or it may be that he finds it a more comforting dream than one in which he converses with a murderer, and it is possible that this would have been the road his life took, had he not been executed.

Does the realisation that Sal does not really exist mean that Dickie actually visits a prison on at least three occasions, and talks to himself while the staff, inmates and visitors stare in amazement at him? This cannot be ruled out, but it is more likely that his presence in the prison is another part of the hallucination, conjured up in order to make it more believable to himself.

Sal is to Dickie what Jennifer is to Tony later: a friendly and supportive confidant to help him navigate the perils of the Mafia lifestyle. Unfortunately for Dickie, Sal is actually much more like Isabella, the unreal product of trauma and stress. Even the types of people who murder their family members and live off the suffering of others sometimes need someone to talk to. The intention of Chase is to put the viewer inside the mind of the central character of the film and to see his emotions at work. In this way, his inner turmoil is experienced in a more powerful way than relying only on his reporting or demonstrating it. To be taken in by a hallucination, as Dickie is, means that the reveal that it was only that has a greater impact, even if the truth is not explicitly proclaimed, but has to be inferred on the basis of subtle clues. No published commentator has managed to do this, although, as *The Many Saints of Newark* was released only a few years ago, this is more forgivable than the failure to spot the other hidden stories from the television series discussed in this book, some of which are over twenty years old.

There are numerous more subtle allusions to the overall theme to buttress the stories of the main characters. In a scene in the Soprano household, the 1948 film *Key Largo* is on the television, and Frank McCloud helps his enemy Johnny Rocco, other characters and those watching to understand that Johnny always wants 'more', and that no amount has ever been enough to satisfy him up to this point. Frank says that he gave up on his own hope of a world where Johnny, and by implication others like him, cannot be found. Later, Tony tells Mrs Jarecki, the guidance counsellor at his school, that every time his father goes to Yankee stadium, home of the New York Yankees baseball team, he comes home and moans about the lawn on their property.

The feeling of dissatisfaction that pervades humanity, that one does not have enough, even if one struggles, like Johnny Rocco, to articulate clearly what would qualify as enough, can be discerned in the activities of those who are drowning in riches and those who struggle to feed themselves, in the major decisions of life and the trivial. *The Many Saints of Newark* adds much to the analysis of this phenomenon that is offered in the original series.

Chapter Six
Oh Yeah?

In House Arrest, the eleventh episode of the second season, three of the main characters, Tony, Junior and Jennifer, find their freedom curtailed by a combination of forces external and internal to themselves. Their varying responses to their situations say much about how their stories develop during the rest of the show. The hidden story in this episode is at the same time the shortest and the most eye-popping of all those discussed in this book. Its author is Tony, and as such bears the hallmarks of his psychological profile. It is a mental and emotional response to the cage in which he finds himself, and serves as one of the smaller pieces of evidence offered that he has a limited ability to take on board and follow sensible advice.

Tony visits Mink, a lawyer of questionable integrity and a desire for the finer things in life. He gives him some champagne as a mark of his gratitude for support given during the recent investigation into the murder of Matthew Bevilaqua; this was committed by Tony and Big Pussy to avenge his attempted murder of Chris in Full Leather Jacket (2.8). In return, Mink gives him a 'lecture' about how close to arrest he was, and says that if he wants to give him a real gift he will heed his advice: 'insulate yourself from these shenanigans'. He suggests that, for the time being, it would be prudent for Tony to lay low and spend time at one of his front companies, ostensibly legal ones, such as Barone Sanitation.

It is Junior's situation, meanwhile, that in literal terms is the source of the title of the episode. Although he is advised to recuperate at home following a medical procedure, he has a more pressing reason to remain in his place of residence: the house arrest that has been imposed upon him by a judge. On leaving the hospital, Junior meets Catherine Romano, an old acquaintance and the widow of a cop he knew. Although he is pleased to see her, he is initially reluctant to socialise with her, partly because he does not want to tell her the real reason why he cannot leave the house, but also because he displays more interest in lively and sexual women. He laments the unwillingness of Bobbi to return his calls, which is unsurprising, given that, in Boca, he shoved a pie in her face and called her a 'stupid f***ing blabbermouth c***', on learning that she had been gossiping about the oral sex he gave her. There is a similar lack of interest in his advances from Tracy, the young nurse who treats him at home. She responds to his clumsy compliments politely, but he hears nothing after sending her a bottle of perfume.

However, as the episode progresses, Junior becomes more accepting of his situation, even after losing all of the manicott brought by Catherine to Bobby's endless hunger, enduring six hours with his hand stuck in the kitchen sink, and learning from Richard 'Richie' Aprile that Tony will not allow them to sell cocaine on their garbage routes. He invites Catherine to his home and spends time with her, although she does not appear again in the show.

Tony's first attempt to enact the advice from Mink finds him bored at home. He stares out of the lounge windows and the camera angle from above presents him like a fish in a bowl. On the radio is Dylan's 1979 song *Gotta Serve Somebody*, the lyrics of which state that, no matter who you are, at some point you will have to dance to someone else's tune. He turns to food for comfort, a habit that will not serve him well in the long term.

In a therapy session with Jennifer, before which she consumes alcohol to deal with the stress that this patient is causing her, Tony tells her that he is bored and can see no point in life. He even lost interest while watching the violent and shocking 1995 film *Seven*: 'what's the point? You go to Italy. You lift some weights. You watch a movie. It's all a series of distractions til you die.' Jennifer says that he sounds depressed, and he admits to not taking his medication. The root of his problem, as he sees it, is that he is barred from doing the things that give him pleasure.

As he finally arrives at Barone, his situation is mirrored by a savage, barking dog which is straining at its leash. Inside, Dick Barone, the owner of the company, introduces Tony to Connie DeSapio, who works in the office. He is immediately attracted to her, although there is no evidence that it is reciprocated, and his interest intensifies when Dick tells him that she is a born-again Christian: 'oh yeah?'. It is interesting to speculate on why this is. Perhaps it is because this comment about her morality means that she is in his eyes likely to be nurturing and caring, like Carmela, or even Isabella, his maternal substitute fantasy; or, on the other hand, he might see her virtue as a challenge, the overcoming of which will help to alleviate his boredom, in a manner reminiscent of the treatment of Madame de Tourvel by the Vicomte de Valmont in the 1782 novel *Dangerous Liaisons* by Pierre Choderlos de Laclos.

The next time we see Tony this enthusiasm has vanished. He is attending the Garden State Carting Association 13th Annual Couples Invitational Golf Classic with Carmela, Dick and his wife, Richie and Janice. He looks bored and depressed as Dick talks to him about the business, and the other conversations we eavesdrop on are similarly tedious. Tony interrogates Richie about selling the cocaine, telling him to stop immediately, lest it bring unwanted surveillance from the authorities; soon afterwards, he displays symptoms of a panic attack and collapses. It was not a coincidence that the writers chose the number thirteen for use in this scene.

Returning home from the hospital, where he is impolite to the doctor and receives advice on losing weight in return, his confinement continues. He has to refuse an invitation from Sil to come and see a hoard of World War Two memorabilia, presumably because it is stolen. Perspiring and stressed, he once again turns to food for comfort.

Back at Barone, Tony alleviates his boredom by sketching fish in a bowl on a notepad, thus making explicit the narrative clues from earlier, and scratching an angry-looking rash with a ruler. Unobtrusively, a logo of the company is visible. Connie asks him if he needs anything, but only in a way that is redolent of an amicable employee-boss relationship. He declines because nothing like that will satisfy his needs.

Concerned by the rash, Tony visits a different doctor, who tells him it is caused by stress, advising him to talk to his therapist about how to manage it. This obviously gives him an idea, as the scene cuts to Tony having vigorous and wild sex with Connie in the office at Barone. However, although he has many opportunities for extra-marital sex before and after this episode, there are reasons to doubt the authenticity of this particular instance and to conclude, not for the first or last time either, that the viewer is being fooled into taking the contents of a subject's mind as reality.

The first is the different arrangement of the office. The logo has changed, and the walls, furniture and equipment are much lighter in colour than before, an allusion to the temporary improvement in Tony's mood. An obvious rejoinder is that this could be another office at Barone, one of a number, but watching closely will allow one to spot on the desk the pad he was doodling on earlier, before Connie sweeps it away during the throes of passion; in so doing she is symbolically freeing him from his fishbowl.

Another clue is that Connie's style of clothing has changed. Before this scene, her clothes are standard and monochromatic, what one would expect from a born-again Christian who works in an office. But those she is (partially) wearing now are more striking, more in keeping with the desires of a bored mobster. Her top also has markings like those of a tiger; is this an early expression of Tony's lust for Adriana, which will be revisited in future seasons?

One also needs to consider the narrative isolation of the scene. There is no prior development earlier in the episode to justify Connie's involvement. Of course, this is the sort of thing that Tony indulges in on a regular basis, but it contradicts what has been learned, admittedly over a short period of time, about her. She demonstrated no interest in him beyond what could be interpreted as fulfilling the requirements of her job at Barone.[101] She is a born-again Christian, and although no one needs to be told that even (or especially?) the fervently religious can commit sinful acts, she does not give that impression. Every other time that Tony has sex it is provided with narrative justification or buildup: either it is his wife, a woman he has participated in suggestive chat with, a mistress, or one who takes money for her services. But not here, and before the sex scene Tony himself does not seem particularly interested in Connie when she asks if she can get him anything, so it must be noted that only when being introduced to her does he display any romantic interest. In line with this, soon afterwards life in the office is back to normal: Tony is organising a basketball pool for the office staff, until his relative contentment is buffeted by Dick telling him that the police have one of Richie's guys on video selling cocaine the night before.

The final reason to distrust what is happening is at the same time the most convincing and the likeliest to be missed: Tony's rash disappears! One does not need to be trained in medicine to realise that a rash of that size would take weeks to disappear, even with the correct medication, but there is no reason to believe that weeks have passed since the previous scene, and it was only then that the doctor diagnosed it. Even if that were put aside, and it is a big 'if', the rash is visible again in the final scene in Satriales, as Tony applies an electric shoe-cleaner to it in the hope that it will provide relief.

Taken together, these factors are a compelling justification for interpreting the sex scene between Tony and Connie as a fantasy on the part of the former, one of a number of ineffective

---

[101]Contrary to what Schirripa says at 01.05.03 in *Talking Sopranos* 24.

ploys to combat stress and boredom that he draws upon in the episode. It is likely that he imagines it as he is sitting in the doctor's consulting room at the end of the previous scene. None of them, bar the disappearance and reappearance of the rash, are impossible, but their cumulative weight means that the viewer is inside Tony's head as he is conjuring up a more appealing version of reality. This is, therefore, a similar type of hidden story to those discussed in previous chapters, a deceptive state of consciousness masquerading as a standard narrative; like them, it has been overlooked by commentators who universally take the sexual encounter between Tony and Connie to be as real as the other events in the episode. The intention of the writer, Winter, is to throw into stark relief the sheer boredom that plagues Tony, by showing what depths his mind will go to in order to experience pleasure.

During the fantasy there are, in addition to Connie's screams of pleasure and the sound of Tony slapping her thigh, also to be heard loudly the dog barking and a telephone ringing. The former is a clue that indicates that Tony is still on his leash, no matter how things look. His desires are still frustrated and so he is forced into an imaginary release for them. The latter is more ambiguous and open to different readings. Is it a sign of the limited persuasiveness of the fantasy, in that the boring tasks of everyday life will not stop nagging Tony, that the real world and its obligations are still there? Or is the unanswered call an indication that he is not getting the message, in other words, misunderstanding his situation? Or is it actually part of the joy of the fantasy, in that he is keeping this pretty young woman away from her dull duties? More than one, or all, of these could be accurate.

In the final scene, Tony succumbs to temptation and gleefully returns to Satriales and his crew. They are distracting themselves from the monotony of existence by chatting about moisturisers, eating, looking at pornography and gambling. Tony returning to them shows his limited ability to follow the sensible and informed advice of Jennifer and Mink, and the probable long-term consequences of this are seen when Agent Harris and his new partner turn up 'for a chat', which symbolises the ongoing interest of the FBI in the illegal activities of his crew. The last shot places the 'suckling pigs' prominently in the shot, suggestive of the uncontrolled greed which rules their lives and ruins those of others. The song that is heard is You Can't Put Your Arms Around a Memory by Johnny Thunders from 1978, the lyrics of which are expressive of Tony's experience: 'Feel so restless, I am...beat my head against a pole...'.

There is a more positive story in House Arrest to balance against Tony's fitful and ultimately unproductive resistance to his impulses. Not for the first or last time, Jennifer is presented as a realistic role-model in how she makes a decent effort to follow advice and deal with her issues sensibly. Her mind grounds itself more securely in reality in the way that that of her patient does not; ironically, it is he who is the source of her stress.

In her own therapy session with Elliot, Jennifer confesses that she is consuming alcohol between sessions on the days she sees Tony, something she is seen doing first-hand earlier. Treating him is taking a significant toll on her: 'I can't take it.' She likens it to 'watching a train-wreck. I'm afraid and repulsed by what he might tell me, but somehow I can't stop myself from wanting to hear it.' He strongly advises her to refer her patient to another therapist.

Jennifer is facing her own idiosyncratic form of house arrest, on a higher psychological level than those of Tony and Junior. Whereas they are constrained by external forces with which they have no sympathy, her predicament is the result of tension between different parts of her psyche. These include, but may not be restricted to, professional concern for her patient, morbid fascination by his confessions, and, although it is not explicitly mentioned at this point, sexual attraction towards him (as evidenced by her dream about him in Two Tonys). Unlike Tony, she has a developed sense of how satisfying personal desires may not be healthy or sensible.

The toll that it is having on her becomes clear in how she reacts to a woman smoking at a table next to herself and her son Jason in a restaurant. The practice is allowed in the establishment, but she argues with the woman, insults her and throws a napkin at her. The woman is rightly angry, Jason is embarrassed, and Jennifer is told to leave.

Eliot prescribes Luvox for her compulsive drinking and, despite an initial resistance to the suggestion, she appears to acquiesce and benefit from it. In a session with Tony, he comments that, unlike himself, 'still a miserable prick', she 'looks very mellow today', as if she is 'on drugs'. She is, but on a prescribed one, rather than alcohol. She has dealt with her stress and taken advice better than her patient does. While he is considering suicide ('ready for the George Sanders long walk here') she rediscovers the strength and courage to challenge his behaviour by telling him about the psychological phenomenon of alexithymia, which is common in people like him. They crave 'almost ceaseless action, which enables them to avoid acknowledging the abhorrent things they do.' After a few seconds of silence, Tony mentions

Richie, rather than his own behaviour, to the obvious annoyance of Jennifer. When he sees this, he asks 'what happens when these anti-social personalities aren't distracted from the horrible s*** they do?' She replies that they are forced into self-reflection about 'how what they do affects other people. About feelings of emptiness and self-loathing haunting them since childhood. And they crash.'

There are few people worthy of admiration in *The Sopranos*, but Jennifer is an exception to this. She makes mistakes and can be guilty of poor judgment, but she makes an effort to learn from them and grow. Even when she undergoes the most horrifying of ordeals in the next season, she displays remarkable fortitude and bravery.

Before concluding this chapter, it should be suggested that there is a fourth character who is dealing with their own version of house arrest. This is Richie, but he has no understanding of what it is, even though the door to his cage will be slamming shut in the very next episode, The Knight in White Satin Armour (2.12). Before that, he, Janice, Tony and Carmela are visiting a potential house purchase. A quiet word with him, about the prohibition against selling cocaine on the garbage routes, induces stress in Tony, who goes outside for fresh air. He looks back and sees Richie through a window, the bars of which make it look like he is in prison. 'Oh, you poor b***ard', laments Tony, but even he does not comprehend just how quickly life with Janice will bring Richie down.

Part Two

Satanic Black Magic

Chapter Seven
Focus on the Good Times

How certain characters behave is the next piece of evidence that points to Made in America being a dream that Tony has in the safehouse. More precisely, each of them acts in a manner that is inconsistent, either with how they have in recent episodes, or in the entirety of the time we have known them. No satisfactory explanation is offered for why this happens, and for this author this is the clearest indication that the nature of the narrative in the finale has been misunderstood. It is not a standard episode depicting events in the waking world.

As one expects in a drama, throughout *The Sopranos* changes are evident in all of the main characters. Sometimes this is in response to specific events. After the murder of her ex-boyfriend Jackie, Jr. in Army of One (3.13), Meadow becomes depressed, angry towards her father, and more aware and questioning of the influence that organized crime has in the life of her family. When Artie, Tony's friend since childhood, learns that it was he who ordered the burning down of his restaurant in the Pilot, albeit because he thought it was in his friend's best interests, given the plan of Junior to execute someone there, an understandable temporary dip in their relationship ensues, which sees Artie pointing a gun at Tony.

Other more significant changes can be discerned by looking over the entire run of the show. Chris begins as a young associate in the crew run by Tony, with ambitions of making a name for himself as a Hollywood screenwriter, and his story takes in serious drug abuse, his rise through the ranks to become a capo, two major relationships, the birth of a daughter, and finally murder at the hands of the man he once naively idolized. Despite his worry, expressed in The Legend of Tennessee Moltisanti, he does indeed have an arc. The same is true of Carmela, who is first seen as the mother of two teenaged children, who puts up with the infidelities of her husband because of the lifestyle she enjoys. Her story includes aborted infidelities of her own, including with her priest, attempting to wrest some of the responsibility for the family finances from her husband, growing resentment at his behaviour, which leads to them living apart for a while, and ending up as a widow.

What happens in Made in America, though, is quite different. Main characters who are integral to either the Mafia war, or Tony's personal life, behave in ways that are surprising or even startling. What is even more unusual is that no explicit reason is given for the changes. As noted before, one of the many strengths of *The Sopranos* is the quality of the writing from both the showrunner Chase and those he assembled to support him. Although some episodes are better than others, none are poor, and all are of a standard that puts the entire output of most other shows to shame. The writing in the finale, though, looks amateurish by comparison when judged by the standard of character consistency. So, what are these changes, why do they occur and why is there no obvious explanation? A clue is offered by Freud, when he states that dreams ' show a clear preference for the impressions of the immediately preceding days'.[102] What he means by this is what is referred to as the continuity hypothesis,[103] that dreams are perhaps most concerned with experiences that their author has had very recently, particularly in the time since they last slept: 'in every dream it is possible to find a point of contact with the experiences of the previous day.'[104] Therefore, to explain the inconsistencies, we should pay close attention to what happens to Tony in the run-up to the commencement of Made in America.

Perhaps the most noticeable change is that of AJ. Although in the first season he is presented as a fairly happy, although spoilt and mischievous, boy in his early teens, over the following seasons his personality gradually takes a turn for the worse. It is worth remembering that in the Pilot he celebrates his thirteenth birthday, which in hindsight is an omen for him.

He does not grow into the son that Tony hoped for. His behaviour at home and school deteriorates. In The Telltale Moozadell, he, along with some friends, break into their school one night and proceed to smash a glass cabinet of trophies and throw things from a nearby office into the swimming pool. Following his expulsion from school, after being caught cheating in a test in Army of One, he is on the verge of being sent to a military academy by his parents before collapsing from a panic attack, which causes them to reevaluate their decision. This first happens when he is playing football in Fortunate Son (3.3), the title of which is an ironic statement about what he has inherited

---
[102]Op. cit., p. 247.
[103]Michael Shredl 'Characteristics and contents of dreams'.
[104]Freud, op. cit., p. 249.

from his father's side of the family. He also has a panic attack in Johnny Cakes (6.8), after he fails in an attempt to take revenge for Tony by killing Junior, although the precise trigger is when he is later asked to help someone settle a dispute by bringing in his father. The attacks are related to a fear of responsibility and growth, and possibly a conviction that he will never be the son that Tony wants him to be, and are to be borne in mind during the events of Made in America. AJ also falls into full-blown depression, and attempts suicide, after he is dumped by his girlfriend Blanca Selgado in Chasing It (6.16).

As the story develops, his behaviour and personality become more and more reminiscent of his grandmother, somewhere between Borderline Personality Disorder and psychopathy. This is evident back in the first season, when Meadow comments on his lack of concern for his father after the failed murder attempt in Isabella, and in less noticeable ways, such as when he gives Carmela for her birthday the DVD of the 1999 science fiction film *The Matrix*, something he would have more interest in watching than her, in The Telltale Moozadell. It reaches a nadir when, in Walk Like A Man (6.17), he helps a group including Jason Gervasi and Jason Parisi, sons of members of Tony's crew, to hold down a student who owes them money, while they pour sulphuric acid on his toes; but the unpredictability of his personality means that when, in Kennedy and Heidi, the same group beat up a Somalian youth, his initial enthusiasm turns to shock and sadness at the human condition.

This downward curve for his personality continues right up until the penultimate episode. When Tony tells him and Carmela that they need to leave the house because of the war breaking out with the New York Mafia, he reacts like a scared and self-absorbed child. It is important to remember that this is Tony's last experience of his son before he retreats to the safehouse, and the memory looms large over what follows.

It is all of this that puts a huge question-mark over his demeanour and behaviour in Made in America. Before this episode, he very rarely appears in the dreams of his father. This is undoubtedly because of the disappointment of how he has turned out; indeed, he is most visible briefly in The Test Dream, when this is verbalised. Anyone who has been paying attention to his arc will be very surprised at what they see in the finale.

His relationship with Rhiannon is blossoming, despite him telling his parents they are only friends. In his car they listen appreciatively to the Dylan song and attempt sex. He enjoys TV and snacks on the couch with her, but does not forget to respond to Carmela's greeting when she enters. He is doing chores as requested. He is interested in the state of the world, and not afraid to call out its hypocrisy using a quote from W.B. Yeats' 1919 poem The Second Coming. He jogs. He has the confidence to consider joining the army, not only because it will improve his career prospects, but also because 'this country is in a crisis', not fazed by the prospect of being sent to Afghanistan. He buys CDs to learn the Arabic language, a skill that we later see Agent Harris has. This is all in stark contrast to the horror he expressed at the thought of being sent to the military academy when he was younger, which led to a panic attack.

When his parents berate him for the loss of his car he takes it calmly, stating that their refusing to buy him a replacement is a good thing, because of America's dependence on foreign oil. Later, he tells his therapist that he feels 'cleansed', but not because of it not being able to pollute the atmosphere anymore;

he does not say why exactly, but gives the impression that he has realized that contentment does not consist in owning such things. He participates meaningfully in his therapy sessions. He takes part in a mature conversation with his parents about their resistance to him joining the army. This is doubly surprising because they too manage to keep their heads, something that is unusual in the Soprano household when delicate subjects are being discussed. He thinks carefully about the offer to work on the development of a movie under Little Carmine, and takes it up.

All of this culminates in the positive outlook he evinces in Holsten's. He has called to tell his parents that he is on his way. Although he gripes about being given unfulfilling tasks at work, he does not reject out of hand their more upbeat interpretations of his employment status. Even when his 'focus on the good times' leads to his father telling him to not be sarcastic, he takes the misreading of his intention in good spirit, and echoes the advice that Tony gives to him, Meadow and Carmela, when they are sheltering from the storm at Artie's restaurant at the end of the first season: 'try to remember the times that were good'. An alternate phrasing of this is used by Carmela in conversation with Tony in Live Free or Die (6.6): 'accentuate the positive.'

Something is amiss here. For a writing team that has received so much praise, during and after the initial run of *The Sopranos*, this is poor, and doubly so given Chase's own experience of therapy. AJ's deep emotional problems and mental illness have been brushed aside, without his remarkable and speedy recovery being given due treatment and explanation. Is the viewer expected to conclude that all that someone in his position needs is a new girlfriend and job, a session with a friendly therapist, and a meal with the family for a quick turnaround? The idea is laughable and suggests no understanding of what is faced by those suffering from emotional and mental turmoil.

One thing is clear and that is that the writing team are not this bad, so how should the marked difference in AJ, in such a short space of time, be interpreted? As wish-fulfilment on the part of his father. We are not seeing AJ as he really is, but only as Tony wants him to be; the AJ we see in Made in America is a creation of a dreaming mind. Even though Tony is not a trained medical professional, if he were thinking clearly about his son he would know that the scale and speed of recovery presented in this episode is just not possible. But he is not. He is asleep on the bed in the safehouse, where he has remained since we saw him drifting off at the end of The Blue Comet.

His most recent memory of AJ was him crying like a child, when he was told that Bobby had been murdered and the family needed to go to safety. As the boss of a Mafia family who is expected to display strength and courage in the face of adversity; as a therapy patient who expresses loathing for those modern American men, including himself, who do not live up to the standard of the strong, silent type set by Gary Cooper; and as a father of Italian heritage, with the cultural value placed on sons, there is no possibility that he would not react vehemently to this. He drags AJ out of bed to the floor, berates him for his weakness, and later his dreaming mind expresses the hopes for his son that, when awake, he knows there is little chance of ever being realized.

As part of the process, his subconscious picks on details and regurgitates them in a haphazard way. For example, AJ's interest in global politics comes from Tony seeing the website of the

Jamestown Foundation on the computer in his bedroom as he leaves, but not realizing that Rhiannon was the one reading it. When she earlier recounts to AJ a story about the transportation of nuclear material, his only response is a lethargic 'f***'. In a similar way, in the previous episode, after returning home, he watches a war documentary on television, but one that is characterised more by action and explosions than thoughtful analysis. The AJ of Made in America is in truth partly Rhiannon because of a simple mistake on the part of Tony.

A trace of the waking despair over his son seeps through in the penultimate scene. In the room when Tony visits Junior is a young man sitting nearby. Dressed shabbily, unshaven and with unkempt hair, he gives the impression of someone suffering greatly from mental illness. He is perfectly framed in the mirror on the far wall, and is also in shot as Tony is leaving; this implies that he is not just there to make up the numbers. He bears a strong resemblance to AJ, and is therefore an expression of Tony's ambiguous feeling towards his son. He wants his son to grow into a healthy adult who would do him proud, hence the implausibly optimistic depiction of him that dominates this episode; but he fears that there is no chance of this happening, and this generates the appearance of AJ in the psychiatric facility where his mind has also placed Junior.

Chase has not done an amateurish job of writing this episode, or left the staggering difference in AJ, his discovery in the space of one episode of joy in life, manners and a new personality, unexplained. He just has not given a straightforward answer to the questions raised about these characters, but it is one that, if the viewer is paying attention, is in line with artistic techniques used often before by him. Let us use this discovery to see what light it sheds on two other conspicuous cases of unexplained character change, the boss of the New York Mafia Phil and his underboss Butch.

Phil first enters the narrative at the beginning of the fifth season when he is released from prison, along with Tony's cousin Tony B, Michele 'Feech' La Manna and Angelo Garepe. At this point he is a capo, but it is not long before events and his own ambition conspire to make him the boss of the Lupertazzi family. Two bosses are moved out of the way in quick succession: Carmine, Sr. dies of natural causes, then his underboss and successor, John 'Johnny Sac' Sacrimoni, is arrested and dies in prison from lung cancer.

Phil is an intense and determined man with a nature unsuited to compromise, who tends to dwell on perceived insults and injustices. The nickname 'Shah of Iran', used because of a resemblance to Mohammad Reza Pahlavi and which is only uttered behind his back, riles him. He is ruthless in his support of the bid for power of Johnny Sac, and even more so in pursuit of revenge against Tony B for the murder of his brother William 'Billy' Leotardo. Even once Tony B is dead the resentment lingers, and is not helped by the discovery that Vito Spatafore, a capo in the Soprano family who he is related to by marriage, is homosexual. Phil hunts him down and watches him being beaten to death, even though he knows that this will do nothing to improve relations with Tony.

A heart attack causes him to stand back from operations for a while, but an insult by the presumptive boss of New York, Faustino 'Doc' Santoro, provides him with fresh motivation. He arranges for him to be murdered and becomes the boss himself. Things turn sour with the Soprano family when Coco intimidates and sexually harasses Meadow while she on a date with Patrick, and in revenge Tony gives him a vicious beating which includes a curb stomp. In response, Phil launches a war against the New Jersey family, 'nothing more than a glorified crew' in his eyes and those of his predecessor Carmine, Sr., in The Blue Comet.

Butch first appears in Kaisha (6.12) as a capo, but is promoted to underboss when Phil takes over. He is of a similar mindset in that he is not one to give ground, and leans towards action rather than negotiation to solve disputes. In the aftermath of the murder of Vito, Butch favours killing Tony or another member of his crew, and, when Tony visits Phil in the hospital after his heart attack, Butch needles him. In The Second Coming, Tony and Little Carmine visit Phil's house in the hope of reconciliation, but Butch takes great delight in refusing them entry. He is perfectly suited to serving under the current head of the Lupertazzi family.

The war promises to be short and disastrous for Tony. His brother-in-law and underboss Bobby is murdered while buying a toy train, a Blue Comet, which also provides the episode with its title. There is a very apposite double meaning to this: comets throughout history have been believed to be harbingers of doom, and blue is often used to connote depression; as such, it is one of many subtle clues in the final season that things are not going to end well for Tony. Not long afterwards, Sil and Patsy are attacked on leaving the Bada Bing!, with the former being shot multiple times, about which Paulie later reports that the 'doctors don't think he'll recover consciousness'. This leaves Tony with a skeleton crew of only Paulie, Carlo Gervasi, Dante 'Buddha' Greco and Walden, five men against the might of a New York Mafia family. Others, including Patsy and Benny, are presumably out there, but they are not seen at this point as they retreat to the safehouse.

This is the context for an analysis of the presentation of Phil and Butch in Made in America. Despite the fact that they have severely weakened Tony's position, there is a very surprising change in their attitude. The first time we see them is when Phil calls Butch, who is in the Little Italy area of New York. Phil is worried that there has been no progress in finding Tony and is disappointed in the efforts of his underboss. Butch then suggests offering a truce, which Phil rejects out of hand, saying that they 'can't go back', which sounds like it is based more on believing that Tony would reject it, rather than it being ridiculous, given the strong situation they are in. Phil puts the phone down on him mid-sentence and clearly their relationship is souring. We hear from the FBI listening to Tony's phone call with George Paglieri, the boss of one of the other New York Mafia families, that Butch is not happy with Phil and is open to being reached out to.

A meeting is arranged by George, and with him present Tony and Paulie discuss terms with Butch, Little Carmine and Albert 'Albie' Cianflone, who is consigliere to Phil. George has never been seen or even mentioned before, so his appearing out of nowhere to do something that is very helpful to Tony raises the suspicion that he does not exist outside of this dream. His surname is also that of a famous Italian perfume company[105], a possible allusion to his helping to make things smell artificially sweeter for Tony. That the meeting is happening at all is odd enough, but the tone is even stranger. Tony has the upper hand, criticizing the management style of Phil, and talking to Little

---

[105] www.paglieri.com/en.

Carmine like he is a lackey. Butch concedes that 'it has gone too far'. Tony says that his price is them helping him to find Phil, which Butch says he cannot do, but nor will he get in the way of the payback. The position of strength enjoyed by Tony in this meeting, that it is him naming his price and not Butch, and that he also gets restitution for his sister Janice because of the murder of her husband Bobby, is completely illogical.

The execution of Phil happens at a petrol station. He is spending time with his wife and grandchildren, acting like he does not have a care in the world, rather than participating in a war between Mafia families. He does not mention it, pays no attention to his surroundings for fear of attack, and only gives instructions for his wife when she is at the drugstore. Again, this makes no sense at all. In the previous episode he was ultra-cautious, going into hiding approximately 'four or five days', according to Sil, before Tony decided to go to war, but here he is careless in the extreme and pays with his life.

As an aside, a similarly careless attitude is demonstrated earlier by Meadow, who is leaving the family safehouse as Tony arrives because she is meeting Patrick in the city. She, AJ and Carmela are concerned for their safety, but she is going into New York, where the enemy are based, and neither of her parents comments on this. If there is no reason to be worried, then why are they in hiding?

There is a profound but unexplained difference in Phil and Butch. At the end of The Blue Comet, they were already in a commanding position in the war, having quickly taken out two of their three targets, so it makes no sense at all that they are now unsure of themselves and at odds with each other. Either the writer of the episode has had a lobotomy, or there is something the viewer is missing. Phil and Butch behave in Made in America in noticeably different ways than at any time they have appeared before; it is as if they have had personality transplants without any accompanying explanatory mechanism. But an explanation has been provided, if the viewer is watching sufficiently closely to spot it: the change is due to the fact that Tony is dreaming. What we are seeing is not the real Phil and Butch, but only distorted memories of them taking part in an exercise in wish-fulfilment.

There are behavioural anomalies in Made in America not just with major characters, but also with ones who have never been central to the plot previously. Agent Harris plays a key role in helping Tony to win the war, but this is a new side to him. In The Sopranos, he is initially assigned to the task force tackling organized crime, in which he has an on the ground role that makes him the most senior figure that the New Jersey Mafia usually meet face to face. He executes search warrants, makes arrests and oversees the bugging of the Soprano family home in Mr. Ruggerio's Neighbourhood. He is at all times calm, professional and polite with those he is investigating, even when they are insulting in return to him or his team.

He is respected by his colleagues in the FBI, and, after the September 11th, 2001 attacks, he is reassigned to counter-terrorism and makes requests of both Tony and Chris to pass on any relevant information they come across. Any positivity shown towards Tony and his crew is within the context of his commitment to his work and never undermines that. In Kaisha, he tells Tony that he has heard that he or someone in his crew might be in danger, but this is not a special favour, rather, standard practice by law enforcement agencies in the USA and other countries when they receive information about a threat against the life of a criminal or anyone else.

Towards the end of the show, a certain amount of mutual respect is evident between Agent Harris and Tony, and it may be that if they had met in different circumstances they could even have been friends. In the Blue Comet, Tony sees Agent Harris in Satriales and asks him what happened to 'the Arabs' from the Bada Bing! he passed on information about, but he does not know and nor does he give the impression he would tell if he did. Despite Tony saying 'go f*** yourself!' and walking off, he catches up with him outside and tells him that his life in danger. This is important for his depiction in Made in America, but what Tony does not see is that Harris looks to be in two minds inside before he decides to pass on the information; his dreaming mind only has the warning to play with. As with AJ, the construction of Harris in the finale is based on limited information.

The Agent Harris that appears in Made in America is something different entirely. He meets Tony secretly at night and asks 'what's up, my friend?'. His polite front to the Mafia in the past was not to be confused with friendship. He is highly professional in his pursuit of criminals, never before either treating Tony as a friend or referring to him as one. It is soon evident from a phone call that he has domestic troubles, but this too is a new side to him, and an unjustified leap from him telling Tony in the previous episode that his counter-terrorism work is limiting the time he can spend with his children. After Tony has visited Janice, he receives a phone call from Harris, telling him about 'multiple calls traced back to a payphone at Oyster Bay, Long Island', which is probably at a gas station. We immediately see Benny and Walden watching one. Harris made this call from what looks like a hotel room, where he has just had sex with a female colleague, from which it can be concluded that he is having an affair, although they do not seem to be enjoying each other's company. He calls while she is in the bathroom and ends it as she comes out, so his help for Tony is a secret both from his job and mistress.

In short, Agent Harris is not the professional, calm and self-assured man that we have come to know before this episode. How can this be? Because this is not the Agent Harris we are familiar with, rather, it is the man that Tony needs him to be. He is in a desperate situation and his sleeping mind is crying out for help. That is why Harris is suddenly his friend, greeting him as such, and later gleefully reacting to the news of the death of Phil with 'damn, we're gonna win this thing!'. He is keeping a dangerous secret from his colleagues and mistress. That is why he is so pleased with the tip about possible terrorism, it means that he is benefitting from this relationship with Tony and is therefore more likely to continue giving his valuable support.

More evidence that all is not right with this portrayal of Harris is very easy to miss. When he is given the news about Phil, his desk calendar gives the date as March 28th 2005, which is over two years ago, if this episode is taking place on its date of broadcast of June 10th 2007. No news items from that date seem to have any significance to the storyline, but this can at the least be taken as an indicator that the highly professional and organised FBI Agent is missing in action.

Harris is under pressure, harried and struggling to meet the demands that his life is making. He needs a win from anywhere, and this is not the first time this has been true of acquaintances of Tony, whether they be other law enforcement officers, such as Vin Makazian, or people he has known for a long time, such as

David 'Davey' Scatino. Why would anyone with options choose to spend time or make deals with a murderous, lying psychopath? The possibility that Tony may not have any real friends, only people who need him or want something from him, is explicitly raised by Carmela in All Happy Families... (5.4). It is sad to see, but not surprising given what we know about him, that his best friends might be imaginary.

The final example of a character presenting a new side to the viewer is Mink. He is Tony's lawyer and is good at what he does, although he displays no qualms about helping criminals out of trouble with the law, or even advising them on how to avoid it in the first place. He is insistent on the need for Tony to limit his exposure to surveillance from the authorities and pass these risks on to his subordinates. He enjoys the finer things in life, such as expensive suits, cigars and liquor.

Although Made in America is not the first time that Mink visits Tony at the Bada Bing!, the majority of their previous meetings are in his office or at a golf course. He is not here the professional lawyer, focused on the job at hand, that we are used to seeing. His attention is distracted by getting the ketchup out of the bottle, the waitress who brings their food, and the naked women on the security monitors overhead. A lack of continuity that is very easy to miss is that the security monitors are a new addition to the room, not there in the previous episode during the conversation between Tony and Sil, or at any time before. The food Mink is eating is out of keeping with his preference for the finer things: as with Carmela in Holsten's, as will be discussed later, he is being served from Tony's menu.

Like the appearance of Agent Harris, this too is not as it seems. This is not Mink, but a representation of him in Tony's sleeping mind. His subconscious is crying for help, in the face of the terrible situation his life has come to, and generates positive images. There is less creative licence required here than in the representation of Agent Harris, because, unlike him, Mink has helped Tony in the past and been happy to do so, albeit on receipt of the payment of his fees. That is why the viewer must look beyond Mink simply offering Tony help for evidence that something is amiss.[106]

There is therefore a pattern in Made in America of characters that have appeared previously, some significant and others less so, behaving in ways that we are not accustomed to. Unless we are prepared to accept that Chase and his team have suddenly had their minds wiped and forgotten about who their characters are, an alternative explanation is necessary. Thankfully, this episode provides one that is based upon story-telling techniques that have been used numerous times before in the show, either in dreams or in waking life, but it is overlooked by commentators, who see nothing unusual in the differences in AJ, Phil, Butch and Agent Harris, and do not even spot that in Mink at all.

As the references to Freud suggested, the appearances of these characters are at the mercy of the emotional responses by Tony to his recent experiences, and the situation he finds himself in, as he lies down on the bed at the end of The Blue Comet. The intention of Chase is to put the viewer inside the head of the central character, and in so doing to make evident

---

[106] Bernard makes the claim that 'it somehow feels very typical of him' that he should be distracted by the women, even though he has never behaved like this in the past. He also misses the fact that the monitors are an unexplained new addition to the room; *op. cit.*, 'Made in America'.

the desperation that he is feeling. Tony has nowhere to turn and no one who can save him from the attack by Phil and Butch; he is resigned, even though he does not know it, to being taken in by sleeping fantasies.

Chapter Eight
A Beautiful, Innocent Creature

One of the factors that finally leads to Jennifer ending her therapeutic relationship with Tony is reading the research on criminal personalities by Samuel Yochelson and Stanton Samenow.[107] This study suggests that therapy can actually help people like him to become better criminals, in that they play along and simulate emotions to beguile their therapists, and then apply these insights to their criminal lives. In Meadowlands, Tony tells Jennifer that he learns 'a lotta good ideas here' and uses her advice, about giving elders the illusion of control, to solve the problem of who will lead the New Jersey family after the death of Jackie Aprile, Sr. The study also points out that criminals like Tony exhibit excessive sympathy towards children and animals. Right at the beginning of The Sopranos, he develops an attachment to a family of ducks that have made a home in his swimming-pool, and he collapses at AJ's birthday party after he sees them flying away. During In Camelot (5.7), we learn that in his childhood he had a dog called Tippy, who is seen in The Many Saints of Newark, and that he was very sad when

---

[107]The Criminal Personality, Volumes I-III.

he lost her, but he learns that she was given by his father Johnny Boy to his mistress Fran Felstein, because Livia was tired of her. In Made in America, this attitude towards animals is manifested through the protection of the cat from Paulie and, although it is a dream and therefore not truly him, it turns out that this is not the first time that an animal is an element of antagonism between the two of them.

Pie-O-My is a racehorse owned by Ralphie. He is a made man in the crew that had been run by Richie, before his murder by his wife-to-be Janice. Ralphie earns well, but is prone to violence and has a big mouth. He makes a joke about Ginny Sacrimoni, the obese wife of Johnny Sac, which leads to the latter demanding his execution. Part of the reason why this does not happen is that Ralphie is making a lot of money for both Tony and Carmine, Sr. through the Esplanade project. In University (3.6), Ralphie beats to death Tracee, a stripper at the Bada Bing!, who is carrying his child. Tony then attacks him, about which he complains vociferously, because made men are supposed to be above that sort of treatment by those higher in the pecking order. Tony initially passes Ralphie over for the role of capo of the Aprile crew, in favour of the calmer and more reliable Gigi, but, after he dies of a heart attack while on the toilet, Ralphie is reluctantly promoted.

Pie-O-My is only important as a source of revenue to Ralphie, but Tony quickly demonstrates affection for her. The veterinary costs for her are substantial and, late one night, Tony receives a call that she is sick and the veterinarian will not treat her unless payment is made. Ralphie has refused, so Tony pays and rushes to the stables to comfort her. In Whoever Did This, Ralphie's son is hospitalized after being seriously injured by an arrow to the chest. The medical bills promise to be significant. Not long afterward, a fire breaks out at the stables and Pie-O-My does not survive. Tony leaps to the conclusion that Ralphie started it, so that he could collect the insurance money, but he denies it. Their argument leads to a fight and Tony kills him. In explicit terms, the question of whether Ralphie really did start the fire is not given a definitive answer. However, the viewer who is aware of the panoply of story-telling techniques used by The Sopranos team will discover the truth secreted in the next episode, The Strong, Silent Type.

When Tony, Sil, George 'Georgie' Santorelli, Chris and Paulie are playing pool at the Bada Bing! and discussing the disappearance of Ralphie, Paulie shows no interest and even seems happy about it, joking that perhaps they should check out the Gay Men's Choir. Tony opens a delivery, which turns out to be the painting of himself and Pie-O-My that he had commissioned earlier. He leaves without saying a word and Paulie shows no understanding of why. Not long after, Tony calls Sil and tells him to burn the painting, later pouring out his grief to Jennifer, who remarks that the only other time she has seen him like this was when the ducks left his swimming pool, and not after his best friend Big Pussy disappeared, or his mother Livia died.

A few days later, Paulie reports to Sil his surprise that Tony looked like he was on the verge of tears when he saw the painting, and then comments that there is still no word from Ralphie, seemingly drawing a connection between the two. When he sees Benny and Little Paulie burning the painting as Tony ordered he stops them, citing the monetary value of it. It is not a coincidence that Pie-O-My died in a fire, but here Paulie saves the painting of her from one. He hangs it in his living room, but the boxing commentary on the television is used to hint that all is not right: 'at this stage the fight is getting closer and closer and closer'. He clearly cannot settle because when the scene continues he is cleaning, and it is at this point that what is being heard from the television becomes even more important. We hear George Foreman advertising his grill and no less than three mentions in quick succession of its countdown timer feature, including that the user can 'set the timer and walk away'. It is clear that the viewer is meant to pay attention to it because the volume does not drop as the camera moves to Tony in the painting, then his eyes and Paulie's expression that he feels he is being watched. Our hearing the words 'grilled to perfection' is synchronised with the camera focusing on Pie-O-My. The fact that Foreman is an ex-boxer reinforces the point that violence is part of the equation.

Paulie later goes to a studio to ask if the painting can be altered, specifically Tony's appearance, and when we see it next he is wearing the garb of a military leader from the past, but his eyes still bother Paulie. The final clue is the drums that begin and play over the end credits. They are an execution drum roll, as would have been heard in times past in accompaniment to the taking of a life. Tony is believed to have killed Ralphie over the death of Pie-O-My, as we hear during the conversation between Sil, Patsy and Albert 'Larry Boy' Barese, and now Paulie fears it too. But why should he? What has he done wrong to merit the ultimate punishment?

The answer has already been given implicitly, although it is not one that has been spotted by commentators. Paulie started the fire that killed Pie-O-My, doing so deliberately. Ralphie did not do it and therefore Tony killed an innocent man (of this crime at least). This is the only possible conclusion to draw from the evidence. Paulie dislikes Ralphie intensely. He was unaware of the affection his boss held for Pie-O-My. He saves the painting of the two of them from the fire, but the sight of it bothers him, particularly as he hears timers being promoted on the television. Put all of these together and the finger of blame points squarely at him. One could be forgiven for attributing the paranoia Paulie demonstrates to a fear that his passing on of secrets to Johnny Sac will be discovered. There is probably an element of that in there, but to explain it solely by that is to overlook important clues.[108]

Paulie is one of the best characters in a show full to the brim with ones that are carefully constructed and intelligently acted. He is by turns hilarious and psychopathic, a loving son and a nasty bully, a good friend and a backstabbing traitor. He is insecure about his position in the crew and this drives his leaking of secrets to Johnny Sac. There is a deep neuroticism about him, which comes out in his furniture still being in the original packaging, superstitious beliefs, and his habit of cleaning when he is under stress, as is seen in this episode. He views the world very much as the colour of his hair: black and white. He has some awareness of his psychological weaknesses, as in I Dream of Jeannie Cusamano, he admits to having visited a therapist in the past. More will be learned about him later, as he is also the subject of a second of the hidden stories.

His hatred for Ralphie stems primarily from the amount of money that the latter earns for Tony. Ralphie does not appear

---

[108] In their article on The Strong, Silent Type, Seitz and Sepinwall relegate the entirety of the involvement of Paulie to one footnote, and, not surprisingly, completely overlook his relevance to the Pie-O-My storyline. Op. cit., p. 180 footnote 42.

in the first two seasons because he is in Miami, looking after the real estate interests of the family. This experience allows him to be responsible for the Esplanade construction project, which makes him the highest earner of all the capos. This is why, although Tony also dislikes Ralphie intensely because of his behaviour, the money he brings in cannot be overlooked, and is the reason why he finally runs out of reasons not to make him a capo. This plays on Paulie's insecurity about his status within the family,[109] and so, when Ralphie makes the joke about the weight of Ginny in No Show, he reports it to her husband Johnny Sac. Ralphie narrowly avoids being executed by the Lupertazzi family for this, and when he decides that it was most likely Paulie who informed them, he makes a prank call to his mother Marianucci 'Nucci' Gualtieri, which distresses her greatly.

This is a different kind of hidden story to those revealed so far. It does not rely on a surreptitious change in the nature of the narrative, from a standard one to a deceptive state of consciousness, such as a dream or hallucination. What is hidden are events that are part of the main storyline, but which are not shown to the audience; instead, in classic whodunnit style, subtle clues must be pieced together to find the answer. The task, however, is made much more difficult because identifying the culprit is not a concern of the characters, and therefore the plot moves on and away, and also there is no sleuth, no Jane Marple or Frank Columbo, on hand to lead us in the right direction.

---

[109]Bernard attributes Paulie's odd behaviour to this, not spotting that it is he who starts the fire that kills Pie-O-My. He notes that some viewers see a parallel between this fire and the one the painting is saved from, but takes this no further. *Op. cit.*, 'The Strong, Silent Type'.

There is one counterargument to this revelation of Paulie as the culprit, and it comes from a source no less important than the creator of *The Sopranos* himself. In the final *Talking Sopranos* podcast, Schirripa asks him whether Ralphie killed Pie-O-My, to which he responds: 'yeah...yeah...I think so...yeah, Tony had it right...'[110] This was a great surprise to me: surely my argument had been shot down in flames? How could I hold and defend a contrary position to the man with overall responsibility for the story and the show? But something does not feel right about Chase's response. For one thing, it is too vague and mirrored in his body-language. 'Yeah...yeah...I think so...yeah...' is hardly the most definitive of responses. If this was a different show or creator, I would point to the fact that he did not write Whoever Did This (it was Green and Mitchell Burgess), although he had a hand in The Strong, Silent Type (Winter, Green, and Burgess wrote the teleplay, based on his story). But Chase was well-known for being in control of as many different dimensions of the show as he could be. Writers would not be able to get something he was not aware of, or did not agree with, past him. Green and Burgess have stated that they are unaware of who or what started the fire,[111] but this is highly unlikely.

Something else to be considered is the consternation of other fans of the show. The Sopranos Club on Twitter / X posted on December 22nd 2021: 'CONFIRMED...Ralph DID kill the Horse. After 4 years of fighting the argument that Ralph did not kill Pie-O-My, I have no choice but to concede...I can't go against the words of creator genius David Chase, after he

---

[110] 91, 22.01.
[111] Imperioli and Schirripa, *op. cit.*, p. 301.

so adamantly confirmed it...'. This, though, does not prove anything, as my argument that Made in America is a dream goes against the stated opinions of the vast majority of fans and commentators. Nor, because of the less than decisive nature of his response to Schirripa, would I agree that Chase 'adamantly confirmed it'.

The authority that can be drawn upon to most convincingly show that Chase's confirmation, that Ralphie being the killer of Pie-O-My is not correct, is, it turns out, Chase himself. He has a track record of being evasive or even misleading when answering penetrating questions about the show, as was demonstrated earlier. He does this to maintain both the artistic integrity of his show, a key part of which is the uncertainty which reflects the real world, and also the possibility of our enjoying it. An artist who reveals the hidden depths of their work to their audience, rather than allowing them to discover it all for themselves, is doing them a great disservice. Most do not realise that to properly understand this show requires navigating public pronouncements by its creator, including ones which contradict others he has made, even a few seconds previously: in response to being asked if Ralphie started the fire he says 'no...*Wait*...I take that back! I think he did'.[112]

Pie-O-My is another of the animals in *The Sopranos* that comes to symbolize the emotional state of one of the characters, but whereas the ducks in Tony's swimming-pool are treated well because they represent his family, she, unfortunately, comes to be associated with the hatred felt by Paulie towards Ralphie, and pays the ultimate price for it.

---

[112]Seitz and Sepinwall, *op. cit.*, pp. 365-366.

Chapter Nine
I'm Not Most Guys

The next pre-Made in America implicit storyline which centres on apparently unexplained behavioural changes is on a lighter note than the death of a horse in a fire, although it still involves a certain amount of unhappiness. It focuses on the social circle of Meadow during her university studies.

In the early seasons, Meadow is going through a rebellious phase. She is impolite to her parents, sneaks out of the house to see a boy, takes ecstasy, and, in Toodle-F***ing-Oo (2.3), organizes a party, which gets out of hand, at the house Livia has recently moved out of but still owns. Compared, though, to the challenge AJ presents to Tony and Carmela, and in the context of growing up in a Mafia family, she is very manageable and could have been much worse. Meadow certainly looks to have been the lucky winner in the Soprano and de Angelis genetic lottery: whereas AJ has the temperament of Tony and Livia and the work ethic of Carmela, Meadow has the temperament of her mother and the intelligence of her father. She achieves a place at Columbia University, an Ivy League institution in New York City.

Noah Tannenbaum is a fellow student and soon becomes her boyfriend. He first appears at the Soprano family home, sitting on the couch with Meadow watching a movie, in Proshai, Livushka (3.2). Despite being a friend of hers, something about Noah sets off alarm bells for Tony and his worst fears are confirmed: not only is he black (mixed race, as it turns out), but Jewish too. The fact of someone with those ethnicities being in his house is bad enough, although he graciously excuses Herman 'Hesh' Rabkin, an old friend of his father, but the suspicion that he is dating his daughter is intolerable. He insults Noah, making it clear that he should leave his house quickly and have no more to do with her. The stress of this situation, and what it might entail, bothers Tony so much that he has another panic attack and collapses in the kitchen, the final trigger being the sight of the black face on a packet of Uncle Ben's rice.

It is unlikely that Meadow would not be aware of how Tony would react to her seeing someone with Noah's racial and cultural heritage, so there is at least an element of a desire to express her independence from her family and their values. Still, she is obviously emotionally involved with him, and for a father who is concerned that his daughter should choose a life-partner sensibly, Noah is in an important sense a good catch, as not only is he intelligent and polite, but his father is an entertainment attorney in Hollywood and he exudes a worldly confidence. Nevertheless, the relationship between Tony and Meadow is strained for a while.

Caitlin Rucker, also a student at Columbia, shares a room with Meadow. She first appears in Mr Ruggerio's Neighbourhood, the episode before Noah enters the story. Unlike Meadow, Caitlin is experiencing life in a big city for the first time, as she comes from Bartlesville, Oklahoma. Initially it seems to sit well with her, as she is in a lively mood, but she boasts about getting drunk, telling

Meadow that she had her last cocktail at 11.30am. A wall on her side of the room is covered with posters of alcohol brands, which adds to the suspicion that her confidence is based on alcohol misuse. This is borne out as the next time we see her she is depressed, has trouble swallowing, and has been prescribed a medication to combat anxiety. She reports not having drunk alcohol for a week, and obsesses about a man she saw on the subway eating chicken and spitting out the bones.

Both of the Noah and Caitlin storylines reach their joint conclusion in University, but part of it is only told implicitly. The viewer must piece together some of the events from subtle suggestions and hints, and in so doing a comprehensive understanding of their storylines and motivations is possible. The episode as a whole is a comparison of the life experiences of two young women: Meadow and Tracee, a stripper at the Bada Bing!. The episode was first broadcast on April 1st 2001, but the events are no laughing matter for either of them.

Although both have bad experiences, those of Tracee are on a different level to those of Meadow. She tells Tony that as a child her mother would hold her hand on a stove, which she uses to justify burning her own child with cigarettes. She also tells him that she is pregnant with Ralphie's baby, and his advice that she should have an abortion is not completely without merit or sympathy, given how Ralphie treats her. She exists only to satisfy him sexually, and he laughs when Sil hits her because she has not been turning up to work. After an argument at the Bada Bing! he mocks her, saying that if their baby is a girl they will call her Tracee, so she will grow up to be a 'c***-sucking slob just like her mom'. She slaps him, after which he punches her in the stomach and beats her to death. University is a poignant story, with Allen Coulter nominated for an Emmy in 2001 for his directing of it.

To return to the main concern, Meadow and Noah are lying on her bed making out, when Caitlin walks in and does not leave. She has watched Todd Browning's 1932 movie *Freaks* and cannot get it out of her head. Noah points out that she is developing a habit of deliberately exposing herself to things she finds upsetting; another she has is pulling strands of her hair out. Noah leaves, then Meadow and they meet in his room. She is impressed by how tolerant he is with Caitlin, to which he replies 'I'm not most guys'. They have sex.

Caitlin later chides Meadow because she did not call her, imagining her having had her throat cut. As she walks out to see Noah, Caitlin cries 'well, at least you have a boyfriend!'. They take Caitlin out for her birthday, but it does not have any effect on her mood. She obsesses over a homeless woman, to whom she tries to give money, but is repulsed when she sees that she has newspaper stuffed between her buttocks. When they return to the dormitory she is still upset and starts drinking. Noah leaves, because apparently a friend is arriving tomorrow morning and they are going on a trip, but Meadow does not seem to believe him.

While Meadow is visiting her family, Noah is in his room studying when Caitlin comes to visit, ostensibly to ask if she is there. She seems very cheerful and is dressed smartly. She asks him if he would like to 'hang out', and although he says he has a paper to write, she persuades him to let her stay there and study too. As they talk, the camera continues to focus in on the two of them, a technique used to highlight that special attention to their interaction needs to be paid by the viewer, because there may be more going on than meets the eye.

The next time we see Caitlin and Meadow in their room her positive mood is continuing, and she says that she will be spending the weekend in Vermont with her family. Meadow goes to see Noah, who is not so happy because he received a C- for his paper, for which he blames Caitlin distracting him. We later learn that his father is filing a restraining order against her. This seems excessive, which does not mean that people motivated to succeed would not do it in such a situation, but if it were purely about distraction from study then Meadow as his girlfriend would surely deserve it more, as he would have spent much more time with her. It is not long before, while they are working together in the library, Noah tells Meadow that they have been 'seeing too much of each other', and that he is ending their relationship because she is 'too negative' and cynical. He then puts his glasses back on and resumes studying, as tears well up in her eyes. Although he does not express it, there can be little doubt that Noah's father was not satisfied with the vague and euphemistic response given by Meadow to his question about how her father makes a living. It is hard to believe that pressure from him over this, as well as the C-, did not play a role in the ending of the relationship, this mirroring, from the point of view of the writing, Tony's treatment of Noah.

There is something else that does not receive explicit attention. What could connect the jealousy felt by Caitlin towards Meadow over her having a boyfriend, the camera focusing on Noah and Caitlin when she asks to spend some time with him, which turns into six hours, the upbeat mood of the latter at that point and when we see her next, talking to Meadow about her trip to Vermont, and the restraining order filed against her by Noah's father? Taken together, these elements point to a sexual liaison between Noah and Caitlin in his room. Having a male show interest in an insecure and jealous young woman would put a smile on her face, and her responding by becoming overly fixated on him would properly explain why she, and not his ex-girlfriend, is served with a restraining order.

It turns out that in this respect Noah is just like many other guys. Any feelings he has for Meadow are secondary to his own pleasures and goals. He dumps her in a clinical and emotionless manner, attempting to justify it to her by using tired old clichés. He is not the higher level of male that his evolution t-shirt implies he might be. The black Jew that Tony feels is not good enough for his daughter is more like him than either of them realise.

This hidden detail in the story of the relationship between Meadow and Noah is one of the less significant ones, both from the point of view of the narrative of *The Sopranos* as a whole, and their breakup. It does not affect any other character, main or supporting, apart from those involved, and none of them, including Meadow, even know about it. Moreover, Noah does not end the relationship because he has found a better option than Meadow. It is clear from the restraining order that Caitlin is no more than a brief episode of extracurricular fun, that quickly becomes more trouble than she is worth to him. The anger of Noah and his father over the obstacles his libido has created to his academic success is all the explanation that is necessary for the ending of the relationship, and this is supported by his detached countenance when doing so.

Nevertheless, the brief encounter between Noah and Caitlin is one more piece of evidence to show that the writers, led by Chase, have an ongoing habit of secreting in the storyline details, for which the viewer must pay extra attention in order to see. The practice of utilising disguised narratives is present at all levels of the show, from murders and significant milestone episodes to more everyday matters. The liaison is unlikely to be spotted on first viewing, but no commentator has even to this day, over two decades since the episode was initially broadcast. As with the involvement of Paulie in the death of Pie-O-My, it does not require a switch in the nature of the narrative, from a standard one to a dream or hallucination. A comprehensive and fully accurate understanding requires us to dig a little deeper at times because of this, even on a show as erudite as *The Sopranos*. In this way, it is important for viewing not just it as a whole, but the finale specifically, which aired over six years later.

Chapter Ten
Beware! Children Playing Under Leaves

By definition, dreams deal in unreality. Although they may contain people we know or have known, or recount events that did happen to us or others, they remain psychological constructions. The events either are not happening at the time we are dreaming or have never happened. This is one of the reasons why they can have such a hold over us and why they are used so often in art. In the first scene of the fifth act of *Macbeth*, the wife of the title character sleepwalks as she is plagued by guilt over her part in the murder of King Duncan: ' here's the smell of the blood still: all the perfumes of Arabia will not sweeten this little hand'.[113] Much more recently, Christopher Nolan uses the phenomenon of lucid dreaming as the basis for the film *Inception* in 2010.

A dimension of dreams that is also common is when they go beyond portraying things that have not happened and into the realm of the unlikely or even impossible. This is probably the most distinctive element of them, both in personal experience and again in art, such as that of the painters Hieronymous Bosch

---
[113]Lines 53-55.

and Salvador Dalí and the aforementioned filmmaker Lynch. The fact that we usually do not question or even notice the surreal aspects of our dreams at the time we are having them, which is possibly due to reduced activity in the dorsolateral prefrontal cortex during sleep,[114] is used by Michel Gondry in his 2006 film *The Science of Sleep*.

The dreams in *The Sopranos*, those of Tony and others, share these characteristics. Those involved in oneirology, the scientific study of dreams, refer to them and others as disjunctive cognition because aspects of cognition, such as memory, imagination and facial recognition, do not function harmoniously. It results in events and behaviours being shown which are unlikely to happen or impossible. If Made in America is a dream, as the central thesis of this book proposes, then things of a similar nature should be discernible in it: characters acting in ways that are unusual or ludicrous, events occurring in an unrealistic manner, and so on. It turns out that this is indeed the case, as has already been demonstrated in the analysis in Chapter Seven of the depictions of AJ, Phil, Butch, Agent Harris and Mink. Those, and the content of this chapter, are not as obvious as in other dreams; why this is so will be explained.

The narrative of dreams is often not straightforwardly linear, like events in the waking world. Things do not always happen in an ordered sequence, or they jump over periods of time, leaving out those that are not emotionally significant to us, to focus on those that are. A woman may dream that her husband is demanding that they have a child and immediately she is showing

---

[114]Rowan Hooper 'Dreams decoded: 6 answers to the mysteries of the sleeping mind', *NewScientist*.

off a newborn. A person may appear old and then younger later. Their sequence is more chaotic even than non-linear works of art, such as the films *Reservoir Dogs* (1992) and *Pulp Fiction* (1994) by Quentin Tarantino.

A careful inspection of Made in America shows that this is true of this episode repeatedly. It skips like a faulty Compact Disc in the same way that happened in Isabella, when the lunch Tony is enjoying with the titular character gives way abruptly to Meadow calling him to dinner. The first scene jumps too fast from Tony in bed in morning daylight to sitting in a van with Paulie at night, causing a jarring transition between the two songs that are heard; Agent Harris' tip about multiple phone calls being traced to a gas station at Oyster Bay gives way to Walden and Benny immediately watching one; and AJ and Rhiannon surveying the remains of his car to him being lambasted by his parents.

The call from Tony to George, suggesting he reach out to Butchie, is not even finished before the hoped for sitdown is beginning; the time between it ending and the family moving back into their home is also brief. There are two skips during the sitdown itself: from the beginning to Butchie saying 'we started it?', and from his 'you do what you gotta do' to Tony adding 'one more thing, you hit my brother-in-law'. The sense of unreality is reinforced by the subtle way that the water bottles move around and disappear from the table at random throughout the scene, sometimes placed in front of characters who refused them earlier.

Other examples of skips are Janice visiting Junior to Uncle Pat sitting in front of Tony warning him about her; the strangely composed face of Carmela in the bath, being told that AJ is planning to join the army, to the face of his therapist as his parents discuss his plans with her; and Tony standing by Sil's bed to being in a chair without moving from one position to the other. In a similar way, Tony enters Holsten's and in the blink of an eye he is sitting at a table. In a classic demonstration of dream logic Meadow is there in Holsten's before she even arrives: a young woman who is strikingly similar to her is sitting against the far wall, under the picture of the football player Michael Shea, and has her order taken by the dark-haired waitress.

In amongst all this, there are too many quick changes from day to night and back again, and changes in the weather, for this episode to be taken as a conventional narrative. Every piece of fiction cuts corners, in order to focus on what is most important from the point of view of the author, but a professional storyteller does this in ways that do not grate with the audience. That is not the case here, and if Made in America were not a dream then the artistic credibility of the editing team would be in tatters.

These are by no means the only unusual aspects of the episode. Why are Carmela and the children hiding, of all places, in an old house that smells of urine? They have plenty of money to afford something better, or a hotel, or even to fly far away to another country. When AJ is being scolded over the loss of the SUV, Carmela makes a very strange comment: 'if there were children playing under those leaves you would have run them over!'. Most people would not be able to manage his restrained 'I guess' to that one but, as mentioned above, when she is told of his plans to join the army there is no reaction from her at all, as if Tony had just told her that their son had changed his footwear. She is soon back nearer to hysteria when she suggests that AJ will end up having his legs blown off, to which he responds with an uncanny impression of Livia: 'always with the drama!'.

Carmela choosing Holsten's as the location for the family meal is another break with character. It is not her sort of place at all, as whenever we see her eating out, whoever the company, it is always at the fine-dining end of the spectrum. When the family eat the type of fare that Holsten's serves it is at home as takeaway. This sort of meal, however, is a big favourite of the author of the dream that all this takes place in, having already appeared in the episode when Tony met with Mink, and, after Paulie rises from his seat after his conversation with Tony at Satriales, a large sign mentioning hamburgers and patties is visible. It is no surprise that he cannot get burgers off his mind, as it has been seen repeatedly that he is a food addict who eats to relieve stress.

Throughout the finale, the type of meat that is sold at Satriales is frequently mentioned. In the safehouse, Tony is eating a pork sandwich and comments approvingly that he has not eaten any green vegetables for days, in response to which Benny asks whether they can go to the pork store, instead of staying where they are. As the family return to their home, after the war is resolved, Tony is carrying a canned ham. The gathering after Bobby's funeral begins with an overhead shot of the food on offer, akin to an aerial view of a mountain range, and, among the hordes eagerly sampling the fare, Tony can be heard talking about chicken and fish, and Jason Gervasi excitedly tells his father Carlo that roast pork is available. On the contrary, Paulie, the person whose loyalty Tony is wrestling with throughout the dream, is more concerned with the price of cauliflower. As well as the food in itself, there is an emotional connection for Tony to Satriales, a place where he has spent a great deal of time with his family and friends, from childhood onwards.

It was demonstrated earlier that the events of Made in America offer an unrealistic ending to the arc of AJ. This is also true of Meadow, although not to the same extent, as her life is in better order than that of her brother. She is going to marry a successful and caring man, is offered a new job out of the blue even before she has finished law school, and what a starting salary - $170,000 per annum!

The new therapist that AJ sees is curiously familiar. She is demurely attractive, has shoulder length hair and dresses professionally. Her intelligence is obvious, although she does not show it off, and she talks in a calm and measured tone. In short, she is extremely redolent of his father's long time therapist Jennifer, even down to her apparent age. Neither Tony nor Carmela treats her as someone familiar, with Tony telling her things about his mother and childhood that are known to Jennifer, so it should be concluded that she is not meant to be her. Still, she holds Tony's gaze and smiles at him, echoing the feelings that he had for his therapist. This new one is a combination of Jennifer with the visual aspect of Evelyn, the psychiatric facility staff member that he and Carmela met in The Blue Comet when visiting AJ. This will not be the last time in this dream that characters appear who are composites of multiple others from the waking world.

Second-hand evidence masquerading as first-hand about the deteriorating relationship between Butchie and Phil is offered in the shape of their telephone conversation regarding the failure to locate Tony. They speak for only forty-seven seconds, but Butchie somehow walks between the Little Italy and Chinatown areas of New York. The distance between them is very manageable, roughly half a kilometre, but it would take longer than the time he does it in if it were to happen in the waking world.

During the scene when Tony and his crew are watching an episode of *The Twilight Zone*, another of them walks into their safehouse without anyone inside commenting, but when Walden does it later in the same scene, either through the same door or a nearby one, he is shouted at and has a gun pointed at him by Dante. No explanation is offered for this inconsistent behaviour. Furthermore, it is absurd that members of the crew are out on the streets, doing collections and bringing the money back there, during a war, as it offers the enemy the opportunity to follow them and discover the location of the hideout. Similarly, Carlo says that he is going to accompany some of the others to the hospital to visit Sil, something they would not be doing if they were fearing for their lives, as that would be a place that Phil and his men would be watching.

The nearest that Made in America gets to portraying the downright ridiculous is the death of Phil. It has already been noted that there is something extremely odd about him being on a relaxing day out with his wife and grandchildren in the middle of a Mafia war, but what happens as he dies is something else entirely. After he is shot twice, including in the head, by Walden and is lying dead on the ground, the SUV starts to roll forward. The tyre begins to go over his head, but we are mercifully spared from seeing the rest. There is, however, a strange loud sound, as if his head explodes like a balloon.[115] The gruesomeness of the spectacle that we are imagining seems to distract viewers from the simple fact that a human head would not explode like that if a heavy weight were applied to it. There are a number of gases in the

---

[115] Bernard inaccurately describes it as a 'crunching sound'; *op. cit.*, 'Made in America'.

head, such as nitric oxide, used for communication by nerve cells in the brain, and of course air, itself partly composed of oxygen and helium, but these are in nowhere near the concentration required to generate an explosion. Even if there were, then being shot in the head beforehand would either cause the explosion, or allow the gases to escape and therefore prevent it. Heads which are rolled over by cars or other suitably heavy objects are squashed and the skull shattered, and therefore the sound that accompanies what happens to Phil is unsuitable.

As well as killing Phil and thereby putting an end to the war, the icing on the cake for Tony's subconscious is that it signals the rescue of his enemy's grandchildren from him. Remember that, according to the Yochelson and Samenow text read by Jennifer, a sentimentality towards children and babies is a trademark of some types of criminal personality; this will not be the last time in the episode that Tony's anxiety about Phil's malignant influence on the young is evident. This care is, however, qualified by his imagining the grandchildren witnessing the murder of their grandfather; the sentimentality of a man like Tony exhausts itself quickly. Earlier, a clip from the 2006 film *Little Miss Sunshine* is seen by him when visiting Sil. In it, the young girl, Olive Hoover, screams in excitement when she learns that she has a place in a State beauty contest. His old friend being gravely ill is a heavy burden for Tony to bear, and exuberant joy from a child is how his mind tries to give him an emotional lift.[116] He also nags Meadow about her becoming a lawyer rather than a paediatrician and,

---

[116] Some commentators misinterpret the scream as one of horror, presumably because they have not taken the time to watch the film; see, for example, MasterofSopranos op. cit., Page 4, Part VI (4).

remembering that his sentimentality also extends to animals, protects the cat from Paulie.

No dive into the subconscious of Tony would be complete without an appearance from his racism. The black characters who appear before the final scene are undignified and border on the comedic. Among those who witness the execution of Phil are a cripple and one who vomits. When Tony visits Junior, the scene begins with a short man with bulbous eyes, who shuffles off as if he too is a cripple, then Tony looks disdainfully at the orderly who politely asks him to move. The racism that he and his peers demonstrate towards black people throughout *The Sopranos*, even to those they are working with, is again in evidence here. Two very minor black characters, both of them women, do appear and represent ones who Tony had more or less positive relationships with. One is the nanny working for Janice, and she is based on Perrilyn, who briefly helped Livia in her home, in 46 Long (1.2). Tony liked her, although he felt the need to warn her in advance: 'no ganja!'. The other is at the entrance to the facility where Junior is staying, and she politely deals with unspecified difficult behaviour from Janice. She is Fiona, one of the nurses who treated Tony in The Fleshy Part of the Thigh (6.4) when he came out of his coma, and his knowing her name and using it is noteworthy in itself.

Although Junior talking to Tony about visits from 'a man from another galaxy' sounds like his subconscious being dismissive of people with serious mental illness, this is actually a recent memory from the previous episode, of Janice telling him that Junior thinks his accountant is 'from outer space' because of his artificial voice box. At the beginning of this scene, Junior looks out of the window and the chirping of birds can be heard, but when in anger Tony says "enough with the f***ing birds", it stops immediately.[117]

Paulie enters the rear part of Satriales carrying a box containing numerous pairs of barber's scissors. When he offers them to those present, they respond with no less enthusiasm than that observed when Chris offers DVD players to the crew in 46 Long. Of all the gifts and bribes that change hands during *The Sopranos*, none achieve an effect more out of proportion to their value. This is Tony's subconscious expressing a suspicion about Paulie's loyalties: in the previous episode, Albie and Butchie, on the orders of Phil, meet at the Flatbush Bikini Waxing and Beauty Shoppe, a place where, amongst other things, hair is cut, to order their men to execute Tony, Sil and Bobby. Interestingly, they answer a question about including Paulie in the negative. Tony would not know about this meeting, but it can be assumed, from the appearance of the scissors, that he knows about the location being a haunt of the Lupertazzis.

Tony's paranoid suspicion about who is working against him even falls on Rhiannon. In previous episodes there is nothing at all to suggest that she is anything other than what she says she is: the ex-girlfriend of AJ's friend Hernan O'Brien, who he later meets again as a fellow patient in the facility where he recovers after his suicide attempt. Most of what viewers and commentators remember about her comes from Made in America, but as a dream of AJ's father it is untrustworthy as evidence. Her main function there is as part of the implausible

---

[117]This point is made by Clark / @cynss in a comment on my 2018 YouTube video.

wish-fulfilment edifice that Tony builds around his son: she enters into a sexual relationship with him, which helps to boost his outlook. Nevertheless, when Tony arrives at the house his family are staying in, she is there with AJ, and as she is leaving Carmela, or, more accurately, the version of her constructed by the sleeping mind of her husband, gestures to her and says 'this kind of bothers me', to which he replies 'who's she gonna tell?'. This means that somewhere in Tony's mind is the consideration of the possibility that Rhiannon might be hiding something, but he is not sufficiently convinced for it to come out of his own mouth. The same baseless suggestion might also explain the briefest of glances that Rhiannon makes towards Carmela, when she tells AJ that the family will be eating at Holsten's later. A balanced examination of the evidence leads only to the conclusion that there is nothing truly about Rhiannon that should worry Tony; one of the consequences of the life he lives, though, is that no one is above suspicion. There is, therefore, a modicum of truth to the theory, expressed by some on social media, that she is secretly working for the Lupertazzi family. A problem with this, although not the only one, is that it fails to recognise that Made in America is not a standard narrative.

At the gathering for Bobby, his son, Bobby, Jr., looks surprisingly lighthearted for someone whose father is being mourned. This is the second parent he has lost in the space of a few years, as his mother Karen died in a car crash in Christopher. There is a much more remarkable recuperation from trauma, though, in the shape of Little Paulie. Only four episodes ago, in Walk Like A Man, he was thrown out of a third-floor window by Chris, breaking six of the vertebrae in his back. Even if a month or so has passed since then, his being out of hospital and back at work, albeit looking the worse for wear, is as unbelievable as the rehabilitation of AJ.[118]

During the tipoff to Tony, Agent Harris makes the suggestion that Phil is using the payphone because 'he may not be able to put his hands on a clean cellphone'. Things have got so bad so quickly for the Boss of one of the Five Families in New York that he cannot even access a new cellphone? Even in 2007, these could be purchased easily anywhere by anyone, a consequence of this being that, according to the mechanic interviewed by Little Paulie while posing as a police officer, there are hardly any gas stations that have payphones anymore. He could most likely have bought one at that very gas station where he was using the payphone, so the logic does not hold up.

The next scene to that one is generated by the random association that is common in dreams. Paulie tells Tony that Carlo's son was caught selling ecstasy, and up pops Meadow's friend Hunter, who flunked out of her initial university studies because she was partying too hard.

It has been suggested that AJ's car catching fire is also unrealistic. It happens because he parks over dry leaves, which are set alight by the heat from the underside of the car. This is actually possible, even for cars such as SUVs which sit higher above the ground than others, according to firefighters who dealt with a similar incident in Mundelein, Illinois, on November 19th 2023.[119]

Returning to Paulie, in his final scene he stakes a claim for the award for the most ridiculous feature of an episode that is full

---

[118] 'Spinal Fractures', North Bristol NHS Trust, especially p. 10.
[119] 'SUV bursts into flames after driver parks it on pile of leaves', www.firerescue1.com.

of contenders. His account to Tony of his vision of the Virgin Mary at the Bada Bing! is prefaced with the disclaimer: 'I never told this to another living soul.' Even the most casual of viewers will know by now that there is little chance of this being true, as this neurotic gangster cannot help but prattle on about anything that matters to him, whether or not others think it significant: the hygiene of shoelaces, the welfare of his mother, his muscle definition, and on and on. Obviously, he did confess to the vision to someone, or Tony would not be including it in his dream here.

As dreams go in *The Sopranos*, other works of art and those experienced by the average person, the one in Made in America is at the more realistic end of the scale. The surreal and bizarre aspects are toned down more than in, for example, that in The Test Dream. There, Tony explicitly encounters deceased acquaintances such as Carmine, Sr., Vin, and his horse Pie-O-My, which he rides inside the family home, and he has sex with Charmaine while her husband Artie eggs him on. Made in America is different because it is obviously the intention of Chase to keep secret the fact that it is a dream. There is no such necessity with all of the other dreams because they are overtly acknowledged as such, with two exceptions. The phantom therapy appointment that Tony imagines with Jennifer, in Isabella, is kept secret, and therefore contains nothing obviously ridiculous, with the most unlikely elements being the alleged location of her office and the increasing of his dosage on the basis of the symptoms he is reporting. The sexual encounter with Connie, in House Arrest, is treated similarly, with the temporary vanishing of the rash on Tony's arm being difficult to spot. All of the other dreams are acknowledged as imaginary, even in cases where this is not done so immediately, as is the case with the visions of Isabella.

It is extremely surprising that very little of what has been presented in this chapter has been noticed by other commentators. How is it that Made in America has been watched countless times by those who have published material, without spotting the sheer absurdity of the execution of Phil, or the recovery of Little Paulie, nor what these imply about the nature of the narrative? The nearest to proper recognition any of it receives are comments about certain of the oddities, such as Carmela hearing about AJ planning to join the army, or Butchie ending up in Chinatown after his phone conversation with Phil,[120] but even these are not flagged as strongly as they should be. There have been, and remain, serious weaknesses in scholarship for The Sopranos.

---

[120] Bernard interprets this as Chase highlighting 'the shrinking of Little Italy'. Op. cit., 'Made in America'.

Chapter Eleven
The Governor of Maryland

Russ Fegoli is a minor character who appears only in Marco Polo. He does not appear before or after, is not integral to the plot of the episode, and is therefore quite an insubstantial character. It was remarked earlier that one of the many strengths of *The Sopranos* is the depth of its characterization as it relates both to primary and secondary characters, so in itself his appearance is not unusual. What does need explaining, though, are the subtle connections to a character who is much more significant, given that this is his only appearance, disappearing afterwards like a ghost in the night, never to be seen or heard from again. The context is a party being held to celebrate the seventy-fifth birthday of Carmela's father Hugh. At a family meal beforehand, her mother Mary expresses her worry that Tony will behave in a way that embarrasses her in front of an old friend, a sentiment she expressed before, in the hospital while she and Carmela were waiting for Hugh to be treated following his fall from a roof.

The person in question is Russ. He possesses a Ph.D. and has retired from the Foreign Service. Carmela is not a fan of him and his family, citing the five-page letters that his wife sends out at Christmas that she perceives as bragging about their achievements; Mary suggests her dislike is more to do with his children finishing college. Russ was awarded a medal in California for unspecified reasons. He served in the State Department, and in Rome was Career Assistant to the Ambassador to the Vatican; he received a medal from the Pope, although it is not clear whether that was the one that was awarded in California. Hugh, however, paints him in a different light for AJ: 'when we were kids together in the Navy he had such a bad case of the crabs [slang for pubic lice] we used to call him the Governor of Maryland' (this American State is renowned for its crab dishes). Later on, we learn from Carmela that Russ grew up on Arthur Avenue, a street in the Little Italy area of the Bronx in New York City, which indicates that he had a working-class upbringing.

On the day of the party, Mary anxiously informs Carmela that Russ has an allergy to tomatoes, which developed after he was given radiation therapy for prostate cancer. In response to Tony joking 'a doctor in the house? That's good because somebody usually goes down at these things' (a reference to his own collapse in the Pilot), Russ says that his doctorate is in international affairs, to which Mary adds 'from Princeton'. Hugh tells Tony that he had an audience with four Popes. Russ is a little stiff and reserved, but polite. After Hugh has opened his present from Tony, a Beretta shotgun, Russ comments that he has been to the Beretta studio in Brescia and that they do not export their best guns. Tony and Hugh take offense at this perceived slight to the gift and Carmela later describes him as 'pompous', although Russ does not seem to have intended it to be taken that way. This lack of tact in social interaction is worth remembering.

The appearance of Russ does allow the snobbery of Mary to be highlighted, but this could have been achieved without the necessity of introducing a character for that purpose alone. There is more to him than this, but to discover what it is we have to wait until the next season, a length of time that means that the subtle clues to come will pass the first-time or casual viewer by. The task is not made any easier by the fact that the information is presented through the prism of another character, even though it is one who is much better known to us.

The sixth season is one of turbulence for Paulie. In the fourth episode, The Fleshy Part of the Thigh, he visits his Aunt Dottie, an elderly nun who is on the verge of passing away. She specifically asked to see him and is desperate to tell him something: she was 'a bad girl' during the war when she was a novice, and met a soldier called Russ who was 'so lonely'. She tells Paulie that she got pregnant and had a baby, a story which he at first does not believe and puts it down to her suffering from Alzheimer's. She persists and tells him that he was that baby, revealing that she is his mother and Nucci is actually his aunt.

He rushes over to the Green Grove retirement home, where Nucci has just come back from a trip to Atlantic City. He grabs her arm roughly and begins the interrogation; this is already the worst we have seen him treat her. Usually, she is on a pedestal, although, in Mergers and Acquisitions, the face he pulls when he learns from the manager at Green Grove that she does not always wear her false teeth is one of the funniest things the show delivers. He swears profusely when he sees that she is unable to lie to him. 'You're a fraud and a phoney! And she's even worse! She's a whore!' He feels that he has been lied to and victimized all through his life.

Later, when he visits Tony at the hospital, he is still angry and distracted. He receives a call informing him that Dottie died. During a later visit, he tells Tony what he has discovered about the nun he believed to be his aunt: 'some c***sucker GI knocked her up during the war. Russ...Who the f*** even knows who this Russ b***ard is?' He again visits Nucci at Green Grove, who says he was wrong not to attend Dottie's funeral. He is still angry, which is not helped by her saying that Dottie is stained by the sin of her pregnancy outside of Holy Matrimony; it seems to be a family trait to be tactless. Paulie makes it clear that he will no longer pay the residential fees that keep her at Green Grove, throwing an expensive television he bought her out of the window. Nucci is upset and scared because she has probably never seen this side of him before, or, at least, not directed towards herself.

In the next scene, there is an echoing of Paulie's complaints when he and Tony berate Jason Berone for his actions concerning the sale of his father's company. 'How was I supposed to know? My family kept me in the dark!' is Jason's excuse, but Paulie does not see the hypocrisy of his angry rejection of what he is hearing from the young man. In a conversation between Paulie and Tony, we learn that the cost of putting Nucci in Green Grove is $4000 per month, which he says he will be paying no longer. Tony reminds him how much Nucci did for him, including being a loving mother and repeatedly getting him out of trouble with the law. With his own lack of self-awareness, he criticises Paulie for being stuck inside his own head and ignoring the suffering of others: 'you're part of something bigger, when you going to learn that?' (one of the many times Tony parrots knowledge and wisdom from others which is not applied to his own life). Further evidence that Paulie is deeply wounded by the recent revelations is provided by Jason's mother Helen visiting Tony and begging for him not to hurt her son. Paulie is moved to tears and leaves before anyone can see, but any sympathy that is felt for him disappears when we see his response to the spectacle of a caring mother. He visits Jason again while he is rowing and proceeds to beat him with an iron bar, calls him 'f***ing Momma's boy' and demands he pay him $4000 per month, presumably to recoup the money he feels he wasted on Nucci over the years.

This particular arc is completed later in the season in the ninth episode, The Ride (6.9). As Paulie enters his local church, his lack of proper respect for the faith is shown by the fact that he does not kneel and cross himself as Patsy does, talks loudly and disturbs the prayers of an old woman, making a joke about St. Elzéar of Sabran, whose feast is approaching. His humour, however, disappears when the new priest suggests that his donation of $10,000 should be increased to $50,000, citing the costs of charitable work being done by the Church. The priest is suspicious that Paulie and Patsy are making a healthy personal profit out of the festival, but Paulie is unimpressed, pointing to the huge amount being paid by the Catholic Church to settle paedophilia lawsuits. He refuses the new demands and, as a consequence, the statue of St. Elzéar goes without his golden hat. Paulie watches the procession sitting in his expensive car with a smile on his face.

Later at the feast, his doctor calls him with the results of a recent test. He asks him if he has a history of prostate cancer in his family – perhaps his father? Paulie does not know and the doctor recommends a biopsy. There is a malfunction on a ride that Janice is on with her daughter Domenica and Bobby, Jr.: a woman breaks her wrist and a boy loses some teeth. Paulie takes no responsibility when informed by Little Paulie, refusing to leave his home to take care of it. However, when Bobby tracks down the owner of the ride, he is told that Paulie would not pay for a proper repair crew. The greed that has infected the festival is represented in the gluttony of a cannoli-eating contest, which Paulie enjoys watching. Bobby confronts him and, after he is escorted away by police, the locals who heard the accusations stare at him.

After calling the doctors to be told that his results are not available yet, he is visibly stressed. His neuroticism about cleanliness appears when he orders an espresso and tells the vendor to avoid touching the lemon rind with his fingers. He bumps into Nucci who is there on a trip from Green Grove. In the absence of his paying the fees the home has been supportive, and her other son is trying to make a financial arrangement to keep her there. She says he was to blame for the accident because he allowed St. Elzéar to go without his hat, but for a change he rejects this superstitious explanation. His anger at Nucci and Dottie is still very obvious, but, at Chris' bachelor party with the crew, Bobby is still angry with him and leaves early. Tony criticises Paulie for the ride incident and tells him to settle things with Bobby. After hearing his fears that he may have cancer, Tony points to his 'germaphobias' and tells him that he is probably worrying for nothing: 'you're too susceptible to the psychics and the dream messages and dirty f***ing toilet seats.' But he is still bothered and cannot sleep, so in the middle of the night he calls the doctor but, not surprisingly, his result is not available.

Paulie goes to the Bada Bing! as instructed by Tony, but, after entering, he has a vision of the Virgin Mary, hovering over the stage where the semi-clad dancers are usually seen. This unusual occurrence can be taken as an indication of his emotional needs, for the next time we see him after leaving the club he visits Nucci, but, instead of arguing, he says little and sits down to watch television with her. She is not seen again before her death, in Kennedy and Heidi. In Moe 'n Joe (6.10), Paulie informs Tony that the test was positive and that he has been diagnosed with prostate cancer, and in Stage 5 (6.14), the episode in which Johnny Sac dies of lung cancer, it is revealed that that his treatment was successful.

There is no doubt that Paulie is a highly insecure person, and this is evident in a number of ways. He is not confident about his status in the crew, alternating between fawning over Tony and passing on secrets to Johnny Sac, such as Ralphie's joke about Ginny's weight and the Housing and Urban Development scam in Watching Too Much Television (4.7). He takes insults very personally and sees them where others would not, such as Vito's homosexuality, about which he exclaims: 'I feel like I've been stabbed in the heart!' (Live Free or Die). He is obsessive about cleanliness. In Mr Ruggerio's Neighbourhood, he is observed by others in the crew washing his hands twice before eating, explaining that this is because he tied his shoelaces after the first wash, following this up with a graphic lecture on the merits of women's toilets over men's. He holds all sorts of superstitious beliefs and approaches Catholicism in the same way, behaving however he wants to as long as he makes regular donations to the Church.

Various explanations are possible for his insecurity. Both his biological mother Dottie and maternal aunt Nucci could be argued to take a neurotic attitude to Catholicism. Even though the latter also seems to be a genuinely compassionate person, she lives surrounded by images and artifacts of the faith. Anxiety is a familial trait and, even if he did not inherit this from Dottie, he was raised by Nucci: nurture and possibly nature also. Added to this is his possibly growing up without a father. Other children of Nucci are mentioned in The Fleshy Part of the Thigh, but it is unclear whether their father treated Paulie as if he was one of his own; does her supporting him when he was in trouble with the law imply that the husband had no interest in him? This can cause long-term anxiety in a male of any background, but in the patriarchal culture of the Italian-American Mafia he would be even more likely to believe that his status was diminished. Serving not only under Tony as boss but his father Johnny Boy too, with the family surname being used for the crew after the former took over, would not have helped.

It is at this point that the dots can be properly connected. Russ is Paulie's father. The distinguished and learned civic servant and Catholic is the father of one of the most dangerous and feared gangsters in New Jersey. The lonely young soldier who the novice nun Dottie took pity on was named Russ. Hugh and his friends would not have given Russ the nickname 'the Governor of Maryland' if he was not showing a marked interest in the opposite sex. The timeline is plausible too. Dottie said that she had the baby during the war and, as there is no reason to think this means anything but the Second World War, this would put it sometime between 1941 and 1945, the period of American involvement. The Fleshy Part of the Thigh was broadcast in 2006, which would make Paulie in his early to mid-sixties; Tony Sirico, the actor who plays him, was born in 1942.

There is more: although at face value there is nothing obvious to link the two men, there are in fact similarities between them. Both suffered from prostate cancer and there is some evidence to suggest that it can be hereditary, although many times it is not.[121] They are both witnessed speaking indelicately. On the one occasion Russ appears, he offends Hugh, the person the birthday party is being held for, and Tony, at whose house it happens; Paulie is abrasive on a number of occasions. Both men appear to do it unintentionally, although Paulie is also very capable of doing it at will. Both of them are very religious in their own way: Russ is a Catholic traditionalist and Paulie takes his Catholicism with an extra-large dose of superstition.

There is something else that has not been spotted yet in commentaries. The Fegoli surname sounds like it should be Italian, but in fact it is not. It is not common at all anywhere in the world, being held mostly by a very small number of people in Argentina.[122] Why, therefore, was it used by Imperioli in writing Marco Polo? One could accept his statement that Fegoli is the name of the man who delivered him at birth, 'our family paediatrician';[123] but that would be to ignore the compelling evidence which begins with the use of an anagram. There is a rare neuropsychiatric phenomenon known as Fregoli Syndrome, sufferers of which believe that two separate people, usually one of them being known to them, are actually the same one. For example, a man might be convinced that a woman he passes on the way to work often is in fact his wife in disguise, even if she

---

[121] 'The Genetics of Prostate Cancer', Prostate Cancer Foundation of Australia.
[122] 'Fegoli surname', Forebears.
[123] Imperioli and Schirripa, op. cit., p. 367.

looks nothing like her and his wife would have no reason to be where this woman is every day. This was named after an Italian actor Leopoldo Fregoli, who had a reputation for quick changes of costume.

Fregoli is an anagram of R Fegoli. Giving the character this name is a clue, along the lines of those used in cryptic crosswords, that there is a connection between Russ and someone else. For those who are familiar with this type of puzzle, it could be expressed as follows: 'the Governor of Maryland, confused, believes himself to be a quick-changing Italian actor (7)' ('confused' is a clue that an anagram is required). Irony is used here in a very subtle way, in that someone with Fregoli Syndrome believes in a link between two people that is false, whereas a mixed-up version of Fregoli takes us to R Fegoli, a character who does have a deep connection to another, but one that the viewer cannot see yet, and will only be able to a season later if they are highly observant.

It is well known that *The Sopranos*, in line with the preferences and style of Chase, is an extremely carefully constructed show. Nothing is left to chance or included without reason. Therefore, even if Dottie did not name the man who impregnated her, the connections between Russ and Paulie are too strong to dismiss; the fact that she did makes it undeniable. There is still work for the viewer to do in pulling together the pieces of the puzzle, because Paulie being the son of Russ is never explicitly stated, and the relevant information about his father is presented before the question has been raised, so one is less likely to retain it. This is demonstrated by the fact that most people who have watched the show even more than once do not spot the hidden story, and as a consequence do not understand why so much attention in Marco Polo is given to an apparently unimportant character.[124]

This is another hidden story that does not require the insertion of a type of narrative other than the standard sort that is being utilized. It is included by Chase and the team of writers to bring an added layer of intricacy to what is already a highly complex exercise in storytelling. This is in line with the theme of connectivity which Bernard argues convincingly to be an ongoing theme in the show, used by Chase to counter the idea that existence has no purpose or value.[125] Although Bernard believes that 'Fegoli being Paulie's father would be just way too much of a coincidence', he does allow the possibility that it is there 'as a fun little easter egg'.[126]

---

[124] In their article on The Fleshy Part of the Thigh, Seitz and Sepinwall spend little time on the question of the paternity of Paulie, not even mentioning the name Russ. *Op. cit.*, pp. 247-250.
[125] *Op. cit.*, 'Home', 'Isabella' and 'Made in America'.
[126] *Ibid.*, 'The Fleshy Part of the Thigh'.

Chapter Twelve
You're A Natural

The context for the next hidden story is the revelation that Vito, a capo in the New Jersey crew, is homosexual. In the patriarchal world of the Italian-American Mafia, being a man in the traditional sense is valued very highly. A real man does not cry at anything, at least in public, so, in Mr. and Mrs. John Sacrimoni Request..., when Johnny Sac bursts into tears at the wedding of his daughter, as the US Marshalls take him back to prison before the newlyweds can leave, the displeasure of his acting boss Phil and other gangsters is plain to see. Crying is a sign of weakness and, if a man cannot control himself in this regard, he cannot be relied upon at other times, such as when pressure is applied by the police and FBI. He marries a woman, has children and particularly a male heir, and provides for them. Tony does not want Carmela to work, and is angry at Finn DeTrolio, Meadow's then boyfriend, when he pays for a meal, in Unidentified Black Males (5.9).

A real man certainly does not stray from women as providers of sexual pleasure; that is what mistresses, prostitutes and wives are for (in that order, it appears). Homosexuality is one of the gravest of sins amongst the men of the Mafia. Common terms of abuse relating to any type of misdemeanour are grounded in homophobia: faggot, c***sucker, and so on. Rather than referring to homosexuality as something natural and common, mocking euphemisms are used: taking it up the Hershey highway, ass-muncher, playing for the pink team, fanook and pillow-biter. Carlo, Paulie and Carmela all assume that someone who is gay is highly likely to have AIDS. Richie suspects his son to be gay, although the only evidence that the viewer is made aware of is that he is a talented dancer, and his sensitivity to this is a primary factor in the argument with Janice, which ends with her killing him. In Cold Stones, Sil declares that being in the closet makes gays 'devious', and praises Richie for disowning his son. Lesbianism appears to be another matter, although it is not really. Women who conform to the alpha male standard of attractiveness, indulging in simulated sexual activity with each other for money, is popular with the men of the Mafia, as is demonstrated by the Icelandic airhostesses in For All Debts Public and Private (4.1), but that is hardly the same as the relationships of everyday women with each other.

It is against this backdrop that the arc of Vito comes to a close. In Unidentified Black Males, Tony arranges for Finn a job as a labourer. At the construction site, Vito tells him that he looks like Joe Perry, the guitarist in Aerosmith, but what might have been a casual comment turns out to be indicative of something else. Arriving early to work one morning, Finn sees Vito performing oral sex on another construction worker in a car. His attempts to intimidate, then bribe, him into silence demonstrate that this is not something that anyone else should know about. In Join the Club, on hearing of the suicide of Eugene Pontecorvo, a fellow capo, Vito suggests that he was 'a homo' and felt he had no one to talk to; there is no evidence that he was homosexual, so Vito is really talking about himself. In the next episode, he meets Meadow and Finn at the hospital while Tony is in the coma, surreptitiously running his hand down the young man's arm.

In Mr. and Mrs. John Sacrimoni Request..., Vito attends the wedding of Johnny Sac's daughter Allegra. During the ceremony, he holds his wife's hand and looks at her wedding ring, but he clearly has things on his mind. When he greets Tony and his family later, he describes Finn as 'all handsome in his Calvin Klein', with the object of the compliment looking uncomfortable in his presence. When dancing with his wife, Vito appears distracted and takes his family away from the wedding early, using the excuse that he is not feeling well. Phil is not impressed at this. Back at home, Vito tells his wife that he has to make collections, even though it is late. In a subtle hint about her husband hiding something important about himself from her, she is watching a scene from the 1959 film *Imitation of Life*, in which a young girl called Sarah Jane pretends to be white when she is in fact mixed-race. Vito is later spotted in a gay club by two acquaintances of the Soprano crew who are making collections. On seeing him, dressed in leather biker gear and leading another man by a leash, they berate him, calling him a 'fag' and his friend 'cupcake'; they leave in disgust and he is mortified at being found out. He goes home, takes a gun and retreats to a motel. Very worried, he calls Sil at 3am, asking vaguely how things are. In the next episode, Live Free or Die, Chris and James 'Murmur' Zancone inform the rest of the crew about the allegations towards Vito. Paulie is very upset, and when Patsy says that he is not bothered, he asks him if it is because he is gay.

Benny, Dante and Terry Doria finally locate Vito at his beach house and tell him to come in to see Tony, but he drives off at speed. After stopping off at home later, for money and to kiss his sleeping children, he drives north. A fallen branch on the road damages his car, so he walks to a nearby town, the fictional Dartford in New Hampshire, and rents a room. The town is sleepy, friendly and picturesque, and in a diner Vito sees that two men who seem to be a couple are accepted in the community. Vito is attracted to Jim, the male chef, and later looks thoughtfully at the motto of New Hampshire on a license plate: Live Free or Die.

The truth about Vito is finally confirmed to the crew when they become aware of what Finn saw. He is taken to Satriales to testify, unsurprisingly looking scared. Paulie is very angry and feels betrayed, and Carlo joins him in calling for Vito to be executed. In a therapy session, Jennifer highlights ambivalence on Tony's part about homosexuality: he finds the idea of two men together 'disgusting', but quite likes what lesbians do; and he is worried about losing the income Vito brings in from construction, but does not mind what people do in private behind closed doors. When she says that his associates who have spent time in jail 'can't be strangers to male / male sexual contact', he replies 'you get a pass for that…There's no women there!', making it clear that he did not do it when he was in jail.

Cold Stones marks the final appearance of Vito. He comes up to Tony unexpectedly in a shopping mall and blames his behaviour on his blood pressure medication: 'it f***ed with my head.' In a meeting with his family, he suggests to his wife that they have another child, a desperate ploy to prove his heterosexuality, but later from his hotel room he calls Jim and is more candid with him: 'I miss you.' Under pressure from Phil, Tony decides to have Vito executed, which he justifies by declaring: 'if Vito wanted to pursue that lifestyle he should have done so quietly.' Sil is puzzled: 'he was, wasn't he?'. After calling Tony to see if he has thought about the offer he made him at the mall, Vito returns to his hotel room, but is accosted by Gerardo 'Gerry the Hairdo' Torciano and Dominic 'Fat Dom' Gamiello from the Lupertazzi family, who beat him with sticks. He is tied up and gagged and, when they turn the lights on, the closet doors open to reveal Phil stepping out. He tells Vito he is 'a f***ing disgrace' and then the others continue the assault. The next day, Bobby informs the crew that Vito has been found dead with 'a pool cue rammed up his ass.'

The story of Vito being outed as a homosexual and the consequences that follow is a welcome addition to *The Sopranos*: it is believable, fascinating and by turns tragic and hilarious. Yet again, the depth of the storytelling demonstrates that this is much more than a Mafia drama. It is an investigation into the human condition, speaking to us all wherever we stand on the spectrum between good and evil. There is, however, a hidden dimension to it. Another story that is only subtly hinted at is attached, and the focus is not Vito, but Phil.

The pieces of this implicit puzzle are as follows. Phil is possibly the person who is most angry at the uncovering of the private life of Vito. At a meal with the New Jersey family to celebrate Gerry and Burt Gervasi becoming made men, in Luxury Lounge (6.7), he compares them favourably to 'faggot-assed corn-holing c***suckers' like Vito. At least part of this undoubtedly comes from his being related by marriage to him: Phil is the cousin of Vito's wife Marie, to whom he expresses sympathy. He also worked with Vito on construction business and so was at risk of financial loss. Despite the potential ramifications of interfering in the business of another Mafia family, he is intent on finding

Vito and meting out justice. Still, as Phil watches him being beaten to death, he grips the bed with his right hand as if he is uncomfortable in some way, which could, of course, be explained by him watching a man with whom he had previously gotten on well being executed brutally. Later on, he has difficulty sleeping.

Other aspects of the story suggest that something about the Vito situation is bothering Phil beyond his prior relationship with him. Before Vito has been found, he says to Marie that 'we can't be in denial'. This can be read as advice about viewing the matter as it is rather than through rose-tinted glasses, but being in denial also has the connotation of not being honest with oneself about being of a sexuality that others do not approve of. As Vito has been outed, could this refer to someone else? At a family gathering for Vito after he is found dead, someone is watching a male bodybuilding competition on television. Phil is saying to Marie that 'you can't let your mind dwell on...', but is distracted by the program and orders it to be turned off. The volume of the television was high, but the writers could have specified any one of thousands of different types of program to be shown, so why images of muscular men?

The final clue that is needed to solve the mystery is provided in the scene depicting the murder of Vito. There is no need for Phil to be where he is, as the room is dark and the others are able to hide behind the door. In the context of a storyline about a homosexual being outed, it cannot be a coincidence that Phil comes 'out of the closet', a well-known saying used when someone becomes open to others about being gay. Vito is already out of the closet, so what could this mean?

When added together, these aspects of the story can only equate to Phil not being a stranger to the homosexual lifestyle himself. He first appears in the show at the beginning of the fifth season, when he is released from prison after serving twenty years. He was imprisoned as a result of the crackdown on organised crime in the 1980s. He refers to this time during a disagreement over business with Tony, in The Second Coming: 'You want compromise? How's this? Twenty years in the can. I wanted manicott; I compromised, I ate grilled cheese off the radiator instead. I wanted to f*** a woman, but I compromised, I jacked off in a tissue. You see where I'm going?'. This is not the first time this story is heard. In Unidentified Black Males, Tony B, who was in prison at the same time as Phil, recounts it to Tony but, in his version, it is a black prisoner grilling the cheese. Here the writers are hinting that Phil is not being entirely truthful about his compromises: he could do without some things, but not sex, and he is now haunted by the choice he made.

This allows us to reconsider two apparently insignificant details from earlier episodes. In Kaisha, Phil says to a woman he is spending the evening with: 'there's something I need to get straight between us.' This may be only a suggestive remark, but it could be a subtle reference to his need to prove his heterosexuality, reinforced by their plans being disrupted by the fire-bombing of their destination, i.e., he is not able to 'get it straight'. In the next episode, after he recovers following his heart attack, a party is thrown for him. Doc Santoro welcomes him back by singing 'young and tall and tanned and lovely', a not completely accurate rendition of the first line of The Girl from Ipanema (1962)[127]. Phil does not display any anger at this, so

---

[127]Lyrics originally in Portuguese by Vinícius de Moraes and translated to English by Norman Gimbel.

perhaps he does not understand the joke, or it may be an allusion to his homosexuality only intended for the audience.

In the language of psychoanalysis, Phil is 'projecting' in his response to the Vito situation. This is when, because something about ourselves causes us so much emotional pain that we cannot process it properly, we project it on to another person, who it may or may not also be true of. What makes Phil uncomfortable about himself is also true of Vito, the person he projects on to, so he vents his anger on him, while not admitting that he too is 'guilty'. In essence, projection is an expression of weakness even when it manifests as strength. Extreme hatred for something in others that is also in us is believed to be a common phenomenon. In 2006, Ted Haggard, then President of the National Association of Evangelicals in the USA, was revealed to have been paying for sex with a male prostitute for three years. In 2009 came a further revelation that he had been in an ongoing relationship with a young man in his church. Haggard had been a vocal defender of the traditional Christian understanding of marriage as being between a man and a woman, and supported a movement that would ban same-sex marriage in Colorado.[128] His story is a complicated and fascinating one, and its equivalents in the experiences of Vito and Phil no less so. Secreting in the narrative another story of hidden events and motivations allows Chase and his writers to once again demonstrate the complexity of human affairs. He confirms that the hints about the sexuality of Phil are intentional, and, therefore, that the revelation of this

---

[128] Documentary by Not The Good Girl 'The Scandalous Life of Pastor Ted Haggard...And His Dark Return'.

hidden story is accurate;[129] as reason has been provided to not automatically trust what he says, this is one instance of his commentary being validated by evidence.[130]

There is one more character who, it is hinted, may be hiding homosexual leanings. As previously mentioned, Richie reacts extremely negatively to the possibility, for which no evidence is made available, that his son might be gay; this, therefore, looks like a similar level of overreaction to that of Phil regarding Vito. After Richie is released from prison, he is given a present of private time with two of the strippers from the Bada Bing!, which happens with the lights off, but he appears unsatisfied afterwards. During his relationship with Janice, it is learned that he enjoys holding a gun to her head during sex. These indications about Richie are more subtle than those regarding Phil, and less time is spent on their development. He is a violent man, even by the standards of the other characters, so the use of the gun with Janice might be due to that, or his feeling that he is not receiving proper respect from her brother Tony, rather than him finding the activity uninteresting, or because he took other men by force during his ten years in prison. The greater ambiguity here means that this is not a hidden story that drives the narrative in the way that others do.

---

[129]*Talking Sopranos* 91, 25.51.
[130]Seitz and Sepinwall raise the possibility of the homosexuality of Phil only in a brief footnote, and overlook key information, thereby failing to properly explain his motivations and the events which they propel forward. *Op. cit.*, p. 269, footnote 45.

Part Three

Going Home

Chapter Thirteen
On Entering This Diner Please Check in Your Weapon

The position that Tony finds himself in before Made in America begins is desperate. He makes what he believes to be the first move in a war with the Lupertazzi family, but it could hardly go worse. His men are sent to execute Phil but target the wrong man, the father of his mistress, and it is revealed that they never truly had the opportunity, as their target had gone into hiding 'four or five days before', according to Sil. The retaliation begins before Tony can get his men to their safehouse, and it is swift and deadly. Bobby is murdered, Sil is shot multiple times and unlikely to regain consciousness, and this signals that Phil's plan to 'decapitate and do business with whatever's left' of the New Jersey family is already almost achieved. A dark shadow is cast over Made in America that encroaches upon the efforts of Tony's sleeping mind to 'focus on the good times'. He is fearing for his life, livelihood and associates, with his most recent memory of his son, crying on his bedroom floor, doing nothing to help. When the Corleones went through a similar experience in

The Godfather in 1972, the youngest son, Michael, stepped up after the deaths of his father, Vito, and brother, Sonny, to save the family and become the next Don Corleone; but the disgust that Tony shows for his son indicates that nothing of the sort will happen here.

The themes of pessimism and death are there right from the beginning of the show: Tony's illness which takes him to therapy with Jennifer, the violence inherent in his lifestyle, and his belief that he missed the best times of the Mafia. As it begins, so shall it end: the spectre of death haunts him throughout the final season and his realization of this is demonstrated repeatedly in the finale from the beginning. The opening image is of Tony asleep, but framed in a way that is reminiscent of someone deceased in a casket. Compare how Karen looks in her casket in Christopher, Chris in Kennedy and Heidi, his father Dickie in *The Many Saints of Newark*, and both Raymond 'Buffalo Ray' Curto and Eugene in Members Only. It is also very similar to the views of Tony lying on the floor after he is shot by Junior in Members Only, and, prior to that, having a biopsy in Irregular Around the Margins (5.5). The organ playing, although it is not traditional funeral music but rather the beginning of You Keep Me Hangin' On by Vanilla Fudge from 1967, adds to the impression that we are with someone who has passed away or is at risk of doing so.

Again with the Corleones: in the trilogy, oranges are associated with death or its proximity. When Vito is shot in the first movie, he is buying oranges and they fall to the ground with him; when he dies, he is playing with his grandson and has put peel into his mouth as a joke. In the sequel (1974), Michael receives an orange from Johnny Ola not long before his house and family are attacked, and, in a flashback scene, the local gangster Don

Fanucci eats an orange just before he is murdered by Vito. In the final movie (1990), Michael drops an orange as he dies. There are many more examples, and the reason behind them is that the colour orange was first chosen so that its brightness could contrast the darker sets and costumes, but this evolved into oranges being used in a more indicative sense.[131] In *The Sopranos*, as noted earlier, eggs are the preferred signal that death is approaching; but the use of oranges does appear too, no doubt as a nod to *The Godfather* trilogy. In Isabella, when the attempt on his life takes place, Tony is buying orange juice and the bottle is smashed by a bullet; in Made in America, he eats an orange when he visits his family in their safehouse.

The cat is also of an orange-like colour and it represents a person who was murdered on his orders: Adriana. She has a fondness for clothes and shoes modelled on tiger and leopard markings, as can be seen in No Show. In the previous episode, For All Debts Public and Private, Danielle Ciccolella, the undercover FBI Agent Deborah Ciccerone, drinks from a wine glass decorated in that way in her apartment, and there is also an orange cat fridge magnet in the home of Chris' mother. In Long Term Parking, the last time that Tony sees Adriana alive before he orders her execution, she is wearing a full-body tiger print outfit, and she is crawling on all fours the last time the viewer sees her, before she is shot by Sil. According to the design plans for the beach house that Tony examines in the finale, the name of the architect is Aryeh Siegel – Aryeh is Hebrew for lion.

---

[131] Gilbert Cruz 'The Anniversary You Can't Refuse: 40 Things You Didn't Know About The Godfather: What's with All the Oranges?', *Time*.

The final appearance of the cat is outside Satriales, after Tony has finally convinced Paulie to take over the running of the Aprile crew. What is incredibly hard to spot is that Adriana's fiancée Chris is also present briefly, despite being murdered three episodes earlier. After Tony in exasperation says 'you don't want the job? You don't want the job', the camera retreats to a longer shot of the two of them and a silver car goes by, obscuring them briefly. Replayed slowly, it can be seen that the driver's face is completely visible, i.e., he is breaking the fourth wall by staring to his left at the viewer and not the road ahead. This is worthy of comment in itself, but even more so is that the driver looks very much like Chris. It is perhaps not surprising that he flashes into Tony's mind by association at this point, because Paulie is disappointing him in refusing to take over the Aprile crew, and Chris consistently failed to meet his expectations to an even greater degree; soon afterwards, also by association, the cat appears.

When Janice visits Junior she finds Uncle Pat there too. He spots what he refers to as a double-breasted robin through the window, but there is no such variety of this bird. The robin signifies transformation, renewal and new life in many cultures. Junior almost put Tony into the next life twice, in Isabella and Members Only, so the presence in this scene of both he and the robin is important. During his sweeping of leaves in the garden of the family home, Tony looks at the sun. The last time that he paid particular attention to a light in the distance was in the coma dream, in Join the Club and Mayham. This experience is explained in more detail in Chapter Fifteen, but, for the purposes of this point, the traditional practice of using a bright light to symbolise the afterlife should be remembered.

In From Where to Eternity, the dream that Christopher has while he is in a coma carries a message for Tony that he will die at three o'clock. This probably comes from the Catholic teaching, that both would be familiar with, that Jesus died at that time: 'And at three in the afternoon Jesus cried out in a loud voice, "Eloi, Eloi, lama sabachthani?" (which means "My God, my God, why have you forsaken me?"). When some of those standing near heard this, they said, "Listen, he's calling Elijah."...With a loud cry, Jesus breathed his last' (Mark 15:34-37). In line with this, the number three recurs throughout Made in America. At the truce meeting, the bottles of water are arranged in three rows of three. The car that the young men are standing in front of, as they watch the execution of Phil, is a 2003 BMW 3-series. After his SUV explodes, AJ is bought a BMW M3; he spoke enthusiastically about this car when visiting his father during his coma in Join the Club, so the implication is that it registered with Tony on a subconscious level then, and reappears during this dream in connection with his son. In the first and only scene in which AJ drives his BMW, the theme of the War on Terror focuses on him: the company he is working for is revealed as Lone Wolves Productions, a lone wolf referring to a terrorist who is operating by themselves[132], and his licence plate contains the letters RDX, the name of an explosive otherwise known as hexogen.

When Tony is raking leaves in his garden, three tall trees stand behind him. In Holsten's, there are three lights visible behind him as he enters; three boy scouts; three lights and pictures on the

---

[132] The name of the company is therefore probably intended to be a malapropism of the sort that Little Carmine is known for: by definition, lone wolves cannot be working together.

wall behind him and Carmela; three sachets of cream served with the drink to the man in the USA cap; three people at the Soprano table, three cokes served and three onion rings eaten; and three attempts at parking by Meadow in a car with the licence plate of 39F LGP (three and three times three). One should also consider that the bathroom, where Tony fears the Man in Members Only jacket will retrieve his gun from, is on his right, i.e., his 3 o'clock; but if the dream representation of Holsten's is representative of how it really is (*The Many Saints of Newark*, and photos posted online, including by customers and fans, suggest that it is), then this is probably a coincidence caused by the internal layout. The increased frequency with which the number three appears in the final scene is part of the greater intensity characteristic of it that will be discussed in the following chapters.

There is more to the car, a Lexus IS250, that Meadow arrives in: like AJ's BMW M3, it is a reference to when Tony is near to death in a coma. In the dream, when Tony is asking the barman if he remembers Kevin Finnerty, who he believes has his briefcase, another man jokes that 'he drives a Lexus', i.e., a rival car to the Nissan Infiniti. In driving a Lexus, Meadow is working futilely against infinity, the approach of the afterlife.

Attention should also be paid to the overt reason given for the family eating at Holsten's. Carmela tells AJ that they are not having mannicott because she has a meeting about the spec house with carpenters. It sounds plausible, but could it have another meaning if this is a dream? It certainly could: the Sopranos are a Catholic family and Jesus' trade before he turned to preaching was carpentry. Catholics hope to see Jesus again in the afterlife, so this is Tony's sleeping mind worrying about whether he and his loved ones will live to see another day. This is reinforced by the song that is heard: The Lifeboat Party by Kid Creole and the Coconuts, from their 1983 album *Doppelganger*. The title speaks of the aftermath of a disaster, and the lyrics of the chorus state that the party is 'only for the rank and file',[133] so Tony, as the boss of the Soprano crew, will not be celebrating, and neither will his underboss and consigliere, both taken out in the previous episode.

The scene in Holsten's is crammed full of subtle references to death. After Tony enters, he stops and looks at the customers and staff as a whole, which allows for a complete view of the mural on the far wall. There is no evidence that Holsten's has ever been decorated in this way, and, although the interior of the shop is seen in *The Many Saints of Newark*, the far wall is not. Given that the mural is unmissable here, but obscured in the prequel film, these decisions by the production team must be connected and deliberate. The rationale is that the former is in a dream sequence which is to be unacknowledged, the latter not. The mural was deliberately put in by the production crew and then taken out once filming for Made in America had ended: in a program with such attention to detail this choice must be explained fully.

The centre is a painting of a large building of residential appearance with the caption 'Bloomfield, New Jersey'. It is flanked on the left by the face of a tiger with the words 'Go Bengals State Champions 1973' and a football player with the information 'Michael Shea Class of 1977', and on the right by another, identified as '"Super Dave" Phillip Class of 1971'. Michael Shea has already been identified as a reference to a porn movie

---

[133]Written by August Darnell and Ronnie Rogers.

from 1977 called The Secret Dreams of Mona Q, and also Shea Stadium, where the New York Jets played at that time. The significance of 'Super Dave' Phillip lies in the man who is sitting below this picture, and this will be explained later.

The players have the numbers 38 and 22 on their shirts, which are not references to football but to common calibres of guns, the weapons that Tony and the other criminals he spends his time with make such deadly use of[134]; his final visit to Junior in the previous scene took place in Ward 22. Their being football players adds to the pessimistic flavour of the scene in that they are a reminder to him of one of the many missed opportunities of his life. He showed promise in the sport while at school, but, as Coach Molinaro reminds him in The Test Dream, he threw it away and is left only with Junior repeatedly telling him that he 'never had the makings of a varsity athlete', a comment which he finds 'very hurtful' and 'undermining' (Where's Johnny? (5.3)).

The tiger looks very much at home on a mural celebrating American football. The team of Bloomfield High School are called the Bengals. The Cincinnati Bengals in the NFL take their name from this magnificent creature, as do numerous teams at the College level and below. In 2017 four of them – Clemson, Auburn, Louisiana State and Missouri – even formed the Tigers United University Consortium to support the protection of tigers globally.[135] However, in a dream nothing is to be taken at face value or as the role it has played in the past. Remembering that we are watching a private showing of Tony's subconscious mind, what else could the tiger represent? It is a large cat – a Big Pussy.

---

[134] MasterofSopranos *op. cit.*, Page 3, Part III.
[135] https://www.clemson.edu/tigers-united/consortium/index.html.

Big Pussy had been an associate of Johnny Boy and a close friend of Tony for a long time. It is revealed in Do Not Resuscitate (2.2) that he is an FBI informant, after being caught selling heroin. The corrupt cop Vin tells Tony that he thinks Big Pussy is a rat, and he is, as expected, deeply troubled by the possibility that his old friend is a traitor. Big Pussy avoids discovery in the first season when the suspicions of the crew fall on James 'Jimmy' Altieri and he is executed instead, even though it is never made clear whether he is actually an informant. Various factors in the second season contribute to the deterioration of the friendship between Big Pussy and Tony, including the toll of living a double life and being passed over for promotion when Tony becomes acting boss. Tony's suspicions about the loyalties of his friend resurface and he finally confronts them in the dream in Funhouse, the second season finale. He later discovers a listening device in Big Pussy's home, at which point the fate of his friend is sealed. Tony, Sil and Paulie take Big Pussy on a boat ride, and, once they get him to admit the truth, he is executed. This is not the last we see of Big Pussy, because his murder affects Tony greatly. An image of him appears in a mirror briefly at a gathering at the family home following the funeral of Livia, in Proshai, Livushka. In The Test Dream, he sits silently in the passenger seat of the car being driven by Johnny Boy in the dream sequence. It is not a surprise, therefore, that he turns up obliquely in Made in America; anything more literal would risk revealing that it is a dream. But he still refuses to speak to Tony.

The psychological mechanism at work here is repression, which amounts to consciousness doing its best to avoid thinking of things which cause it emotional pain, burying them under distortion and distraction. Freud spotted it in the behaviour of those he was treating: 'if my little daughter did not want an apple that was offered to her, she asserted that the apple tasted sour without having tasted it. And if my patients behaved like the child, I knew that they were concerned with an idea which they wanted to *repress*.'[136] This is what happens to the suspicions Tony has about Big Pussy in his dream in Funhouse, although by the end of it they seep out. In Fortunate Son, Jennifer helps him to understand that he has repressed a memory of seeing his father chopping off a finger of someone who had not repaid a debt. The greater the emotional pain caused by a memory, the more the mind has to do to distance itself from it: 'the stricter the censorship, the more far-reaching will be the disguise'.[137]

The mural is completed by the painting of the house. Holsten's is a real diner that is located in Bloomfield, New Jersey, so that explains the title, but the house itself is a mystery. It is not Holsten's itself as that is much smaller, nor is it a notable residence or visitor attraction in Bloomfield. It needs to be analysed in the same way as the rest of the mural: what could a large house mean to Tony? A personal link comes from the fact that his grandfather was a stonemason who came to America from Avellino in Italy. But is there anything more than this? Does he visit such a building in a previous episode? He does so twice, and on both occasions it is during a dream.

The first time is in Calling All Cars. Tony dreams twice and in the second he appears, as he imagines his grandfather would, as an Italian stonemason who speaks barely any English. He follows Ralphie, who he murdered two episodes before, to a

---

[136]*Op. cit.*, p. 222.
[137]*Ibid.*, p. 224.

house where he believes there is work to be done. He sees inside a black silhouette of a female figure descending the stairs. She does not respond and just stands there: there is no reason to believe that she represents anyone but his deceased mother Livia. As he begins to enter the house, he wakes up, unnerved.

The second is in the final part of the extended dream sequence that he undergoes while he is in a coma, after being shot by Junior in Members Only. He appears as a precision optics salesman, repeatedly mistaken for a man named Kevin Finnerty who he resembles. At the conclusion of the dream, he travels to a Finnerty family reunion being held at the Inn at the Oaks, which is not dissimilar at all to the large residential building pictured in the mural in Holsten's. Tony is greeted there by a man who looks identical to his dead cousin Tony B, who informs him that the people inside are waiting for him. At the top of the steps in the doorway, he sees a glimpse of a woman that is very reminiscent of what he saw inside the house in Calling All Cars.

The appearance of Tony B in the coma dream brings added potency to the mural in Holsten's, because of the great emotional pain for Tony associated with his cousin. As he admits to Jennifer in Unidentified Black Males, he feels guilt, partly due to the fact that Tony B was arrested and served a lengthy prison sentence because of his involvement in the armed hijacking of a truck, a crime that Tony was not present at because he suffered a panic attack, but which gave him the opportunity to become wealthy and see his children grow up. However, after being released from prison, Tony B's attempts to go straight flounder, and he unwisely becomes involved in a power-struggle in the Lupertazzi family, and murders Billy. In All Due Respect, to save him from torture and death at the hands of Phil, and to re-establish business relations between their families, Tony executes him. It is because of these varying motivations that Tony B does not appear explicitly in Holsten's with other members of their family: the author of the dream cannot bear to look him in the eye.

There is a long tradition in Catholicism and other denominations within Christianity of envisaging the afterlife as a large house or mansion. It goes back to the early days of the faith. John 14.2 reads: 'my Father's house has many rooms; if that were not so, would I have told you that I am going there to prepare a place for you?'. Tony hears Father Phil Intintola quote this at a funeral in Another Toothpick (3.5), and as a Catholic he is likely to have heard it repeated many times. The building in the mural in Holsten's, if we have been paying attention, can only signify the afterlife. It dominates the view and looms over Tony: his mind is expressing a powerful fear that he is near to death.

The bell on the door is heard six times at the entry of Tony, the woman with long curly hair, the man in the USA cap, Carmela, the Man in Members Only jacket followed by AJ, and an unseen person at the end, who many assume to be Meadow as she is running towards the entrance. There is more to the apparent strangers than meets the eye and this will be explained later. The ringing of church bells is traditional when someone has died, and the colloquial phrase 'getting your bell rung' also means to receive a violent blow. There is a further association with religious practice in how Tony, Carmela and AJ put their onion rings into their mouths, whole without a bite. This is how Catholics take the Communion wafer in a ceremony which is a remembrance of the final meal Jesus shared with his followers, before he was arrested and crucified.[138] It is known as the Last Supper and there is therefore an implication that this will be the last time Tony eats with his family or anyone else.

As Tony is looking through the jukebox selections, there is a glimpse inside the kitchen where there are two chefs frying the type of food that he adores. On the wall behind them, in the top right-hand corner, is a handwritten notice with an odd message. It reads: 'Please write all Cake orders down! No exception!!! Complete the circle'. Below is a large C, which could be a way of drawing the attention of the staff to the notice, but, if so, that is a strange way to do it. Examining it through the lens of Tony's subconscious suggests a different meaning. 'The big C' is a colloquial way of referring to cancer. The link between eating excessive amounts of fried food as he does and increased chances of developing cancer is well-known, as is that with other aspects of his lifestyle, including drinking too much alcohol, smoking, insufficient exercise[139] and suffering from anxiety.[140] He would have been informed of this by medical practitioners and been able to pick it up from the media.

In Irregular Around the Margins, Tony has a cancerous mole removed from his head. One of his oldest friends, Jackie, Sr., dies of cancer in the first season, his uncle Junior has a stomach tumour and Paulie is diagnosed with prostate cancer. When discussing Jackie, Sr.'s cancer with Jennifer in Denial, Anger, Acceptance (1.3), Tony is bothered by the painting of the barn in her waiting room, describing it as 'depressing and scary'. She

---

[138] Matthew 26:17-30.
[139] Cancer Research UK 'Causes of cancer and reducing your risk'.
[140] Although the causal relationship in this regard may be more indirect; Canadian Cancer Society 'Does stress cause cancer?'.

suggests that it troubles him because it reminds him in some way of what his friend is going through. This might also be the first time we see the link in his mind between buildings and the afterlife.

In addition to connotations of cancer, there are other ways in which the notice could be read. One is that, following on immediately from the instruction to 'complete the circle', the C looks like an incomplete circle. There is a long tradition in mysticism and philosophy of using the circle to represent perfection or divinity, for example, the Ensō in Zen and the Dharmachakra or Dharma Wheel in more than one Indian religion. In this interpretation, Tony's subconscious in desperation rails against the situation he finds himself in and the likelihood that many of his hopes for the future will be unrealised; the context being a notice about cake orders ties in with his unhealthy eating habits. His mind is telling him to complete the circle because everything is falling apart.

Another possibility comes from Members Only, in which Tony and Jennifer discuss the 'circle of life', the endless procession of beings entering and leaving existence, in relation to the mental deterioration of Junior. In this sense, 'complete the circle' means to die, particularly as Tony has brought new life into the world twice. It can be taken as an expression of the suicidal impulse that he saw in Livia, his mistress Gloria Trillo, and most recently in AJ.[141]

It is very common to conclude from the final scene that Tony is shot by the Man in Members Only jacket and dies as the screen

---

[141] I am grateful to Alan Stevens for his help with these interpretations of the message in the notice.

cuts to black. At face value, there does seem to be some sense to this. The man and Tony glance at each other, and towards the end of the scene he gets up and walks towards the bathroom, in what is without doubt a reference to the famous scene in *The Godfather*, in which Michael executes Virgil Sollozzo and Captain Mark McCluskey in a restaurant, using a gun that had been hidden in the bathroom prior to their meeting by Peter Clemenza, a capo in the family. As well as many other nods to the three movies throughout *The Sopranos*, this scene has already been referenced in The Test Dream, and in Johnny Cakes, AJ refers to it being his father's favourite. It is also a faint echo in Tony's mind during the sit-down earlier in Made in America: trains can be heard there too in the background, representing his desperation to dispose of his enemies and wanting to use force rather than discussion to settle the dispute. Furthermore, it sets up an association with a previous attempt to kill Tony as the two black men enter immediately afterwards – their identity is explained in the next chapter.

There are, however, very good reasons why this is not a valid interpretation. The most important is that this is a dream and there is no Man in Members Only jacket. But there are more straightforward ones, too, which do not require noticing that we are watching an unusual narrative. He does not behave like a hitman: he takes a prominent seat, has a drink and looks over repeatedly at his purported target. Compare how the executions of Gerry in Stage 5, and Bobby in The Blue Comet, are conducted: quickly, with little time for the victims to react, and obscuring the identity of those responsible. Something else to consider is the reason that Michael goes to the bathroom to retrieve the gun: on entering the restaurant for the meeting with those his family are at war with, he has been searched for concealed weapons, something that the Corleones knew would happen and planned for. The Man in Members Only jacket would not need to go to the bathroom to retrieve a gun because he would not be searched as he enters Holsten's. There is no tense meeting between murderous rivals taking place, only members of the public enjoying their meals. To hold that Tony dies in a manner that reflects this scene from *The Godfather* is to overlook that crucial detail.

Still, as it is a dream that we are watching, it does have significance as an insight into how he is feeling. It shows that he is ashamed that the crew that his father built up and inducted him into is falling apart on his watch, and afraid that he will punish him accordingly. His comment that the onion rings are the 'best in the state' echoes Sollozzo telling McCluskey that the veal is 'the best in the city', and demonstrates that, despite everything his mind has done previously in the dream to ease his worries, he fears that it will all be in vain and that he will share the fate of these two, rather than the victory of Michael.

AJ also functions as a reminder of the Grim Reaper throughout the episode. Although his primary purpose is as an example of wish-fulfilment on the part of his father, he has brought little positive to his family for some time. Tony spares Carmela the full truth, but he lays it bare before Jennifer in more than one therapy session. In Cold Stones, he tells her that he 'hates' AJ and 'ought to smash his f***ing face in'; she comments that his 'anger towards AJ has been building for some time.' His son clearly does not conform to his idea of a man, but it is something that Carmela says about him earlier in the episode that is striking: he has 'a dead streak in him. Chills me to the bone.' It takes a lot for a mother to say that, even one whose husband is a mobster, and of the two Carmela is usually the good cop. There is a pessimistic thread running throughout the show linking Livia, the women Tony chases in order to receive the love that she never gave him, and AJ. It is characterized by cruelty, nihilism and a darkness that corrodes and consumes everything it comes into contact with. Tony sees it in the black female silhouette on the stairs in the second dream in Calling All Cars, and it gradually sucks him in too. In constructing the implausibly positive image of AJ, his father is attempting to conquer death.

In the final scene of Made in America, both Tony and AJ arrive in black leather jackets, Carmela is wearing a black top and, although she does not make it in time, Meadow is wearing a black leather jacket and top. In addition, the shirt worn by Tony beneath the jacket is predominantly a very dark colour, looking very similar to the one he is wearing when he is shot by Junior in Members Only. The darkness has a hold of all of them. Other items of clothing are relevant. The red coat worn by Carmela is another expression of association. It is not a colour that she is seen in often, but one of the rare occasions is during a heated conversation with Tony. In For All Debts Public and Private, she sees the widowed Angie Bonpensiero working in a supermarket, which causes her worry to resurface about how she will make ends meet if her husband dies. Later at home, she raises the subject with Tony and, in response to his attempts to persuade her that she is worrying for nothing, she tells him 'everything comes to an end'; in this, at least from the look on his face, she makes her point. Carmela is wearing red trousers here of a hue identical to the coat, and further evidence that Tony's subconscious draws on this memory is that he talks of the stress he experiences because of his job, while eating something that Holsten's is famous for: ice-cream.

Throughout the finale, and nowhere less so than in Holsten's, the distinction drawn by Freud between the manifest and latent content of dreams is highly relevant. The fear of death is constantly present, but it does not make itself known through anything as obvious or crude as hordes of zombies chasing Tony through the streets of Newark. Instead, and in line with scientific understanding and anecdotal experience, it betrays itself through features as innocuous as numbers, colours and a meal with his family. To see this, it is imperative that the nature of the narrative is understood accurately: it is not a standard one, but a representation of the consciousness of a sleeping subject.

Chapter Fourteen
Holsten's

A huge amount of information, that will be new and surprising to many, about Made in America and its precursors in *The Sopranos* has been put forward so far. In this chapter these findings are drawn together in order to focus even more closely on the famous final scene. It has been endlessly studied and parodied, quite rightly earning a place in our cultural history. Those of us who were not able to watch the initial broadcast on June 10th, 2007 still got to experience the shock of the final cut to black on our first viewing. To this day, it provokes a reaction even after many viewings because of that suddenness, in addition to it signalling the end of the show. If what has been argued to this point about the artistic practices of Chase and the rest of his team is correct, then it must pass the final test of allowing for a deep and comprehensive understanding of the scene in Holsten's. It does indeed manage this quite powerfully, as will now be demonstrated. By the end of this chapter, the reader will have come to understand that the common view concerning what is going on, even amongst those who publish widely read material, is way off the mark.

Something that is absolutely fundamental to the correct reading of the final scene is, once again, the distinction between the manifest and latent content of dreams. The visible dimension of a dream can be very different to the underlying affective one, i.e., the emotional source. Freud wrote that it is often the case that '*ideational material has undergone displacements and substitutions, whereas the affects have remained unaltered.* It is small wonder that the ideational material, which has been changed by dream-distortion, should no longer be compatible with the affect, which is retained unmodified.'[142] The imagination twists and distorts the emotions that are feeding the dream into new and unusual forms. As happens so often in the works of Lynch, such as *Blue Velvet* (1986), there is an undercurrent to the scene that is much darker than a family meal in a diner would seem to indicate.

Holsten's does not appear at all, and is not even mentioned, in *The Sopranos* before this final scene, but *The Many Saints of Newark* makes it clear why it would act as the setting for a dream of Tony. The younger and elder versions of his youthful self both visit it, from which it can be concluded that it was a regular haunt. More than that, there is a deep emotional connection to the place because of the man he idolized when he was that age. Dickie had agreed to meet Tony there one morning but did not turn up, and he would soon discover that this was because he had been murdered the night before. The loss of the man, who was often more of a father to him than Johnny Boy, cemented Holsten's into his emotional history. It means that there is a tangible sense of foreboding given to the scene from it being set in Holsten's, but one that was undetectable to the audience until the release of the prequel film.

---

[142]*Op. cit.*, p. 596.

After Tony enters Holsten's at the beginning of the final scene, and before there is a skip from his standing at the entrance to sitting at the table, it seems as if, for an instant, he is looking at himself. This has happened before, in the dream in Funhouse. He is on the boardwalk at Asbury Park, and through one of the viewing machines he sees himself and Paulie playing cards, inside what appears to be a railway station that is empty except for themselves, although the tannoy can be heard. The skip in Holsten's, and all the others that precede it in the episode, show that we have seen everything from Tony's point of view. Chase took this filmmaking technique from Kubrick's *2001: A Space Odyssey* (1968), using it himself to indicate that 'we put ourselves in these positions...Nothing happens by accident. We are the engineers of our destiny.'[143] This can be read as a typically misleading way of saying that the technique is used in narratives which are representations of the sleeping mind of a subject.

On repeated watching, a suspicion develops that the people in the diner besides Carmela and AJ are not just there as extras to fill out the scene. The more they are studied, the more they resemble people from Tony's life: other members of his family, friends and acquaintances, but also figures who he will not be pleased to see. The events in Holsten's occur as he is on the verge of death and represent his life flashing before his eyes: his sleeping mind frantically conjures up a get-together with his family and friends, but his anxiety also extends an invitation to others.

Before these are discussed, a common feature of dreams should be highlighted. It is another form of disjunctive cognition

---

[143] Seitz and Sepinwall, *op. cit.*, p. 392.

and refers to someone we know not looking as they should. Even if it is someone we know extremely well and have seen very recently, they will look like someone else, despite our being convinced that it is them and treating them as such. This is something to remember in what follows, and the names of the actors and actresses will be provided, where they are known, so that the reader can see the uncanny resemblances for themselves. The reason that Chase makes use of this feature of dreams is to support his intention of hiding from the audience the nature of the narrative. He can include in the scene characters who, if they appear as they truly are, would make it obvious that a dream is being presented.

While Tony is standing at the entrance, there is an older waitress with reddish hair on the left. This is Fran, who he met at the funeral of his Aunt Concetta during In Camelot; she was his father's mistress for some while. Although they are friendly at first, this changes when he realizes that his father was with her when his mother had a miscarriage, and he forced him to lie to her to give him an alibi; she also criticizes Livia repeatedly. Fran is played by Polly Bergen. As the waitress is writing, an old man walks away from her to the right. This is Hesh, another character with close links to Johnny Boy. He was his friend and advisor and has a similar relationship with Tony until near the end of the show. In Chasing It, he loans Tony $200,000 because he has lost a lot of money gambling; it is not paid back on time, which causes animosity between the two. The last we see of Hesh is when Tony visits him to finally pay back the loan, but he barely comments on the sudden death of his girlfriend, and quickly leaves. Hesh is played by Jerry Adler. It is not a coincidence that these two characters are placed in the same part of Holsten's. Not only did they both know Johnny Boy, but they also know each other, and Tony is aware of this: at her home, Fran shows Tony a photograph of herself, Johnny Boy, Hesh and his girlfriend, and Hesh also tells him that he did not like Fran.

Four people are sitting together in the first row of tables. The two facing the camera are a woman with dark hair and a man with a moustache. The woman is Angie, the widow of Big Pussy. The two of them were not getting on well when he was alive, and after he is killed, she is told that he has become an FBI informant and disappeared. Tony provides her with some financial support, allowing her to take over Big Pussy's Cleveland Auto Body. Angie is played by Toni Kalem, whose cheekbones are a giveaway to the identity of the woman. The man next to her is Edward 'Duke' Bonpensiero, Big Pussy's brother, who runs Cleveland Auto Body with Angie. This is one of the closest resemblances here, and Chase is able to get away with it because Duke only appears briefly in one episode, Marco Polo, and is therefore not someone that viewers will be likely to spot. Duke is played by Philip Larocca.

Sitting across from Angie and Duke, facing away from the camera, are a dark-haired man and woman. Not being able to view the man from the front makes identification a little trickier, but he is very reminiscent of Bobby, whose funeral is held earlier in the episode. The woman's face can be seen briefly as Carmela enters Holsten's, and her resemblance to Karen, his first wife who died in a car accident in Christopher, is obvious.

To the right of the people on that table sits an old man in a cap. This is Hugh, Tony's father-in-law. He and Tony have a good relationship throughout the show. The same could not be said of his wife, Mary, who is a much more difficult person: opinionated, impolite and snobby, this explains why there is an old woman who looks just like her exiled to a booth by herself, directly behind their daughter Carmela. Tony cannot imagine even her husband, daughter or grandson wanting to share her company too closely.[144] Hugh is played by Tom Aldredge, Mary by Suzanne Shepherd and the old woman by Patti Karr.

At the back wall are seated a bald man and a woman with black hair. These are extremely well-known characters who first appeared in the Pilot, so it is not surprising that they are away from the attention of the viewer. They are Artie and Charmaine, who run a restaurant called Nuovo Vesuvio together, which is often visited by mobsters and their families. Artie went to school with Tony, and they have been friends ever since, with the odd hiccup in the relationship. Charmaine had a brief fling with Tony when he was first dating Carmela, but is sensible enough to do her best to steer Artie away from involvement in illegal activities. Artie is played by John Ventimiglia and Charmaine by Kathrine Narducci.

To the right of Tony is a woman with light-coloured hair. This is Svetlana, who is employed as a nurse for Livia and, later, Junior. She and Tony have a sexual liaison, he admiring her unwillingness to let her tough childhood get in the way of living her life, and demonstrating a respect for her that he does not have for his other mistresses, although her honesty about why she did not want to continue their relationship riles him. As well as leaving an emotional mark on him in this way, when her cousin Irina, Tony's

---

[144]MasterofSopranos comments on this woman, but mistakenly identifies her as a representation of Livia, although he does not continue this line of thought and address the obvious question of why a dead woman is present in the scene; *op. cit.*, Page 3, Part III.

ex-girlfriend, found out, she informed Carmela, which caused their lengthy separation. This explains why his subconscious generates her memory not just here, but also in the first dream in Calling All Cars. Svetlana is played by Alla Kliouka.

On the left of Tony are seated a young man and woman who both have dark hair. The latter faces away from the camera, but the build and hair of the former shows that they are Jackie, Sr. and his widow Rosalie. Jackie is the acting boss of the crew at the beginning of *The Sopranos*, but does not last long as he is suffering from stomach cancer, dying in Meadowlands. His elder brother Richie is released from prison in the second season, and is prone to the use of excessive violence; he manages to annoy a number of people before he is killed by his wife-to-be Janice. Although Jackie, Sr. did not want it, his son Jackie, Jr. follows him into a life of crime, but repeatedly makes poor decisions, culminating in the robbing of a card game run by Eugene. One of the players is killed, Furio is shot in the leg and, not long afterwards, as punishment Jackie, Jr. is executed by Vito. Because of all of these events, the arc of Rosalie is one of great suffering, seeing her husband dying, her son murdered and her brother-in-law disappearing. Tony has known them both since he was young, with the emotional resonance of their shared experiences explaining their appearance here. Jackie is played by Michael Rispoli and Rosalie by Sharon Angela.

Another facet of disjunctive cognition in the dreaming mind manifests when a woman who closely resembles Meadow has her order taken by the dark-haired waitress. Time is not flowing in a linear manner here, as Meadow has not yet arrived outside and otherwise does not make it into Holsten's, but Tony is desperate for her to be there. Meadow is played by Jamie-Lynn Sigler. One of the many small details that are very difficult to spot in this busy final scene is that she is sitting in almost the exact same spot that Charmaine was earlier. The scene appears to recount events that can take no longer than seven or eight minutes, if one goes by the running times of the two songs heard, possibly less, given that only parts of each are heard and the viewing time of the scene is less than five minutes. However, there are implausibly rapid changes to who is sitting where. This is particularly so with respect to the row of counter seats that lead from the entrance to the diner; in some cases, such as when Carmela arrives, the changes are, quite frankly, ridiculous.[145] Either the editing team were replaced by amateurs, or something other than a standard narrative is being utilised.

Shortly afterwards, as Tony is scrolling through the jukebox selections, he looks up to see a woman with long dark curly hair enter. This is Janice, his older sister, whose character arc includes murdering her husband-to-be, the violent mobster Richie, a fling with Ralphie, which is informative about his unusual sexual preferences, and marriage and a child with Bobby. She is very much a younger version of Livia, as evidenced by the despicable tactics she uses to get her claws into Bobby after the death of Karen. At this she succeeds, but here she does not manage to take Karen's place at the table; she can instead briefly be seen seated at the counter with Richie. Janice is played by Aida Turturro and Richie by David Proval.

The next person to enter is a truck driver. When seated later, we see that he is wearing a cap emblazoned with 'USA'. This is

---

[145] It is surprising that MasterofSopranos does not notice this, given his attention to detail in the final scene; Pages 5-6.

Vin, the corrupt policeman in debt to Big Pussy who appears in the first season. The initials on his cap are a clue to his being employed in a civic role. Tony orders him to commit various illegal acts, including following Jennifer. He eventually commits suicide, which bothers Tony, and explains his appearance not only here but also in the dream in The Test Dream, where he is, for no logical reason, the father of Finn. John Heard plays Vin and Patrick Joseph Connolly the truck driver.

The young couple sitting to the left of Tony, enjoying each other's company, are Chris and Adriana. Unlike the other characters listed here, we get to hear something from the young couple and their laughter sounds very much like it was provided by their actors, Imperioli and Drea de Matteo. The young man is played by Henry O'Neill and his companion by Adrianne Rae Rodgers: that the actress has an almost identical name to the major character is further evidence that something out of the ordinary is going on. Neither O'Neill nor Rodgers have any other acting credits apart from this appearance, and that is unusual also. My suspicion is that both names are pseudonyms, but the only additional evidence that can be offered for this is that Chase's middle name is Henry.

When AJ arrives, he walks in behind a man who has garnered much attention in analyses of this final scene: the Man in Members Only jacket. The opening episode of the sixth season is titled Members Only, and because it ends with Junior shooting Tony, many believe that this man kills him, which immediately leads to the cut to black. As should be obvious by now, the theory that this man is the agent of the death of the central character is incorrect. That does not mean, though, that he is not important to the story; there is certainly something about him that draws Tony's attention, and vice versa. The reason for this is that the Man in Members Only jacket is his father, Johnny Boy. Here is another example of disjunctive cognition in dreams as it relates to time, as he looks to be around Tony's age. The Members Only jacket points to it being this man who inducted Tony into the Mafia lifestyle. He even walks into the diner right in front of his grandson AJ, and goes to sit where his mistress, Fran, and old friend, Hesh, are at the start of the scene. As well as in flashbacks, Johnny Boy appeared in the dream in The Test Dream looking to be a similar age as here. There is a strong resemblance between Joseph Siravo, who plays Johnny Boy, and Paolo Colandrea, who plays the Man in the Members Only jacket. The timing of the entrance of Johnny Boy is precise. It is immediately after Tony tells Carmela that Carlo is the informant who has betrayed him and is going to testify. This is the manifestation of Tony worrying what his father would think of the news: as it is a dream, he is able to appear and stare at his son suspiciously.

This character also forms a link to a previous member of Tony's crew. Eugene becomes a made man, in Fortunate Son, at the same time as Chris, although it is later revealed, in Members Only, that he has been an FBI informant for an unspecified length of time. In the same episode he commits suicide, at least partly because Tony refuses his request to leave the crew to retire with his wife and children to Florida. The perceived motivation for his death, in addition to him being physically similar to the man in the Members Only jacket and wearing this item of clothing often, including in the episode which bears its name, is sufficient justification for his presence on some level in this dream. Eugene is played by Robert Funaro.

By contrast, a character who receives little to no attention is the dark-haired waitress. This is a major oversight, because dark-haired women play a huge part in Tony's life as a whole and in key storylines. They are also the focus of possibly his most penetrating insight about himself. In Amour Fou, an argument with Gloria, the mistress he is trying to move on from, makes him realise that 'I didn't just meet you. I've known you my whole f***ing life.' It turns brutal after she threatens to tell his family about their affair; he starts to throttle her, but is stunned when she urges him to kill her, not for the first time echoing things said by Livia over the years. He has finally seen with utter clarity the repetitive cycle he is in, of seeking emotional connection and sexual gratification from women who remind him of his troubled and difficult mother. Earlier in Made in America, at the family gathering following the funeral of Bobby, a niece of his, Tara Zincone, appears for the first time, having never been mentioned before; as yet another darkhaired beauty, and one who could pass as a younger version of Gloria, she could well be purely a creation of Tony's mind.

Livia is one of the most compelling characters in the history of television. Jennifer suggests that she may suffer from Borderline Personality Disorder, but this is extremely generous to a woman who encouraged her brother-in-law to kill her son. In a characteristic example of life coaching to her grandson AJ, in D-Girl (2.7), she says: 'the world is a jungle...Don't expect happiness: you won't get it, people let you down...In the end you die in your own arms...It's all a big nothing'. She has been feeding her family this nihilistic view of existence since she was bringing up her own children, and the effects on them are very visible.

Livia's belief that 'it's all a big nothing' is not without philosophical or scientific precedent. Pessimism recurs often in the history of philosophy. A branch of Buddhist thought holds that impermanence is the most fundamental characteristic of reality, that no being, object, idea or state of affairs can withstand the passing of time. Even we ourselves, who contemplate the pointlessness of existence, are constantly changing: like everything else we are 'no-thing', i.e., not something which remains the same over time. This is the doctrine of emptiness which is a prerequisite of change, growth, decay, creation and destruction. 'All is possible when emptiness is possible', as Nagarjuna wrote in *Mūlamadhyamakakārikā*.[146] The best course to take in response is the cultivation of mindfulness and acceptance of the way reality is.

This strand of Buddhist thought was studied by Arthur Schopenhauer and is expressed in his hugely influential *The World as Will and Representation* of 1818. Through him and others it made its way into antinatalism, which teaches that the balance of positive and negative experiences for living creatures is decidedly in favour of the latter, and concludes that one should not reproduce, as to bring a being into existence is to inflict the greatest of harms upon them. To the philosophy of pessimism can be added the revolution in our understanding of ourselves and all other forms of life instigated by Charles Darwin, through the publication of his *On the Origin of Species* in 1859. He observed an incessant struggle between beings to survive and reproduce, in which cooperation and altruism are only means to those ends. It should be remembered, though,

---

[146]*Root Verses on the Middle Way*, Chapter 24 verse 14.

that as a biologist he was describing how life works, not stipulating how it should.

What comes from Livia is a statement based on emotion, pain and possibly psychosis, as opposed to reason and evidence. There is a poignancy to the fact that she does not lack understanding of the nature of reality, but has not cultivated an appropriate disposition and ethic, unlike the retired scientist John Schwinn, who explains the basics of quantum physics to Tony, in The Fleshy Part of the Thigh. Despite also dealing with a severe cancer diagnosis, he evinces a relatively positive outlook on life. It would be wrong to lay the blame for the lack of maternal warmth from Livia on nihilism or similar philosophies.

It should be obvious by now who the dark-haired waitress in Holsten's is: Livia, the woman who fed Tony real food as well as a diet of psychological harm. As with her husband, disjunctive cognition has made Livia an age that Tony associates with his being a child. She brings onion rings to the table that he and his family are sitting at, and this is important for two reasons. The first is that he can no longer eat onions. Her bringing them for him to eat is fuelled by the memory that she conspired to have him killed in the first season. The other reason relates not to what they are per se, but their shape. They are circular, like a zero: the waitress is feeding the family a big bowl of nothings (earlier in the episode a large circular wreath, the sort commonly seen at funerals, is visible by the door in the crew safehouse). In line with their arcs, father and son show more interest in the onion rings than Carmela does: AJ says 'mmm, onion rings!', and Tony concurs with 'best in the state as far as I'm concerned!'. Livia's personality that is debilitating to those around her has had a more deleterious effect on them because they inherited the 'putrid Sopranos gene', and Tony was raised by her. They both become more like her, increasingly self-absorbed, depressive and cruel as the show progresses. In flashbacks Livia is played by Laila Robins and Laurie J. Williams, and the waitress by Dani Marco.

The waitress is very reminiscent of Isabella, which is not an accident: she represents the emotional turmoil that he is experiencing, a conflict between how he would like things to have been and how they were. Like the Man in Members Only jacket, who is Johnny Boy with a dash of Eugene, the waitress is a mix of different people, a homelier but deadlier version of his maternal fantasy. She is the mother he loves and fears in equal measure. Freud points out that individual people in dreams can be complex constructions of aspects of more than one[147], and this psychological insight is used by Chase in this scene in a fascinating way.

The presence of Livia is a reminder that, even though Tony's subconscious has done its best to generate a soothing fantasy of a gathering of his family and friends, there is a dark undercurrent. It is never any different in his world, as among the family present are his nephew (in truth they are only related by marriage, Chris being Carmela's first cousin once removed) who he murdered, and his fiancée, of whom he ordered the execution. Of all of Tony's family and friends that his dreaming mind gathers together in Holsten's, there are three that appear obliquely, as if he cannot face them directly. As well as Livia, whose face cannot be seen as she delivers the bowl of onion rings, there is his old friend Big Pussy, appearing in the form of the tiger, and his cousin Tony B,

---

[147] *Op. cit.*, pp. 431-32.

associated through the coma dream with the large house in the mural. It should be no surprise, given Tony's history with these three, why his subconscious cannot look them in the eye. Two of them he murdered, and the other tried to do the same to him.

The anxiety that plagues Tony throughout this dream makes other, less welcome, invitations: these final attendees at the going-away party he is throwing for himself represent threats to him. Each of them is filmed from a low angle, or they appear to stand over him, to emphasise their menace. In dreams, when someone we fear appears, they are often presented as larger than or above us, i.e., more powerful, even if this does not represent the state of affairs in the waking world.

The first is the scoutmaster, an older man with grey hair, accompanied by three boys in scout uniforms. This is Phil, his appearance after his death made possible by more disjunctive cognition. He sits under the image of 'Super Dave' Philip and can be seen looming over Tony's shoulder during the scene. He also threatens his daughter, as the SUV that passes just behind Meadow as she runs towards Holsten's in the final few seconds looks exactly like the one that he is driving in his execution scene. As the scoutmaster sits down, he gestures with his right hand as if firing a gun: in this way he is threatening the boys, which equates to a display of the same sentimentality and compassion towards the young from Tony that came out earlier, when Phil's grandchildren are 'saved' from him by the execution; which children are more deserving of protection stereotypically than Boy Scouts? Phil is played by Frank Vincent and the scoutmaster by William Severs.

The other questionable invitations go to the two black men who enter immediately after Tony's father goes to the bathroom. These are Rasheen Ray and William 'Petite' Clayborn who, on the orders of Junior, attempt to kill Tony in Isabella. Somehow the two of them, despite being armed, and Tony not and under the influence of an overdose of Prozac and lithium, fail in the task and one of them shoots the other in the head. Nevertheless, the memory of the experience is sufficient for Tony's subconscious to bring them into the diner, thereby adding to the creeping sense of menace. Ray is played by Touche and Clayborn by John Eddins, while Du Kelly and Sharrieff Pugh play the men in the diner.

Despite how it appears, Holsten's is actually full of people known to Tony. Disjunctive cognition as a typical feature of dreams means that characters known to him not looking exactly as they have done is not viable as an argument against the people in the diner being them. This also allows Chase to avoid making it blatantly obvious that we are inside Tony's head. Although he is surrounded by people he knows, the only ones who acknowledge his presence are Carmela, AJ, the Man in Members Only jacket, and the waitress or waitresses who bring the cokes and the onion rings (because we do not see the faces, it is difficult to tell whether it is Livia on both occasions). This is an acknowledgment of how he has lived his life and his state of mind not long before he dies. Nobody, not the members of his crew or the close family at his table, tries to warn him about the presence of Phil, or Ray and Clayborn, or to block the Man in Members Only jacket from entering the bathroom; nobody reminds him of the risk posed by eating the onion rings. In the midst of a get-together of his family and friends he feels lonely, unloved and defenceless. How the final scene appears, and what is truly happening, are quite different.

Music is used to great effect throughout the entire run of the show, and the same is true here. Two songs are heard: Little Feat's All That You Dream and Don't Stop Believin' by Journey. Both through their titles and lyrics provide more subtle clues about the nature of the events being portrayed. One that is overlooked is the line 'working hard to get my fill'[148] in the latter. Tony has been dreaming about finding his nemesis, trying to 'get his Phil', and this is the sort of illogical connection the sleeping mind makes. Jennifer points these out repeatedly in his therapy, for example, the ducks in his swimming pool and his own family in the first episode. There would be no basis for this claim, but for the fact that the line forms part of the chain of events in the scene. Immediately after it is heard, the young couple, Chris and Adriana, laugh loudly together and at a volume that is unrealistic in a diner full of people. Both of them died because of Tony, so their appearances in his dream are characterised by expressions of resentment. Here he is imagining them sniggering vengefully something like 'oh yeah? Did you really manage to get your Phil?', taking delight in his predicament.[149]

There is, however, a subtle yet crucial difference between the uses of the two songs that are heard. All That You Dream is a pessimistic song, expressing the view of someone who cannot take any more of what life is throwing at them: 'I've been down, but not like this before. Can't be round this kind of show no

---

[148]Composed by Jonathan Cain, Steve Perry and Neal Schon.
[149]Bernard spots the fill / Phil parallel, and the young couple appearing to laugh at it; but not grasping their identity means that he does not realise that they are truly laughing at it and the predicament of Tony. *Op. cit.*, 'Made in America'.

more'.¹⁵⁰ At the point it is heard, Tony is very near to death: in a futile attempt to save himself, his sleeping mind replaces it with the more optimistic and life-affirming Don't Stop Believin'. The latter plays at a greater volume than the former because its function, like all of the final scene, is a desperate attempt to hold on to life; for the same reason, most of All That You Dream is skipped through, as what we hear are lyrics from beginning. Tony cannot bear to hear the bad news at this late stage.

Music also plays a role in this scene through the selections displayed in the jukebox. It was noted earlier that two of them mention magic in their titles, This Magic Moment by Jay and the Americans and Magic Man (Live) by Heart, and therefore are hints about the unreality of this scene. Others are expressive of his being asleep in a safehouse in a war that is not going well: Who Will You Run To by Heart (1987), Only the Strong Survive by Jerry Butler (1968) and A Lonely Place by Tony Bennett (1969). A final one, Rock It, Billy by T. Graham Brown (1986), explicitly names a person whose death is a major part of the explanation for the situation Tony now finds himself in: the younger brother of Phil, who was shot by Tony B in The Test Dream.

The tables in Holsten's do not ordinarily have jukeboxes. Those in Made in America were put in for the purposes of the story and consequently should not be treated as just part of the scenery. The selection on the jukebox at the table Tony is sitting at is suspiciously geared towards his tastes and the time in his life when he would have listened to them. All of the songs are from the 1960s to 1980s, with the latest, those by Sawyer Brown, Heart and Bryan Adams, being from 1987. His selection, Don't

---

¹⁵⁰Composed by Paul Barrere and William H. Payne.

Stop Believin', was released in 1981. He was born in 1959, which means that every one of the songs are from the period covering his early childhood, and would likely have been played in the family home by his parents, to his late twenties. Made in America is set in 2007, which means that there are no songs from less than twenty years ago available, which does not make sense in a commercial establishment frequented by so many young people, even one which deals in nostalgia.[151] In the episode as a whole, the only song that is from outside of this timeframe is that which is there specifically for AJ to represent his turnaround: Scratch Your Name by Noisettes from 2006.

Got a Lot of Woman on Her Hand by the Gatlin Brothers is an inaccuracy: it should be Got a Lot of Woman on His Hands, the B-side to their 1987 single Changin' Partners. Perhaps this is a comment on the unreliability of memory. There is not much of a selection on the jukebox, as many of the songs are listed more than once. Tony turning the page multiple times, and the camera not lingering on them, gives the impression that there are more than there are. This, too, may be attributed to the limits of memory and imagination.

The perfect timing of the beginning of Don't Stop Believin' to coincide with Carmela entering Holsten's does not feel right at all in an episode of *The Sopranos*. It is as if she were waiting outside to give him a thumbs up when he should enter his selection into the jukebox. Carmela arriving at the table as we hear 'just a small-town girl' is similarly unrealistically harmonious; one almost expects the two of them to embrace and the episode to end in a smiling freeze-frame. The music is first used in a diegetic fashion

---

[151] www.holstens.com.

in that Tony selects it on the jukebox, but it then becomes non-diegetic in how it synchronises with the entrance of Carmela; this blurring of the distinction is an interesting way to imply that things are not as they appear. Viewing this from the perspective of a dream allows it to be understood as association, of the sort that earlier linked the appearance of Hunter to the prior news of the arrest of Carlo's son. The first note of a song Tony loves is heard exactly as he sees his wife. His mind is trying to give him a double boost, with a song whose lyrics talk of two young people akin to he and Carmela when they first started dating.

The visible dates of 1973, 1977 and 1971 on the far wall, along with a jukebox full of music that Tony listened to in his earlier years, strongly suggest that his mind has constructed a vision of Holsten's as he remembers it being during his youth. As Freud noted: 'experiences from childhood...play a part in dreams whose content would never have led one to suppose it.'[152] The interior of Holsten's when he is waiting for Dickie in *The Many Saints of Newark* looks identical to how it does in Made in America, and to how it does today. This allows Chase to set the dream back when Tony was younger, while not making it obvious. It is not surprising that his idea of paradise is a meal at a diner offering fast-food that he frequented when he was younger, surrounded by family and friends and the music he loves. This is similar to how playing with toy trains is a step back in time for Bobby; both men die whilst reconnecting with their past. No one in the scene appears to drink alcohol because there are no alcoholic beverages on the Holsten's menu. Customers are informed: 'from milkshakes to classic cheeseburgers to onion rings, we're here to offer you

---

[152]*Op. cit.*, p. 279.

all your nostalgic childhood favourites'.¹⁵³ There is, however, a possible ambiguity in the cokes that are brought to the table, in that Tony is seen on multiple occasions to use cocaine personally, and to profit greatly from its sale to others, so perhaps this is what he truly wants at this point.

Tony's sleeping mind is taking him back to his childhood, hosting a get-together for his family and friends. This is the second time this has been attempted, the first being the Finnerty family reunion that is the setting for the final part of his coma dream in Mayham. But his fear and anxiety here mean that it is gatecrashed by those who would do him harm: the dream reflects the life he has lived too well. Some of these loved ones were killed by or because of him, or they tried to do the same to him, and there are others whose wishes to hurt him are not mitigated by family connection. Although Tony is sitting in a diner, there is an intensity to the events that has not been seen before in the episode, even when AJ's car explodes, or Phil is executed. An emotional crescendo has been reached, more things he loves and fears being thrown at him in a higher tempo by his mind: family, old friends, sexual partners, people he has killed and others who have tried to do the same to him (it is a sad indictment of his life that these groups are far from mutually exclusive), food, music, pornography and football. There is a desperation to it all that comes from the dark underbelly that will not go away.

This anxiety comes through above all in the attention Tony gives to the entrance to Holsten's. Five times he looks up at the sound of the bell: why is he so concerned with who is coming through the door? There are three reasons, two of which were

---

¹⁵³Holsten's, *op. cit.*

available in 2007, but one for which we had to wait until 2021. The first and primary is that this door is a manifestation of another one that is a source of great anxiety to him. At the end of the previous episode The Blue Comet, Tony is in the dark on the bed at the safehouse, staring at the door to his room. If anyone is going to try to kill him, they will have to come through it. The eerie music begins and his eyes become heavy as he starts to drift off. The last thing he sees before he falls asleep is the door in the safehouse, and later on he nervously pays attention to the door in Holsten's. They are the same door, one a dream reconstruction of the other and provoking the same emotions in him. Further evidence for this is that the music is an instrumental version of Running Wild by Tindersticks (2000). The other time that the music of this group is heard is in Isabella, when Tony first hallucinates the beautiful young woman. The lyrics of the original version of Running Wild are about someone whose attempts at sleeping are sabotaged by emotions that his mind cannot control.

The second reason is that, because of this fear of who might be coming through the door to hurt him, his mind conjures up a more pleasant alternative: Meadow. She is his lucky star, his creation beyond himself. In the montage which opens the final season, she appears as the 'guardian angel' and, not long afterwards, it is her voice that calls him out of the coma in Mayham, her face the first thing he sees. Here she does not make it in time to save him from danger. She is running late because of a medical appointment concerning the switching of birth control, thereby still frustrating Tony's desires for grandchildren, and then she has trouble parking. The last thing he sees is her running towards the entrance before it all goes black. What this means is that no dream, no matter how enjoyable, can make the slightest difference to the problems we face when awake, and it is those that are truly the source of Tony's paranoia. Meadow hurrying across the road to be with her father is a deliberate parallel to a scene in The Army of One. At the funeral gathering for Jackie, Jr., her sadness at his death, and suspicions that the criminal element of her family had something to do with it, leads to her drinking too much and leaving early. Tony follows her, but after a brief argument she runs across the road, narrowly avoiding the traffic. She is rejecting him and his lifestyle and risking her life, but at the end of the finale, when Tony is asleep in a safehouse, scared, lonely and near to death, his dreaming mind recalls and subverts that memory. Instead of Meadow running away from him, he dreams of her hurrying to be with and protect him, with an anxious expression on her face that is not justified by being late to a meal with her family.

The final reason why Tony keeps his eye on the door is similar to the second, but is offered fourteen years later, in *The Many Saints of Newark*. The painful memory of sitting in Holsten's, waiting to meet Dickie, is resurfacing. On that morning, approximately thirty years earlier, he waited and waited, but the man he idolized did not turn up, no matter how many times the bell rang and the door opened. Soon afterwards, he would have discovered that he had been murdered. The pain of that memory is a major part of why his dream at this point is centred on Holsten's.

There is another way in which Dickie is remembered in Made in America. When the two sets of parents celebrate the engagement of Meadow and Patrick at the Soprano residence, Donna attempts unsuccessfully to tell the old joke about a horse visiting a doctor and being asked 'why the long face?'. The same joke is told in *The Many Saints of Newark* by Dickie to Giuseppina during a walk on the beach, and she says he already told it to her many times. It is therefore likely that Tony heard him tell it on more than one occasion, associating it with him long after his death.

Using *The Many Saints of Newark* to shed light on the events of Made in America is not the first time that Chase has retrospectively elucidated the meaning of a dream. In '...To Save Us All From Satan's Power' (3.10), Tony thinks back to a meeting he had with Jackie, Snr. and Big Pussy at the Asbury Park boardwalk. He concludes that there were signs of the treachery of the latter that he overlooked, such as talking about business inside a diner where they might be overheard, and his financial situation. This explains why the dream in Funhouse, in which Tony finally realises that his old friend is an FBI informant, takes place there.

The final scene of Made in America is the most symbolically dense in the episode, and possibly in the entire run of the show, but commentators miss the vast majority of these communications and treat it as a standard narrative. To be understood accurately, it has to be viewed as if it is an artistic creation of the filmmakers that Chase is influenced by, something along the lines of *An Andalusian Dog* by Buñuel (1929), on which he collaborated with Dalí, or *Stalker* by Andrei Tarkovsky (1979). Interpreting any of these literally is unproductive, and doing the same with the events in Holsten's will leave one hopelessly floundering with nonsensical questions such as 'does the Man in Members Only jacket have a gun in the bathroom?', or 'will AJ's recovery last?'.

Chapter Fifteen
Weather - Cold, Sunny

In an interview with *The Hollywood Reporter* in November 2021, Chase appeared to confirm that the cut to black at the end of Made in America means what many, including myself, had taken it to: Tony dies.[154] He later denied that he had said that,[155] but the aforementioned slip of the tongue in the interview with Seitz and Sepinwall must be remembered. Whatever the truth is, questions have already been raised in this book about the reliability of Chase as a guide to the correct understanding of his show. Demonstrating that the death of Tony occurs with the cut to black requires much more evidence.

How exactly does Tony die? Is it possible to give a decisive answer on the basis of the contents of his dreaming mind? The evidence could not be more subjective or solipsistic. In the First Edition of this book, I discussed what I believed to be the only two credible possibilities: that he is executed by someone in the safehouse or that he dies of a stress-induced heart attack. My position is unchanged, in that no other outcomes make sense,

---

[154]Scott Feinberg '"Sopranos" Creator David Chase Finally Reveals What Happened to Tony', *The Hollywood Reporter*.
[155]*Talking Sopranos* 91, 49.27.

but I have now seen that Made in America does offer consistent support for one of them, which means that the question of the ultimate fate of the Don of New Jersey can be answered with some certainty. It is the second of the two possibilities that is correct, but, before it is explained properly, it is worth spending time on the other, as it could so easily have been the road taken by the narrative.

Tony barely avoids execution more than once: in College (1.5), at the hands of Fabian 'Febby' Petrulio, who betrayed the crew to the authorities and went into witness protection; and the hitmen acting on the orders of Junior in Isabella. As the events in Holsten's unfold, he is asleep on the bed in the safehouse, which means that someone could enter the room and shoot him as he sleeps. It is unlikely that this could be accomplished by someone sent by Phil, as that would require them to sneak past the rest of Tony's crew, or kill them all in a way that did not disturb his sleep, or convince them all to stand aside in a collective act of betrayal. A more sensible suggestion is that he is murdered by one of his own crew. The war with the Lupertazzi family is going very badly and there are no medals for second place in a Mafia struggle.

Loyalty is a rare commodity in this world. People routinely turn on their comrades and family members, and there is no better example than Paulie, who is there in the safehouse. There is no way that he would die for Tony, and he is the primary candidate for an underhand deal with Phil. Tony has held suspicions about Paulie for a number of years but never acts on them. This underlies the scene in the Funhouse dream where they are playing cards, i.e., engaged in a secretive struggle against each other, and Tony shoots him. Something equally fatal is not far from happening in reality during a boat trip they take in Remember When (6.15).

Tony questions Paulie about how Johnny Sac learned of the joke about his wife told by Ralphie in No Show; it was indeed because of Paulie, but he denies having anything to do with it. Glances at an axe and a knife by Tony are signs that he does not believe him and is considering murdering him, but for unknown reasons he decides not to.

Throughout Made in America, Tony is grappling with these suspicions about Paulie. Although he is the only senior member of the crew present, Tony does not trust him and is sleeping in the same house as him. Whilst dreaming, he tries to appease Paulie by persuading him to take over the Aprile crew, but even though that happens he is more concerned with cauliflowers than meat, distributes barber's scissors, and is seen for the last time in a solo place in the sun. He is also hostile to the cat, and songs heard in the background of these scenes add a subtle emphasis. The first is Pretty Little Angel Eyes from 1961, performed by Curtis Lee, the lyrics of which repeatedly refer to the afterlife: 'angel', 'you were sent from heaven above' and 'we'll be happy for eternity'.[156] Paulie, though, is more of an angel of death from the perspective of Tony. The second is an instrumental segment of the version of I Heard It Through the Grapevine recorded by Creedence Clearwater Revival, from their 1970 album *Cosmo's Factory*. The song is a story of painful suspicion, the perspective of someone who feels that they can no longer trust a person who means a great deal to them, but lacks hard evidence to support this. All of these elements taken together signify that Tony is deeply worried that his trust in Paulie may be his undoing.

---

[156] Written by Lee and Tommy Boyce.

There are aspects of the narrative of The Blue Comet which suggest that Paulie is involved once again in secretive machinations. It was noted earlier that Albie and Butchie decline the suggestion to execute him in addition to Tony, Sil and Bobby. When told to oversee the hit on Phil he is not overly receptive, asking if Tony has agreed to the plan and reminding Sil and Bobby that he only just survived previous Mafia wars in the 1970s. He nominally accepts but passes the task over to Patsy and Corky Caporale; the latter is a questionable decision, as he is a heroin addict whose primary qualification for the role is being fluent in Italian. At the Soprano family home, Paulie is visibly less stressed than Tony, as evidenced by his appreciation of Rhiannon. When Walden, at the safehouse, sits down and puts his gun on the table, Paulie turns around at the noise as if this is particularly interesting to him; is he making a mental note of how each of the others is armed?

Conversely, there is no evidence to suggest that the man who is identified as a traitor, Carlo, is in fact so. The information that his son was arrested the day before, and Mink later telling Tony that he is an informant (although this is not seen on screen), come in Made in America and are therefore a product of a dream. Tony's subconscious may focus on Carlo because his cousin Burt does transfer his allegiance to the Lupertazzis, and as a punishment is murdered by Sil. It could also be an association between Carlo running the crew that Vito used to be in charge of, and the latter 'betraying' Tony by his homosexuality; and, before that, it being run by Richie and Ralphie, both of whom caused him difficulties.

Of the higher-ranking members of the Soprano crew who die at the hands of someone else, most are dispatched by those allegedly on their own side: Jimmy by Sil; Big Pussy by Tony,

Sil and Paulie; Richie by Janice; Ralphie by Tony; and Chris by Tony. Vito would be on this list if Phil had not got there first. Only Bobby is murdered by a rival family, although Sil probably goes the same way due to his injuries. Before all of these, Aldo is beaten to death by his son Dickie, who is later shot on the orders of Junior. The Sopranos did most of the job of their rivals for them, and this makes Tony being killed in his sleep by one of his own a highly plausible hypothesis.

There is another, though, and it too fits in well with what is known about Tony: it may be that he dies of a stress-induced heart attack. There are subtle hints at this possibility throughout the episode, and in fact so many of them that one is forced to conclude that this is how his life ends. Made in America contains numerous elements that are best understood as his sleeping mind trying to make sense of the symptoms he is experiencing of a coming heart attack. These are no different to our own dreams, for example, searching for a toilet, finding one after another being used, closed or unavailable for another reason, and then waking up to discover that one needs to urinate. Freud refers to such sources as somatic and discusses them in depth, including anxiety dreams of those affected by heart illness.[157] In Tony's dream, these take the form of allusions to specific symptoms, as well as more general ones to the heart and the unremitting approach of the afterlife. One should also bear in mind the ways in which information is conveyed in the work of filmmakers admired by Chase: not overtly, but through insinuation and suggestion.

The heart attack wastes little time in beginning. Tony apparently wakes up in the safehouse to the sound of You Keep Me Hangin' On by Vanilla Fudge from 1967, through the organ

---

[157] *Op. cit.*, pp. 314-38.

and then the radio; the lyrics are about desperation and include a reference to a heart breaking. The blurring of the distinction between diegetic and non-diegetic music here, in that what is heard begins by sounding like an example of the latter, but then becomes the former, is a clue that reality is askew. There is then a skip forward in time to night, accompanied by a drop in temperature: it is snowing with an icy wind blowing. Chills and cold sweats, irrespective of the actual temperature, are common symptoms of a heart attack, and this is not the last time that this happens in the episode. It is also a feature of the dream in Funhouse, where Tony's chills are a result of food poisoning and stress; the weather gets warmer in the dream as he recovers and achieves clarity about the hidden truth that is eating away at him. The onset of illness causes his sleeping mind to conjure up Paulie sitting with him in the van; not the greatest compliment one can pay someone. The precise mechanism for this is association, specifically, with the one of the funniest scenes in the show, in Mayham, when Paulie's attempt at patient care sends Tony into tachycardia; like then, Tony is not feeling well and Paulie is complaining, here about Agent Harris' tardiness.

As Tony and Paulie are waiting in their car, a plane above them descends, drowning out all other sounds for a few seconds. The noise is louder than it needs to be to make the viewer aware that a plane is overhead, and it plays no role in the plot, so why is this so? There are two reasons. The first is that the volume serves as a clue to reality not being as the viewer assumes. The second is that the noise outside an aircraft is known to reach as high as 140 decibels[158], and aviation noise can cause a number of different adverse effects on health, including cognitive

---

[158] The National Institute for Occupational Safety and Health in the USA.

impairment, even for the young, sleep disturbance and various forms of cardiovascular disease, including heart attacks.[159] This is not to posit the actual existence of a plane flying at that moment over the safehouse where Tony is sleeping (at that volume it would be near enough to take the roof off), even though there are quite a few airports of various sizes in New Jersey; it does not need to be snowing because he is feeling cold. As this is a dream, what is happening is that Tony is feeling unwell and his subconscious randomly searches for an explanation, ending up with a belief or memory relating to an alleged link between aircraft noise and heart disease. The unnecessary volume aside, an explanation for the appearance of the plane is the evidence that travelling in this manner can exacerbate existing heart conditions.[160] Tony flew to Las Vegas only three episodes before, shortly after a car accident, and not being in the best of health generally. This is not the last time that the sound of a plane can be heard in the episode, although the next time it is not as obvious.

As Tony and Paulie are talking, there is a small, bright light visible in the distance in the centre of the screen. At face value, this looks like the moon, but in the language of dreams previously established in *The Sopranos* it can be read on a different and more significant level. During the coma dream in Join the Club and Mayham, Tony, in his guise as a precision optics salesman, is fascinated by a beacon of light flashing in the distance that he can see from his hotel room. In order to attend the Finnerty family

---

[159] The Civil Aviation Authority of the UK.
[160] Hammadah et. al. ' Navigating air travel and cardiovascular concerns: is the sky the limit?'.

reunion, where he hopes to meet the man who has his briefcase, he is advised to travel in the direction of the light. As previously explained, the Inn at the Oaks, like the house in Calling All Cars and that in the mural in Holsten's in Made in America, represents the afterlife, as does the beacon, in that lights are a staple of accounts of near-death experiences. One would be justified in questioning this equating of the beacon in the coma dream with the moon here, as there is no obvious basis for it yet; something that would support this would be the repeated appearance of such a light.

During the conversation with Agent Harris, Tony specifically mentions a 'branch' of a bank that is relevant to the finances of two Arabs. The beating of the heart is caused by electrical impulses, which travel along a pathway which has two branches called the right and left bundles.[161] Heart disease can be caused by blockages in either of these. Tony then visits his family in their safehouse, where Carmela moans about the smell, which could be 'toxic'. He reassures her that it is not and is more likely to be urine because of the age of the previous owners; he is correct, but in truth it signals bad news for him. Urinary incontinence, the loss of bladder function, often accompanies heart failure. He wets himself while his final dream is occurring.

This is followed soon after by Tony experiencing another chill. As the family and friends of Bobby gather for his funeral, observed by the FBI, the weather is cold and an icy wind blows; the mourners are suitably dressed in heavy coats and scarves. At the gathering afterwards at Nuovo Vesuvio, Tony studies the painting depicting an eruption of Mount Vesuvius. As well as an

---

Hobart Cardiology and Medical Specialists, 'Bundle branches'.

expression of the sense of dread and anxiety felt throughout Made in America, it can also be read as a metaphor for the heart attack he is experiencing, i.e., powerful forces lying under the surface, preparing to cause great harm. The chill continues as Paulie accepts Meadow's invitation to join her table, expressed through the music heard in the background: Winter, from the violin concertos known as The Four Seasons by Antonio Vivaldi, published in 1725.

Another wind blowing when Tony and his crew are back in their safehouse signals another slight to his dignity: Carlo farts as he is watching television. Flatulence is another symptom of an impending heart attack, and Tony then doubles down on this, in response to being asked if he wants to visit Sil at the hospital, by remarking 'there's shit I gotta do'. Thankfully, he is sleeping alone, because as well as wetting himself he is passing wind too. It is not coincidental that, of all the men present at this point, it is Carlo who is making this stinking contribution. Tony's subconscious picks on him as a source of betrayal, without justification, and therefore, within the logic of the dream, he stinks as much as his reputation. In this same scene Benny mentions Tony's gout. Although this condition, the build-up of uric acid in the blood, is not per se a symptom of heart failure, the two are comorbid in that suffering from gout brings with it an increased risk.[162] At this point, during the night when the occurrence of symptoms is more likely[163], he is probably experiencing something like pain in one or more of his joints.

---

[162] Cipolletta et. al. 'Association Between Gout Flare and Subsequent Cardiovascular Events Among Patients With Gout', *Journal of the American Medical Association*.
[163] Jasvinder Singh. 'Gout Attacks Strike Mostly at Night', *Arthritis Health*.

The next time we see Tony he is visiting Janice. The first words out of her mouth, in response to his offer of a pastry, are: 'I need to watch my weight'. Being overweight increases one's chances of heart trouble. As he is leaving, Tony receives the phone-call he has been hoping for from Agent Harris, but in multiple ways it is not good news. As he is listening, the word 'ice' is framed perfectly behind him on the side of the van, a sign that his consciousness is aware of another chill. In addition, the tip concerns a payphone being used in Oyster Bay, Long Island; oysters have traditionally been considered to be high in cholesterol, although, since the broadcast of Made in America, the view of their significance for heart health has become more complicated.[164] Finally, the female law enforcement official present with Agent Harris leaves the bathroom: Tony is again aware of bladder trouble.

A less common symptom of an impending heart attack is a smell of burning. In Two Tonys, Carmine, Sr. asks those he is having lunch with if they can smell 'burning hair' just before he has a stroke. Confirmatory evidence or an explanation is hard to come by, but it is reported by patients, and the occurrence of phantosmia, smelling an odour without the presence of a suitable stimulant, in other words an olfactory hallucination, is generally accepted.[165] In one of the most memorable scenes in the finale, the SUV in which AJ and Rhiannon are getting to know each other is set alight by burning leaves and explodes; they are alerted by the smoke coming through the vents. This scene also acts as a reference to leaves in that many plants are described

---

[164]Heart UK. 'High cholesterol food'.
[165]Katerina Koteska 'Is Smelling Toast A Sign Of A Heart Attack?', *Brussels Morning*.

as having heart-shaped foliage, such as Dutchman's Pipe or the Flamingo Flower, and some, including the Heart-Shaped Hoya and Hearts on a String, even derive their name from the shape of their leaves.

Medically, things are not looking good for Tony, and this is confirmed by the reappearance of the bright light. At the very start of the scene in which Tony meets up with Butchie and others to discuss ending the war, there is a light inside the warehouse that is briefly the only thing visible in the dark. It is nearer to the viewer than the moon was, meaning that his condition is worsening as his entry into the afterlife approaches. To emphasise the point, he once again experiences a chill as it is very cold in the warehouse; those present are shivering, even though they are wearing heavy coats, hats and gloves, and their icy breath is visible.

Perhaps not surprisingly, his heart once again flashes through his consciousness as Uncle Pat, in conversation with Junior at his care facility, points to what he thinks is a double-breasted robin. Ornithology is clearly not his specialist subject because there is no such bird, but the heart symbol, like the leaves of plants, is commonly described as double-breasted. The focus on the heart continues into the telephone call between Tony and Paulie in which they ponder the disappearance of Carlo. The ringtone of the latter is an instrumental version of the first line of the 1970 song Cecilia by Simon and Garfunkel: 'Cecilia, you're breaking my heart...'. During the conversation, Tony's continuing bladder malfunction calls to him through the dream as a bright 'Men's Room' sign becomes visible behind Paulie in the Bada Bing.

Later, Tony pulls up alongside AJ, who is jogging. Exercise is a key ingredient of heart health and Tony says 'I gotta get back at it myself', although he has already sabotaged his son's exercise session by telling him to get in the car. When Tony and Carmela meet with their son's therapist, the latter has to visit the bathroom, another reminder of her husband's need to urinate. In the scene where he is executed, Phil and his family are in a Ford vehicle, with the logo of the company put in the centre of the screen brazenly four times. Henry Ford, founder of the Ford Motor Company, suffered from cardiovascular problems[166], and the hospital which bears his name in Detroit has for decades specialised in, amongst other branches of medicine, cardiology.[167]

As if Tony's health is not in a sufficiently precarious position at this point, it then takes an even more alarming turn for the worse. He meets with Mink at the Bada Bing to discuss his legal situation over a meal. There is something farcical about their failure to get the ketchup out of the bottle, but what it and the agitation it causes him represent is anything but: the blood flow to his heart is slowing. More than a symptom, this is the very definition of a heart attack. This is reinforced by the name of the track that is heard in the background: The Jam by Graham Central Station, from their 1975 album *Ain't No 'Bout-A-Doubt It*. Many jams are red and sticky, and all do not flow as smoothly as substances containing more water. Moreover, a jam is colloquially a difficult situation that is hard to extricate oneself from.

The next scene is dense with symbolism. Tony visits Sil, who is in the hospital following the attempt on his life by the New York Mafia. He is unconscious and looks to still be in a very serious

---

[166] Charles E. Sorensen *My Forty Years with Ford*, pp. 266 and 271-272.
[167] Henry Ford Health 'Cardiology'.

condition. The prominent blue tubes that he is connected to from the right represent the venae cavae, the two large veins, the superior and inferior, that carry deoxygenated blood (hence the blue colour) to the heart for oxygen; they empty into the right atrium and are located towards the right of the body.[168] During a heart attack the organ is deprived of oxygen.

In addition, during the first part of this scene, an advert is heard for a kitchen appliance which mentions, amongst various foods that Tony enjoys, an omelette, remembering that eggs are an ongoing omen of death in the show. Also included in the dialogue are onions and peppers, as ingredients of a 'zesty' meal, and garlic. These can all cause indigestion even in the healthiest of people, but he is particularly susceptible after being shot by Junior; it can also be a symptom of a heart attack. His mind is thinking of things which can cause the chest pain he is experiencing. The name of the appliance in question is the Magic Bullet, an ambiguous yet loaded phrase. It can refer to something which overcomes a difficulty or cures a medical problem, and food is often what Tony turns to when life is getting him down. Relevant in different ways are that 'magic bullet' is the name of an old German myth about a projectile that is incapable of missing its target, bringing an unavoidable death; and a mocking term for the theory relating to the assassination of John F. Kennedy, that he was killed by the same bullet that injured John Connally, the Governor of Texas, who was also travelling in the presidential limousine.[169] These, too, are bad

---

[168] Cleveland Clinic 'Vena Cava'.
[169] Marc Lallanilla ' JFK "Magic Bullet Theory" In Spotlight On Anniversary Of President Kennedy's Assassination'. *Huffington Post*.

omens for the author of the dream and signal an awareness that all is far from well.

Now that, in reality, Tony is in the advanced stages of a heart attack with no hope of rapid medical support, this dire state of affairs is expressed in the dream in another way. Working in the garden, he looks up at the sun, which looms large and bright in the sky: the light representing the afterlife has returned and is nearer than it has ever been. This is anything but the 'moment of contentment' that Imperioli describes it as,[170] even though Tony looks to be at peace. The difference between the surface and hidden truth of dreams has never been more apposite, and this is further demonstrated by the manifestation of the number three in the form of the tall trees behind him.

His sleeping mind reacts in panic by grasping at aspects of his life that hold emotional value. The first attempt is to Junior, but the anxiety that has him in his grip only allows his imagination to generate an image of his uncle who cannot remember him or anything else about their past. Tony then takes a trip, in some respects back in time, in others remaining in the present, to Holsten's for a party with other family and friends. His life is flashing before his eyes, and it is a sad statement about him that the objects of this grasping include relatives who ordered his execution and who he himself murdered. Behind Junior, the patient information sign on the wall declares ominous warnings for Tony. It says the weather is 'cold', which means he is experiencing another chill; 'sunny', reinforcing the proximity of the light of the afterlife; and that the next meal is supper, the Last Supper that he and his family shortly reenact. Inside Holsten's, the house

---

[170] *Talking Sopranos* 91, 2.03.29.

depicted in the mural, representing the afterlife, dominates the screen and remains right behind him throughout the final scene.

It has already been noted that music by the band Heart appears in the jukebox selections: Who Will You Run To and Magic Man (Live), which the camera lingers on and is visible again a few seconds later. That the word 'heart' finally appears explicitly on screen, rather than being alluded to, is a sign of the gravity of the situation. To make a selection on the jukebox Tony presses the letter K, then a number that is obscured by his hand, but given its position it must be either 1 or 2. Vitamins K1 and K2 are helpful for combatting manifestations of heart illness, such as arteries and valves being clogged with calcium deposits. What is almost laughable, though, is that only in the dreaming mind of a desperate person on the point of death could it make sense to call on the healing power of Vitamin K.

Another symptom of heart attacks is distress, and more of that engulfs Tony's mind: he responds with 'I don't know' to Carmela asking 'what looks good tonight?', and there are diners in Holsten's who represent threats to his life. The Man in Members Only jacket sitting at the counter, his father, worries him even before the beginning of the re-enactment of the execution scene from *The Godfather*; in going to the bathroom he also serves as a reminder of the bladder malfunction that has been plaguing his son since early in the dream. This is followed immediately by the entry of the two black men who botched their execution of him in Isabella; and the scoutmaster, Phil, was in Holsten's as Tony arrived.

His final action in the dream is to eat an onion ring. This can be taken as his mind responding to a terminal stab of pain in his chest by, as he did during the visit to Sil in the hospital, imagining the ingestion of something which could have led to such a reaction; ironically, onions contain Vitamin K. He desperately imagines Meadow rushing to save him, but listening carefully reveals the whine of a jet engine.[171] It is cleverly blended with the noise of the road traffic, but once it is heard it is unmistakable, the final one of many pieces of evidence that he is dying of a heart attack.

Made in America, the dream it presents, and the life of Tony then end as the screen cuts to black; as Bobby suggested in Soprano Home Movies, he probably didn't even hear it as happened. Throughout the episode there are a staggering number of references to the heart and its state of health; once one or two are spotted, the rest jump out in a torrent with little effort on the part of the viewer. Symptoms of heart attacks, some common and others less so, manifest repeatedly: chills, bladder malfunction, flatulence, the smell of burning, agitation, chest pain and restricted blood flow to the heart. A small number of the examples cited could be explained away as coincidence, or this author focusing on particular interpretations to suit an agenda or preconceived theory; but this amount means that the weight of evidence leans strongly towards this thesis. It can only signify an obsession of the sleeping mind of Tony caused by the onset of serious ill-health. The burden of proof now shifts to those wishing to falsify this reading.

Chase has his cake and eats it, understanding that even though the world often does not tie things up neatly, there are features of it that are beyond negotiation. He depicts the death of the

---

[171]MasterofSopranos comments on the 'roar' but does not spot that it is not characteristic of anything as small as a car; *op. cit.*, Page 3, Part III.

central character of his show, is precise about what causes it and the specifics of how it happens. He takes us inside Tony's body and mind, showing the stages of the malfunctioning of the former and how the latter reacts and tries to make sense of it, before both shut down permanently. Chase talks about his past experiences of being told to take anything offensive out of whichever program he was working on,[172] but here he has the last laugh, spending an hour focusing exclusively on a man slowly dying, and unpleasant associated phenomena such as him wetting himself and farting. All of this is achieved, however, without sacrificing his commitment to ambiguity and other artistic principles that he learned from the filmmakers he adores. He hides the momentous event in plain sight so effectively that it is being revealed here for the first time.

The idea that Tony's heart might be his downfall is a recurring theme from the early days of the show; the toll that stress is taking on his health is the premise of the narrative. His over-indulging in food, alcohol, tobacco and other drugs is made very clear. In The Strong, Silent Type, Chris, during his drug intervention, tells Tony that he is going to die of a heart attack because of his addiction to food; his weight steadily increases and his breathing becomes heavier.[173] In Members Only, Tony eats alone at a sushi restaurant that he and Carmela usually go to together and shows signs of poor digestion; his being there without her points to his prioritising of his desires above his relationships, a parallel to the 'eating alone', not sharing the spoils fairly, that the crew accuse

---

[172]Seitz and Sepinwall, op. cit., p. 331.
[173]Chase, in a Sisyphean struggle against his own evidence, does his best to persuade us that this is not intentional. Seitz and Sepinwall, op. cit., p. 370.

Junior of in Pax Soprana (1.6). Tony also experiences something similar when eating at home with his family in Stage 5, as they are discussing the cast and crew screening of Chris' movie *Cleaver* and the christening of his daughter; both topics relating to someone who has greatly disappointed Tony means that this is not coincidental. All of this fits with the lesson that comes out of many of his therapy sessions with Jennifer that some, perhaps most, of his troubles are of his own making. This man, who loves to emphasise his Italian roots, is very much a modern American in his caving into his desires.

Made in America is the account of a man dying of a stress-induced heart attack, told from the perspective of his sleeping mind. There is no trace of an understanding of this amongst commentators: Seitz and Sepinwall do mention a 'coronary' as one of a number of possibilities of how Tony might die, but without any supporting evidence, only pointing to what they mistakenly see as the ambiguity of the ending which is not exhausted by any explanation.[174] Tony experiences an early death, in pain, scared, lonely and hungry in a safehouse. On the surface level, in what is manifest, things appear to turn out well for him; but the truth that lies beneath, latently, is much worse. He leaves Carmela a widow and does not live long enough to see any grandchildren, or to attempt to enjoy a peaceful old age. His opportunities for redemption in the final analysis are spurned, including those offered by therapy: the 'dark irony' is that he 'learns to become more self-deceptive'[175], represented appropriately in his dying

---

[174]*Op. cit.*, p. 316.
[175]Kevin L. Stoehr, 'The Sopranos, film noir and nihilism' in Steven Sanders and Aeon Skoble (ed.) *The Philosophy of TV Noir*, p. 157.

whilst dreaming. Moreover, in the final scene he gives in to the same type of pointless nostalgia that he criticised Paulie for, six episodes earlier: '"remember when?" is the lowest form of conversation'. He cannot stop himself from becoming like the man he suspects of betraying him.

Chapter Sixteen
It's Done

One of the many reasons why *The Many Saints of Newark* was so eagerly anticipated was the hope that in focusing on the character of Dickie Moltisanti, the father of one of the central characters in *The Sopranos*, light would be shed on his murder and the events that led up to it. The film does just that and indicates that there is a hidden story during the show, some of the details of which have been overlooked by commentators. In the opening episode of the fourth season, For All Debts Public and Private, Tony tells Chris that 'your father was like a mentor to me'; Dickie, murdered when Chris was a baby, 'was a legend.' Later, in a conversation with Adriana, Chris declares that he is worried that Tony compares him unfavourably to Dickie: 'you never know, I could be on the endangered species list.' There is definitely some truth to that observation, both at this point and ongoing.

After celebrating the Esplanade deal, with the help of some Icelandic stewardesses, Tony and Chris go for a drive. They park opposite a restaurant, and Bobby pulling up behind in another car makes Chris agitated, but he will not die tonight. Gesturing to the restaurant, Tony says: 'the guy in there killed your father. Barry Haydu, Detective Lieutenant in the Clifton Police Force'.

The party going on inside is for his retirement. He goes on to explain that Haydu did the hit for Jilly Ruffalo: Dickie stabbed Jilly in the eye because in prison Jilly stabbed Dickie's cellmate to death. 'Loyal, your old man'. Chris says that he was told that Dickie was killed outside his house as he was bringing home a crib for him, which Tony confirms, except to say that it was TV trays. 'That rat f*** was in uniform then. Gambling like you wouldn't believe. He did it on contract.' He has been spared thus far because he has been useful, but has now 'outlived it'; Tony gives Chris the address at which he can find Haydu after the party ends.

When Haydu arrives home he is knocked unconscious, and on waking finds himself handcuffed and Chris watching an episode of *Magnum P.I.* on the television. Chris asks him if he remembers Dickie, to which he says no, asking if he was a friend of his; 'he was my father.' Haydu also denies knowing who Jilly is: 'you're being set up! He's lying to you, whoever he is!' The response from Chris is interesting: 'wouldn't make any difference. He wants you dead.' He is obviously open to the possibility that Tony might have not been completely honest with him. Haydu breaks free and crawls away, but Chris shoots him dead. He is next seen at his mother's, where pictures of Dickie in Navy uniform and with Chris as a baby are visible. As he leaves, he attaches a twenty dollar bill, taken from Haydu's wallet, to her refrigerator.

At face value, these events lead one to conclude that Dickie was murdered as the latest in a series of retaliations with Jilly, and the contract was carried out by Haydu because he was a corrupt policeman. This seems plausible, as this type of behaviour is common in the real and fictional worlds of the Mafia; numerous untrustworthy policemen appear in *The Sopranos*, from Vin to the officer who takes part in the threesome with Ralphie and Tracee in University. To Captain McCluskey in *The Godfather* can be added Louis Eppolito, a real-life corrupt detective in the New York City Police Department, who had a minor role in the 1990 Scorsese film *Goodfellas*.[176] However, the guiding principle of this book is that, for an accurate understanding of events in *The Sopranos*, it is a mistake to fail to delve below the surface, so we should consider whether other relevant information is made available.

The scene which follows immediately upon the murder of Haydu presents Carmela in bed, watching a television news report about a successful armoured car robbery in Pennsylvania. Two men were shot dead and one of them had links to organised crime in New Jersey. The two scenes being in succession raises the question of whether there is a link between them: is it no more than a coincidence that Tony gives Chris the opportunity to kill Haydu on the same day that this robbery occurs? No further evidence is provided, but it is possible that Haydu is either one of the robbers who escaped, or provides inside information, and now that the job is done he needs to be silenced. There is certainly little doubt from the television dialogue that intrudes on his execution that he is corrupt: Magnum is heard asking 'police? In a Ferrari?', which can be taken as an indication that Haydu has profited illegally from his career. In this scene, the episode of *Magnum P.I.* functions in the same way as the advert by George Foreman in The Strong, Silent Type, masquerading as simply a part of the scenery, but actually playing a more significant role.

---

[176]Ed Shanahan 'Louis Eppolito, Police Officer Turned Mob Hit Man, Dies at 71', *New York Times*.

Just before Chris shoots Haydu, he repeatedly apologises, but this too is not definitive proof that he is guilty of the murder of Dickie. He may be apologizing because of something else, a mistake he has made or another way in which he has let Tony down. He appears to be completely ignorant, and he could be, in which case the apologies could be a desperate attempt to save his own life. People under pressure from authorities often say or do whatever they are told to, as the numerous false confessions signed by suspects all over the world testify. When Chris is driving Tony earlier in the episode, the latter is suspicious about a Chevrolet Caprice that is behind them. It is suggested that it might be the FBI following them, but later the car that Haydu returns home in is the same make and model. Of all the different cars that are out there, the fact that the Chevrolet Caprice appears twice is too unlikely to be a coincidence; does Tony suspect that Haydu is planning to do him harm, or even that he is an undercover cop masquerading as a corrupt one? There is certainly something about the car that makes him uneasy.

The Many Saints of Newark brings to light another piece of the puzzle. It turns out that the murder of Dickie is ordered by none other than Junior. Not for the first time, Tony's uncle is presented as a jealous man, who believes that he has not been given due respect; he feels overshadowed by both his younger brother, Johnny Boy, and Dickie. The final straw with respect to the latter comes when Junior slips on wet steps when leaving the wake for Lino 'Buddha' Bonpensiero, father of Big Pussy, the sight of which Dickie finds hilarious, although he does offer to help him up. The identity of the gunman is unknown, and therefore may or may not be Haydu, but neither of them are mentioned in the credits. Immediately after the execution,

Junior takes a furtive call from a public telephone near to his house, and all that is heard is a voice saying 'it's done'. The identity of the speaker is unclear, but this is a phrase that has been heard before, during a call from Paulie in A Hit is a Hit (1.10), when he informs Tony that the robbery and murder of the Colombian drug dealer was successful. It is also used by both Corky and Patsy in The Blue Comet, with regard to what turns out to be the failed execution of Phil. Earlier in the film, Paulie is angry when he gets blood all over his new suit after Dickie tells him to torture someone.

Furthermore, Dickie is not the loose cannon and addict that we have been led to believe. He is a highly successful gangster, makes little or no use of drugs such as heroin or cocaine, and has no more of a drink problem than many of his contemporaries. He is prone to violent outbursts, murdering both his father and his mistress, Giuseppina, but in this regard also he is not out of place in the company he keeps. The understanding of him that Chris arrives at by the time of Walk Like a Man, that 'he wasn't much more than a f***ing junkie', is not accurate. This false rumour begins after he is murdered, when the antidepressant Elavil is found in his pocket, but he had procured this for Livia at the request of Tony. Jilly is mentioned in the credits, but it is very difficult to spot him in the story; the credit may be due to a deleted scene, in which Junior calls him with respect to something that he needs to be taken care of. If he does make a minor appearance, there is nothing in the story to link him in any way to Dickie: they are not observed interacting or even mentioning each other. The most that can be concluded is that they may be aware of each other's existence; there is nothing to indicate any bad blood between them.

It is possible that the account that Tony gives Chris of the murder of his father represents the truth as he understands it. Tony idolized Dickie, so Junior may not have ever let him know what really happened, for fear of how he might react. He would also have had reason to conceal it from the rest of the New Jersey crew; the killing of a high-ranking made man, who was respected and financially successful, would not have gone down well, particularly as it was done out of petty jealousy. There is disquiet in the ranks when Tony beats Ralphie after he murders Tracee; and when it is rumoured later that he has killed Ralphie, because of the fire at the stables which causes the death of Pie-O-My, the response is even worse.

There is another angle to consider. Even if Tony sincerely believes that Haydu killed Dickie on the orders of Jilly, it does not mean that he is not using it for his own ends when he tells Chris. This type of behaviour is typical of him: in this very episode, he pretends to be doing Junior a favour by buying property from him, as he needs the money for his legal bills, but he knows he can make a big profit on it as part of the Esplanade deal. In the therapy session, Tony tells Jennifer that there are only two endings possible for him: 'dead or in the can [prison]'. He needs to minimise the risks he takes, saying and doing as little as possible that can be observed by the authorities or rivals. In the life she knows that he leads, 'you rely only on family...You trust only blood.'

To this end, Tony's aim with Chris is 'bonding him to me inseparably', which equates to transferring as many of the risks he faces as possible on to him; he confirms this in a conversation with Bobby while they are fishing in Soprano Home Movies. There is little or no altruistic concern for a member of both of his families here, this is not about what Tony can do for his family but what it can do for him. One does not need to be a legal expert to see also that, if Chris has the blood of a police officer, albeit corrupt and retired, on his hands, then the chances of him becoming an informant in the future are greatly reduced, and even if that did happen his value as a witness would be diminished. Perhaps the reason that Tony chooses Chris over others in the crew for this role is because he has doubts about him, and is less worried about his loss.

Chris has consistently disappointed Tony because of his drug abuse, questionable decisions, such as hijacking a truck company that pays protection money to Junior in 46 Long, and his wish to sell his story to Hollywood, as expressed in the Pilot. A calmer and wiser head, such as Sil, is of greater value to him, and the death of Gigi in He Is Risen is a significant loss. Neither would have murdered a police officer and been so careless as to leave a cigarette in the ash tray, or touch the television, lights and holster without gloves on; compare the care that Tony takes when cleaning up after the murders of Richie and Ralphie. Like AJ, Chris plays virtually no role at all in the dreams of Tony that are presented in the show, which can be taken as a comment about the disappointment he engenders.

What all of this amounts to is a serious question mark over Haydu being the person who killed Dickie. Not for the first or last time in the show, the viewer is left with the conclusion that nobody knows anything: not the identity of the murderer, how much Tony knows about it, nor his motivations for telling Chris that it was Haydu. It is shown that Dickie is killed on the orders of Junior, but beyond this there are only clues offered in the different strands of a complex series of events.

Part Four

Living in a Dream

A thorough analysis of Made in America has provided a mountain of evidence in support of the theory that it is an unacknowledged dream; not the first to appear in *The Sopranos*, but certainly the first time that an entire episode is devoted to the activity of a sleeping mind. There can be no other conclusion than that the finale is the last dream, both in terms of the television series and Tony's life.

There is one more task that will further strengthen the argument: the dreams that are shown previously need to be examined in the light of these discoveries. If Made in America is indeed a dream, then there should be similarities with those that preceded it, and this should be true not just of those of the character who is the author of it, but also those of others whose dreaming mind the viewer is granted entry into, as they are all artistic creations of the same team of writers under the guidance of Chase. The earlier dreams should be consistently expressed in the same artistic language: they should include the same features, narrative idioms and signs.

This task will be complemented by the examination of a major work from a filmmaker who, by Chase's own admission, has had a significant influence on him. If *Mulholland Drive* by Lynch can be shown to be aesthetically consistent with Made in America, and earlier dreams in the show, then so much the better for the hypothesis that the finale is the product of a sleeping mind, particularly as it was released in 2001, during the time that Chase was planning the later seasons.

What follows is not exhaustive and will be limited to the dreams that are shown first-hand rather than reported, and those that occur while the subject is asleep as opposed to experiencing a waking vision. The aspects of the dreams that are of interest are: matters that the author is emotionally invested in; events that are highly unlikely or impossible; unexplained behavioural changes; characters who have died; inconsistencies; references to dreams or similar cognitive states; and anything else that calls to mind what is shown in Made in America. Other parts of the dreams that have no direct connection, or are repetitive of others, will be omitted.

Chapter Seventeen
We Don't Talk Like That Here

(i) Funhouse

The series of dreams in Funhouse are connected by the suspicions that Tony does not want to face about his old friend, Big Pussy. Their eating away at him can be seen in his unease when Big Pussy explains the callcard scam to Furio in a degree of detail that seems excessive; this is confirmed when Pussy meets his FBI handler, Skip Lipari, handing over a recording.

   The dreams begin at the dilapidated buildings and deserted boardwalk at Asbury Park. It is cold and snowing lightly, despite it being June, and there is the sound of wind but no visible effects. Tony meets Sil, Chris, Patsy, Big Pussy, Hesh and Paulie; Big Pussy is motionless and staring out at the sea. Tony tells them that he was diagnosed with something a month ago, for which nothing can be done, and Hesh adds no clarification at all by adding that 'the various protocols to date are ineffective.' The group express their gratitude that he has promised to set himself on fire and save them the hospital visits. It turns out that Patsy is actually Spoons, turning his head to show the bullet wound from his execution; Tony apologises. Deciding that a mysterious 'they' are not coming, he walks over to a gasoline container, and this action shows that Spoons has instantaneously shifted to sitting on the back of the bench and is having his shoes cleaned by Gigi, who has appeared out of nowhere. It is also noticeable that there has been an absurdly rapid change in the weather, as now much of the sky is blue. Tony empties the container over himself and asks where Big Pussy is, who has disappeared in a split second, but before anyone can answer he bursts into flames and wakes up.

There are parallels with Made in America that are obvious already. These are the suspicions about Big Pussy with those concerning Carlo; unrealistic changes in the weather; appearances from the deceased and associated emotional reactions; dialogue that has no meaning in the context; the flow of events skipping forward unnaturally; and the ill-health of the body manifesting as aspects of the dream, for, as becomes obvious soon after he wakes, Tony is burning up and nauseous.

Tony falls asleep back into the continuation of the dream. The sky is now mostly blue at Asbury Park and he is there by himself. He hears a strange squeaking and sees Junior watching him from a window. The echoey voice of Sil asks him a series of questions: 'where you goin'?', 'I dunno'; 'who you looking for?', 'someone's looking for me'; 'who?', 'I dunno'. Sil then appears, moving as if he is on a conveyor belt, dressed like Michael in *The Godfather Part Three*, repeating one of his memorable quotes, although not quite verbatim: 'our true enemy has yet to reveal himself'. Tony then puts some coins into one of the viewing binoculars and sees himself and Paulie in a railway station playing cards. There is no one else there, but announcements can be heard over the tannoy; Tony watches himself take out a gun and shoot Paulie. As noted in Chapter Fifteen with regard to Made in America, there is a link here between the cold weather and the chills he is experiencing as a result of his illness. As he recovers, the weather in the dream improves.

At this point he appears to wake up and there is another skip to a session with Jennifer. She listens to what he is saying, observing that he has not dealt with his anger, 'and look at the cost'. But it is then revealed that Tony is still dreaming, as Annalisa Zucca, who he met in Italy in Commendatori (2.4), is suddenly sitting in her chair and dressed like her, but in her own voice says 'you are the biggest threat to yourself'. He replies 'but that's what being a human being is', and in Jennifer's voice she says 'but some people are more self-destructive than others'. He then truly wakes up. The similarities with Made in America continue. There is the bizarre behaviour of Sil and a reference to one of *The Godfather* movies. Tony watches himself. His relationship with Paulie is problematic. He appears to wake up but that turns out to not be so, a characteristic of the finale that has contributed to its misunderstanding over the years. There is an instantaneous skip from Jennifer to Annalisa and the voice they speak with.

Tony falls asleep again, sitting in the bathroom moaning about Big Pussy, and the suspicions about his friend that mirror those about Carlo in the finale continue. In the dream he is sitting in Jennifer's waiting room in trousers and a vest; she tells him to come in and he does, but says nothing and has a visible erection. 'So, who's your friend? Pussy?' she asks, to which he replies 'I'm confused'. 'Isn't Pussy your friend?' she asks, at which point a strange creaking can be heard. 'I got Pussy on the brain. I always do.' Tony says he wants to have her and she admits 'I find you immensely attractive, Anthony'; they have sex on her table. After Tony wakes, it is learned that Big Pussy has none of the symptoms that he is experiencing, apart from slight diarrhoea, which suggests that at least some of his illness is a psychosomatic reaction to what he fears about his old friend. In this section of the dream there is a random association between two meanings of the word 'pussy', an expression of his libido, and unusual behaviour from Jennifer, all of which have their counterparts in Made in America.

The dream is completed back at Asbury Park, with one of a row of fish on ice for sale speaking with Big Pussy's voice. 'You know I've been working with the government, right Tone?', to which he replies 'don't say it'. 'C'mon Tone, sooner or later you've got to face facts', 'I don't wanna hear it.' Big Pussy is insistent: 'well, you gotta hear it'. He appears as a talking fish because of two factors. The first is a random association from a large fish being on the table before him as part of the meal at the Indian restaurant earlier. It is also another reference to *The Godfather*: the murder of Luca Brasi, one of Vito's men, is announced by a delivery of fish; Sonny, Michael's older brother, explains its meaning: 'Luca Brasi sleeps with the fishes'. Soon, Big Pussy will be in a watery grave too.

The final parallel with Made in America comes from when Tony is awake. The undignified way in which black characters appear is echoed in his comments about the Indians, who he believes gave him food poisoning. He calls them 'w*gs', 'f***ing ragheads' to Bruce, and suggests that the chicken he ate was 'probably a cocker spaniel'.

(ii) Calling All Cars

In the first part of the dream in this episode, Tony is sitting in the back of an old-style Cadillac like his father had, and The Tears of a Clown by Smokey Robinson and the Miracles from 1967 is playing. The deceased Ralphie, completely bald, is in the front passenger seat reading a map. On his head is a caterpillar; he talks to Carmela, who is driving, but what is said is inaudible. Gloria is in the back and asks Tony if he wants to 'take it for a test drive'. The caterpillar on Ralphie's head has now become a moth. Svetlana is suddenly in the back in place of Gloria. Carmela looks back over her shoulder at Tony, her hair now the shorter style she adopted recently.

Just as the anxieties Tony feels about the war with the New York Mafia are manifested in Made in America, here those that are provoked in him by the desire for greater control in their marriage being demonstrated by Carmela are behind her being in the driving seat, her hair changing to the shorter style he is not keen on, and the conversation with Ralphie that he cannot hear. It is suggested, in the therapy session with Jennifer later, that the car being one his father had highlights the transgression in the eyes of a Mafia male of a woman driving, literally and metaphorically; travelling in this car in the dream equates to moving through life in the way his father taught him to.

Various dead people, including his parents, Chris and Adriana, are present in Holsten's, and Ralphie and Gloria are fellow passengers in the car. The afterlife looms over Tony and his loved ones in the form of the painting of the building on the far wall, and the caterpillar that becomes a moth is similarly suggestive. It has undergone a significant change, as has the man whose head it sits on, and there is an ambiguity to the manner in which this points to the afterlife. It could be 'like a moth to a flame', with light as a common metaphor for Heaven, or it may be more appropriate, given the lifestyles of Ralphie and Tony, to take the dark colour of the moth as instead indicating Hell. The instantaneous transitions of the caterpillar into the moth and Gloria into Svetlana, and the updating of Carmela's hairstyle, are skips forward. The Tears of a Clown was released when Tony was a child and fits with the selection offered on the table jukebox in Holsten's.

Much of the second part of the dream has already been discussed with reference to the building in the mural in Holsten's, but the brief appearance of a woman's leg from the back seat of the car needs comment. The very first appearance of Tony in the Pilot is of him sitting in Jennifer's waiting room, with the camera framing him through the legs of a statue of a woman. This is commonly understood as implying that his problems are connected to the woman from between whose legs he first entered the world, and those others who remind him of her and thus trap him. This central theme of the show is being touched on again here, in that Tony is travelling through life with this problem as a constant companion, and he may not be able to rid himself of it before he reaches the afterlife. Indeed, the waitress hovering around him in Holsten's just before the cut to black shows that he cannot. In the therapy session earlier in Calling All Cars, Jennifer is wearing a skirt that shows off her legs. In addition, there is a narrative skip when, after leaving the car, Tony is still dressed smart casually in shirt and trousers, but this changes to the attire of a manual labourer. Also like the finale, there is a sense of unease in this second part of the dream that becomes more palpable and intense as the black silhouette of the woman descends the stairs; it is no surprise that Tony is distressed when he wakes.

(iii) The Test Dream

The dream in this episode begins with Tony waking in bed in the hotel room in New York he has been staying in. There is nothing to indicate immediately that it is a dream, until the female voice asking him if he wants oral sex turns out not to belong to the prostitute who visited his room, but the deceased Carmine, Sr., lying next to him in bed. The phone rings, which Carmine knew would happen before it does, and a male voice on the phone says to Tony that an unspecified group need him to do something important.

The narrative cuts quickly to a therapy session in which Tony is discussing the dream as if it is over, but it is revealed that he is in conversation with Gloria, who alternately speaks with her own voice and that of Jennifer. Like Carmine earlier, she understands that she is dead; the violence that broke out between she and Tony in Amour Fou is raised. He impersonates Ralph Kramden, the character played by Jackie Gleason in the 1950s sitcom *The Honeymooners*, saying 'one of these days, Alice', and waving his fist. He accuses Gloria of trying to stick a fork in his eye, but in the voice of Jennifer she says 'no, that was your mother', which he finds hilarious. In her own voice she asks him 'are you ready for what you have to do?', to which he replies 'don't sweat, I did my homework'. She then points to a television, on which can be seen Tony dressed in a suit and tie, in a car reminiscent of that from the dream in Calling All Cars, being driven by his father. Suddenly, he is alone in the office and then in the car. His father is the age he was when Tony was a child; he asks Tony if he 'wants to ride up front', i.e., be in control, but he declines. Big Pussy is in the front passenger seat and says nothing; Mikey is in the back with Tony, spattered with blood, but then it is Artie. Tony asks 'where we going?', and it is now Ralphie, wearing his wig, in the front passenger seat who says 'driving you to the job'.

Already in this dream echoes of Made in America are evident. Both begin in the same way, with Tony apparently waking up. The concerns from his waking life are driving the narrative, although he is yet to arrive at a solution. Six dead people have roles, and Johnny Boy appears to be a similar age as when he is the Man in Members Only jacket. The effect of Livia, the waitress in Holsten's, on him comes through in a childhood memory and female acquaintances who remind him of her. There are unfeasibly fast changes to the setting. There is also an association with his cousin Tony B, which grows as the dream progresses, that is at least partly responsible for the reference to *The Honeymooners*. Unusually, this is stated explicitly when Tony says his cousin 'does a mean Gleason', which is demonstrated to Rusty Millio, who seems less than impressed, in Marco Polo.

Back in the dream, the car takes Tony to the home he shared in the past with Carmela and their children. He is then inside dressed in a dark tracksuit and his hair messy; Carmela is dressed in a formal black outfit as if she is going to a funeral, but instead she reminds him that they are meeting Finn's parents and are late. On the television he sees a scene from the 1951 film *Scrooge*, an adaptation of *A Christmas Carol* by Charles Dickens (1843), in which Ebeneezer Scrooge is delighted to discover that he is not too late for what he needs to do. The broadcast then changes to the couple leaving for the lunch with Tony dressed; as he leaves one of his teeth falls out.

The lunch is at Nuovo Vesuvio, where they are greeted by Charmaine, dressed in a style that Tony is very appreciative of. On the television is a scene from the 1952 Western *High Noon*, the star of which, Gary Cooper, embodies the ideal American man for Tony (which is ironic, as he was born to English parents in Montana and returned to England for part of his schooling); he is coming to realise that he will need to get something done, and this is why his subconscious is turning to a suitable image to inspire him. The next products of it are more surprising: Finn's father is Vin, or at least looks and speaks identically to him, and his mother is the actress Annette Benning, appearing as herself. This is an expression of disjunctive cognition: although we do not meet Finn's parents, there is nothing to suggest that they are these two. Annette asks how long Tony can stay and he says he has something he needs 'to take care of'. He loses another tooth. Finn suddenly becomes AJ, dressed just like Tony, but Annette reports, as if he is her son, that they did not expect him 'to amount to much', and Carmela agrees. Vin then serenades Annette with Three Times A Lady by The Commodores (1978), although she does not appear overly appreciative.

Tony and Vin go to the bathroom, where a man watches their entrance on television. Tony goes into a cubicle and searches behind the cistern for something which he cannot find. Vin asks him if he is going 'to be able to come through on the thing?', and he reassures him that he did his 'homework', and to prove the point shows him a paperback copy of *The Valachi Papers* by Peter Maas, a 1968 biography of Joe Valachi, who was the first member of the Mafia in America to become a government witness.

As well as a number of skips forward in the narrative, and strange behaviour from those depicted, in this section of the dream there are other uses of the same techniques employed in Made in America. There are two references to *The Godfather*. The first is when Tony searches for something in the bathroom cubicle, as Michael did before murdering Sollozzo and Captain McCluskey in the scene that is also echoed in the events in Holsten's, when the Man in Members Only jacket heads to the bathroom. The second is easier to miss: Annette says 'I don't want my husband coming out of there with just his cock in his hand', which are almost the same words spoken by Sonny when planning that murder. One aspect of this section that may be interpreted as another link to Made in America, but which probably is not as much as it appears, is the song Three Times A Lady. It is from 1978 and consistent with the time period of the songs generated by Tony's mind. However, the number three here, rather than being an expression of his fear that he will die at three o'clock, is more likely a subtle reference to the fact that Vin has two failed marriages behind him. Annette is his third wife and, judging from her lack of enthusiasm at his singing, if this were not a dream it may not be long before she becomes his third ex-wife too.

To complete the dream, gunfire is heard and Tony B is shooting Phil who is sitting in a car; a man in the crowd asks Tony 'why didn't you stop him?'. Phil gets out of the car and collapses, before Tony B finishes him off with his fingers in the shape of a gun. Tony asks him 'you have any idea what you just did?'. Harold Melvoin, Junior's lawyer, is in the crowd, but for no obvious reason. A black man asks Tony whether his cousin is the guy he should have taken care of to stop this from happening. The crowd, including Melvoin, begin to chase him and it is suddenly dark; Carmela is also in the crowd chasing, as are men in old European dress with torches and dogs. He is saved by Artie calling him into an alleyway, and then they are in a car with Gigi and Richie in the backseat. The scene changes suddenly to Tony having sex with Charmaine in a bed with the encouragement of Artie, and again to him riding Pie-O-My inside the family home. Carmela warns that one of the conditions of him returning is that he does not bring his whores in; 'whores' is deliberately chosen because it sounds like 'horse'. She is surprised that he has not yet taken care of the unidentified task. The final rapid scene change finds Tony walking through a corridor at his school; in the dark changing-room he finds Coach Molinaro, who taught him football, and presumably looks as he did when Tony was young. The coach sees him aiming the gun at him and begins to criticise him. Another attempt to kill him fails when the gun falls apart; he tries to pick up the bullets, but they are smeared with faeces and he retches. 'You're not prepared!' shouts Molinaro, and then Tony wakes up looking stressed.

Like Made in America, and Funhouse before it, the dream in this episode represents the mind of Tony working towards the solution to a problem, one that involves murder, and the attempted overcoming of the stress it causes him, but unlike the finale the conclusion that is reached here is more than simply wish-fulfilment. He knows now what he has to do and carries it out two episodes later. As the viewer discovers from the telephone conversation which follows with Carmela, this is not the first time that he has dreamed of Coach Molinaro: 'were you unprepared as usual?' she asks. It is unknown whether any of the previous ones also involved Tony trying to kill him, but as he and his cousin Tony B, the true object of this dream, are around the same age, the school setting might be an association with him, rather than the coach. It is also unknown whether the coach is still alive, but Pie-O-My is certainly another visitor from the afterlife. Throw in the absurdities, such as those doing their best to re-enact a scene from a Hammer House of Horror film, and more skips in the narrative, and this dream is another major clue to the correct interpretation of Made in America that was provided to the viewer three years earlier.

(iv) Join the Club / Mayham

The extended dream sequence that occurs while Tony is in a coma, following his shooting by Junior, takes up much of two episodes, the second and third of the sixth season. Many viewers did not enjoy this radical prioritising of his inner life,[177] which is surely relevant to the lack of interest in considering the possibility that Made in America is a similar type of narrative. Join the Club opens with the beginning of the dream: Tony wakes on a bed during the evening, and out of the hotel room window he sees a beacon of light in the distance. He has a drink in the hotel bar and the television shows a news report about fires in Costa Mesa, California, where the hotel is situated. He calls his family, and from the answering machine message we hear that they are called the Sopranos, but his children do not sound like Meadow and AJ. The beacon is visible from the bar. As he leaves the hotel, reality briefly intrudes as his stomach feels uncomfortable, and

---

[177] Imperioli and Schirripa, *op. cit.*, p. 448.

the face of a doctor is vaguely visible, with his torch manifesting as a helicopter shining a searchlight above him.

It is immediately daylight. When entering the convention, the reason for his trip, he gives his name as Anthony Soprano, but his identification card says Kevin Finnerty of Kingman, Arizona, with a photo of someone else who looks quite like him. It is obvious now that he is not speaking with his familiar New Jersey accent. He is not allowed to enter the convention as he cannot prove his identity; he realises he must have picked up the suitcase belonging to Finnerty at the hotel, as it contains solar heating brochures. He calls his wife, who does not sound like Carmela, and tells her about what he has mislaid: 'my whole life's in that case.'

Back in the hotel bar, the barman, after declaring that he has no idea where Tony's briefcase is, reports that Costa Mesa is 'dead'. He joins a group in the bar, but only after he sees an attractive dark-haired woman amongst them. During the conversation it is learned that he sells precision optics, and that his sales team have won a number of awards. For no particular reason he says 'I'm forty-six years old. Who am I? Where am I going?', to which the woman replies 'join the club'. As the group leave the bar, on the television he sees the question: 'are sin, disease and death real?', which is then replaced by the Christian cross. While kissing the woman in the car park the helicopter returns, and she says 'they're looking for a perp'. The dream is interrupted to reveal the medical team treating Tony for a seizure; he rips out his breathing tube and, in a semi-conscious state, twice asks 'who am I? Where am I going?'. This concern for the path his life is taking is a recurring theme in the show right from the opening scene in which his therapy with Jennifer begins, and is present also in his interest in the ducklings in his swimming pool, whose new attempts at flight symbolise for him 'the realisation of a natural and instinctual ability to elevate oneself beyond certain limitations'.[178]

Back in the dream he checks into another hotel, the Omni. He uses the card belonging to Finnerty, and two Buddhist monks behind him, on the assumption that he is Finnerty, tell him that they will be filing a suit against him because he has been ignoring their attempts to contact him. They complain that they have had a cold winter, one assumes because of the heating system Finnerty sold them; Tony repeatedly denies being him, and one of the monks slaps him across the face, telling him to 'lose your arrogance.' Afterwards, he calls his wife, saying he wants to come home, and she responds by saying that he is too distracted by work, that his predicament is partly his own fault. There is a skip to morning. The elevator is out of order, so Tony has to use the stairs, but in rushing he slips and knocks himself out. When the dream resumes, he wakes up in a hospital with a bandage on his head. The doctor has ordered an MRI based on things he saw in a CT scan and tells his patient that he is displaying symptoms of Alzheimer's; Tony says 'I'm lost!'. Back in his hotel room, he picks up the phone to call someone, presumably his wife, but changes his mind. The beacon in the distance continues to flash and he looks dejected and lonely.

As in Made in America, this first part of the coma dream presented in Join the Club begins with Tony apparently waking up. It shows his subconscious grappling with issues that are bothering him in the waking world, not least of which are the

---

[178]Stoehr, *op. cit.*, p. 151.

philosophical questions of personal identity and the meaning of life. 'Kevin Finnerty' sounds like 'Kev Infinity' and sets up a dualism between the person that he thinks he is, Tony Soprano, a husband, father and precision optics salesman, and a foundational spiritual nature which is an expression of the infinite. The name of the hotel that has room for him, the Omni, is of Latin derivation and means 'all' or 'universal'; in theistic religions God is often believed to be omnipotent (all-powerful), omniscient (all-knowing) and omnibenevolent (all-loving). Despite complaining to his wife that he wants to return home, he might actually be there already, if he would only take responsibility for how he acts and change his perception of his identity.

The intrusion of reality in the dream, present also in him nervously watching who is coming through the entrance to Holsten's in Made in America, can be seen as the torch of the doctor shines in his eyes and becomes the searchlight of the helicopter; and, before the dream doctor mentions an MRI, Carmela refers to the one he underwent in the Pilot, when she memorably tells him that he is going to Hell when he dies. Unlike that in The Test Dream, there is also less of the absurd here. It is presented in a more realistic style akin to Made in America, and a viewer might not spot that it is a dream if they are new to the show, or if it is not made obvious by frequently returning to the waking world. It is not until the next episode that the deceased appear. The skips in the flow of events are not as obvious as elsewhere and can be easily missed, like that in the finale between Tony standing and sitting in Sil's hospital room.

When the dream resumes in the next episode Tony wakes up in his bed in the hotel. He finds a summons that has been pushed under the door, from a place called Crystal Monastery, and drives there to discuss the matter with the Buddhist monks. Unfortunately, it is not a productive meeting: they believe little that he says and want him to take responsibility for the problem. He says he cannot and wants them to help him 'reach Finnerty'. Later in the hotel bar, he tells the bartender about his diagnosis of Alzheimer's and mentions the mental decline of Junior; he also asks him if it is possible that he is in fact Finnerty. The beacon is visible in the distance.

In his room he takes an invitation to the Finnerty family reunion out of the briefcase; it is to be held at a location called the Inn at the Oaks. He makes a call to get directions and they include heading towards the source of the light. He is disturbed and annoyed by a loud noise from the next room, which turns out to be Paulie, who has come to visit him in the hospital in the waking world. Despite instructions from Meadow to only talk positively, he is soon in a characteristic moaning rant and in the dream the noise from the next room sounds like Paulie muffled. The vital signs monitor shows that all is not well, and Tony enters into tachycardia.

As he drives to the reunion, the shocks from the paddles being used by the medical team become bumps on the road. The Inn at the Oaks turns out to be a beautiful large building decorated with lights. Traditional Italian music can be heard, and a girl and a younger boy, sporting a haircut like AJ had in the first season, run by. Tony is greeted by a man who looks identical to his deceased cousin Tony B, who tells him 'they're waiting for you.' On asking 'has Kevin Finnerty arrived?' the man replies 'we don't talk like that here.' Tony's family are inside waiting for him: 'you're going home'. He glimpses a woman in the doorway who is reminiscent of Livia and the black silhouette from the second dream in Calling All Cars. He is tearful and walks towards the entrance, but the man, referring to his briefcase, informs him that 'you can't bring business in there'. Tony does not want to leave it behind, but the man is adamant: 'you need to let go'. The voice of a girl can be heard shouting 'daddy...don't go, daddy... don't leave us'. After the man tries to reassure him that 'there's nothing to be scared of. You can let it go. Just come say hello', a blinding light erupts from the doorway, and he comes out of the coma, hearing Meadow shouting 'daddy' and seeing Carmela with her. The change in the sound of the flatline monitor as he becomes conscious suggests that he was clinically dead.

Despite the appearance of a man identical to Tony B, this second part of the dream continues in the more realistic style seen in the first. There is more investigation of questions of great personal import to Tony: the ongoing search for Finnerty represents the desire for something beyond the material world to hold on to, and its absence causes struggles that are visible also in Made in America. As in the finale, there are more intrusions into the dream from the waking world, including the hilarious attempt at patient support by Paulie. There are also two ways in which this part of the dream prefigures Made in America. The first is at the beginning of both in the similarity between the camera views as Tony wakes. The second is his understanding of the afterlife, which underlies the final scene in Holsten's where he is surrounded by family and friends. The Inn at the Oaks is where he will find his family, and after he is out of the coma he says to Carmela, when various of them are present in the room with her, 'I'm dead, right?'

Chapter Eighteen
In the Czech Republic Too We Love Pork

As Tony is the central character and lynchpin of *The Sopranos*, it is logical that most of the dreams that the viewer is allowed to peer inside are his. They are not, however, the only ones access is granted to. The show is full of fascinating characters, driven by their individual arcs and how these as a whole intersect. Analysing their dreams will further demonstrate that the techniques utilised in the production of the finale are not new to the series.

(i) Jennifer

The character who ranks next on the list in terms of time devoted to their dreams is Jennifer. This is appropriate because, although she does not appear as often as some of the other characters, there is a case to be made for her being the most important one after Tony. His need for her therapeutic skills is the premise of the story, and the state of his mind its central theme. It would also be a missed opportunity in a show in which dreams are presented regularly to fail to delve into those of someone trained in psychoanalysis. Two of her dreams are of sufficient length to play a meaningful part in the overall argument concerning Made in America.

The first is found in Toodle-F***ing-Oo. The scene in question begins with Tony driving in heavy rain at night, although it is not immediately obvious that it is a dream, as the previous scene ended with him leaving the family home to go somewhere. On closer inspection, however, he left in the daytime and is now wearing different clothes. He begins to have a panic attack and the song Optimistic Voices, from the 1939 film *The Wizard of Oz*, can be heard; he reaches for his bottle of Prozac, but passes out and crashes head on into a truck. Jennifer drives by, and it is at this point that the possibility arises that it is not a dream of Tony that is being shown. She sees him lying on the bonnet having been catapulted through the windscreen; he looks dead, and his medicine bottle is beside him. Jennifer wakes and writes down her experience.

The context for the dream is the guilt felt by Jennifer over no longer treating Tony. Earlier in the episode, they bump into each other in a restaurant; she is more friendly than him, and on leaving she says 'toodle-oo'. This bothers her afterwards and she discusses it with her therapist Elliot. He interprets her use of the phrase as her dropping the therapist façade because she does not want to treat Tony, but she disagrees, viewing it as a way of avoiding responsibility for abandoning her patient.

This dream demonstrates the same storytelling techniques that are evident in those of Tony that have already been discussed, and therefore it is important for correctly understanding Made in America. The emotional foundation, the latent content, is once more an issue that the author of the dream is grappling with, in this case Jennifer's therapeutic relationship with Tony. It aids her in reaching a decision, although it is not one that Elliot agrees with.

The practice of including a visitation from a deceased character is subverted by showing Tony dying in the crash. The song from *The Wizard of Oz* has meaning for Jennifer in the same way that those heard throughout the finale and displayed on the jukebox have for Tony. The lyrics express relief at leaving problems behind: 'you're out of the woods, you're out of the dark, you're out of the night. Step into the sun, step into the light'; but the consequences of this freedom for her professional self-respect are unpalatable. This is one of the dreams in the show that are more in line with how things operate in the waking world, but there are touches of the absurd in the association of a happy, carefree song with a depressive mobster, and the medicine bottle landing where it does after the crash.

The second of Jennifer's dreams is found in Employee of the Month, the fourth episode of the third season, and, given the traumatic event to which it is a response, it is little surprise that the dream portrayed is of a darker bent than that in Toodle-F***ing-Oo. As Jennifer is leaving work, she is brutally raped by a stranger in a stairwell that leads to the parking garage. Her suffering and feeling of powerlessness are compounded both by the rapist being freed because of a mistake by the police in the procedure for charging him, and seeing him lauded as 'employee of the month' on the wall of a shop where she buys a soft drink.

The dream begins with Jennifer working in her office. It is very dark and she hears the sound of her car remote key. On her door is a 'Danger High Voltage' sign with 'New Jersey Gas & Electric' on the bottom. She opens the door and sees herself in her office by an Acme Cola machine;[179] she puts a piece of pasta in the payment slot, but her hand gets stuck in reaching for the drink. A large dog begins to bark and the pasta comes out of the change slot. The rapist appears and grabs her, but the dog attacks him; she then wakes up, looking less stressed than one might expect.

In a session with Elliot, she reports feeling relieved and safe as she woke up, and he adds 'empowered'. She suddenly realises that the dog was a Rottweiler: 'big head, massive shoulders, direct descendant of the dog used by the Roman armies to guard their camps'; as such it represents Tony, who she could set on the rapist for vengeance, and she reports a sense of 'satisfaction' knowing this. But she also knows that if she did it would violate not only their therapeutic relationship, but also the rules of civilisation. Earlier in the episode, encouraged by her husband, she suggests to Tony that he should be moving on to a course of Behaviour Modification Therapy with someone else, the idea of which makes him upset; but when he now expresses more of an openness to the idea it is she who is upset, and she bursts into tears. Tony, dressed in dark colours reminiscent of the Rottweiler, asks her 'you wanna say something?', to which she replies 'no'. The episode ends in a gesture of defiant courage from a woman who has undergone a horrific ordeal.

The dream has clear similarities to the events of Made in America. It is driven by emotional forces, possibly even stronger than those felt by a mobster who is in fear for his life, and the narrative reflects them; here, the manifest content is in tune with the latent. The Rottweiler is her saviour in the same way

---

[179] In the 1964 film *Dr. Strangelove*, a Coca Cola vending machine represents American capitalism; it does so here, too. Chase is an admirer of Kubrick.

that Agent Harris is for Tony. As he does in Holsten's and the Funhouse dream before that, she watches herself as she performs the ridiculous act of paying for a soft drink with a piece of pasta, and as figures appear out of nowhere.

(ii) Chris

The only dream of Chris to which the viewer is given access is in The Legend of Tennessee Moltisanti, and it occurs at the beginning. Chris is sitting in Satriales, drinking coffee and staring thoughtfully ahead. The music playing and the camera focusing on the coffeemaker imply that things are not quite as usual, and when the voice of Emil Kolar, who he murdered in the Pilot, is heard saying 'in the Czech Republic too we love pork. Ever had our sausages?', it is clear that a dream is being presented. Chris moves through the store as if he is on a conveyor belt, as Emil repeats what he said. Adriana is on her knees, being fed a large sausage by a hand from inside the meat counter, and she then becomes Carmela. Chris sees Emil through the window looking very dead, but the view appears to be the blue sea at sunrise or sunset. Suddenly, Chris is behind the counter wearing a blood-spattered butcher's white apron and Emil orders a sandwich, for which the hand passes the meat.

The conversation then becomes more pointed: 'you killed me', 'what do you want me to do about it now?'; 'I want to tell you...', 'tell me what? You come here every night!'; '...you f***ed up.' Emil drops used bullets on to the counter and says that he found 'one in the table, three in my skull. You will have our sausages'. Chris bends down and gives the bullets to the hand to get rid of, but it grabs his arm: 'let go of me! Let go!' He wakes up in bed next to Adrianna, breathing fast and sweating. Later in the episode, with the help of Georgie from the Bada Bing!, he digs up the body of Emil, a risky move for which he is berated by Tony.

Once again, this dream is heavily influenced by the anxieties and desires of the subject. The central theme is the emotional consequences for Chris of killing Emil, and in particular his worry that he made a mistake which could tie him to the crime. His victim is a visitor from the afterlife, and the hand in the meat counter is the typical fare of horror movies. His sexuality comes through in Adriana and Carmela acting in a way that is suggestive of fellatio. Throw in the absurd dialogue, and the beautiful seaside setting outside a pork store in Elizabeth, New Jersey, and all of these features make the dream a precursor of Made in America.

(iii) Carmela

There are two dreams of Carmela that the viewer is allowed to witness first-hand, and both are less than a minute in length. The first is found in Members Only, depicting her reporting to the deceased Adriana, at the spec house, how worried she is. The second occurs in Cold Stones, while Carmela is visiting Paris with Rosalie. In the dream, Carmela is out walking and sees a stylishly dressed woman walking a dog. She turns around and reveals herself to be Adriana; with a smile she says 'look - I found Cosette!' This is the dog that Chris unintentionally sat on and killed, while high on drugs, in The Strong, Silent Type. A French policeman then tells Carmela, in an American accent, that someone needs to explain to Adriana that she is dead. She then wakes up in bed.

The latent content that drives this dream is the suspicion of Carmela that what Chris told her and others about the disappearance of Adriana, that she ended their relationship and moved away, is not true and that something more sinister happened to her; like those already examined, it helps the author of the dream to develop a better understanding. As a precursor to Made in America this dream is also based on fear and anxiety, includes an unlikely, though not impossible, ingredient of a gendarme speaking English with an American accent, and contains two visitations from the dead.

On the basis of this chapter, and the previous one, it can be seen clearly that there is a consistent language of dreams spoken throughout *The Sopranos*, one that is prior to, but in harmony with, that found in the finale. It is a very familiar one that is based on the sleeping experiences of the average person, but to it are added lessons from psychoanalysis and knowledge of the work of influential filmmakers.

Chapter Nineteen
No Hay Banda

To complement the discussion of dreams prior to Made in America the focus will now be moved away from *The Sopranos*. Chase has spoken often of the profound influence that the work of the American filmmaker Lynch has had on him; about *Twin Peaks* he said: 'everything was mysterious… the weather, the trees, the doughnuts. The dream sequences were more nightmare-like than anything I'd seen before… Lynch dug them up from the bottom of his unconscious… Anybody making one-hour drama today who says he wasn't influenced by David Lynch is lying'.[180] The impact on Chase of the 2001 film *Mulholland Drive* is of special relevance to this argument. It was released only six years before Made in America; this would have given him plenty of time to digest it and allow it to inform what he was producing. Investigating this connection allows for the shedding of light on their common interests as storytellers in a way that supports the conclusion of this book.

The majority of *Mulholland Drive* is a dream, quite similar to the finale of *The Sopranos* and other dreams in the show in many

---

[180] Eliana Dockterman 'Creators of *Lost, Fargo, The Sopranos* and Other Shows on How *Twin Peaks* Influenced Them', *Time*.

ways. It is a 'nice dream' like Made in America, but has a different structure in that it shows both dream and waking reality. As a one-off story about the characters, it would have been difficult, although not impossible, for Lynch to make it completely a dream if the reality which underlies and generates it is to be understood. Made in America can be a dream throughout because it is preceded by eighty-five episodes of mostly waking reality.

At face value, *Mulholland Drive* is about two women, Betty Elms and Diane Selwyn, who appear identical even though their behaviour and lives are very different. Betty is an aspiring actress who arrives in Hollywood to realise her goals; she is beautiful, compassionate and humble, and possessed of acting talent that immediately begins to open doors for her. Diane is also an actress, but her career is going nowhere; she is unhappy, needs drugs to cope and cannot get over the failure of her relationship with another actress. Understood as a traditional narrative, the film is very confusing because of multiple inconsistencies. A number of characters besides Betty and Diane are physically identical but act in different ways, such as the amnesiac woman, who survives a car crash and takes the name Rita from a poster of Rita Hayworth, and Camilla Rhodes, the ex-lover of Diane. The latter is the second person to be called Camilla Rhodes, the first being another actress who, for an unspecified reason, is supported in her career by mobsters. An elderly couple who chat pleasantly with Betty at the airport later demoniacally terrorise Diane. There are also unusual thematic changes, and sections which would not be out of place in the detective, comedy, horror and romance genres. If there is a straightforward chronology of events it is not easy to discern.

The point of this discussion of *Mulholland Drive* is not to attempt to explain in-depth its structure and meaning and the intentions of Lynch in making it, but to go some way along each of these paths in order to understand even better Made in America. Both work on more than one level and cannot be grasped properly if this is not taken on board. The narrative presented on the surface of the film concerns Diane. The most recent events in her life that are learned about are her trying to develop a career as an actress in Hollywood, and entering into a relationship with another woman, Camilla, who has the same goal. Unfortunately, she has no success in acting while her lover does, and then their relationship ends, leaving her depressed and angry; in response, Diane hires a hitman to kill Camilla, but once it is done, her mental and emotional condition worsens, and she commits suicide.

Like Made in America, *Mulholland Drive* cannot be understood properly on first viewing, even for those who are familiar with the previous output of its writer and director. Initially, one falls into the habit of approaching it from the standpoint of a traditional narrative structure which is characteristic of most films, but it is not long before the shortcomings of this approach become clear. The flow of events is not smoothly linear, characters behave in unusual or inconsistent ways, dialogue does not easily fit the context, and music appears inappropriate for what is being depicted. In short, the impression is given, not for the first time in a work by Lynch, that things are not quite as they seem and that the true message is not coming across clearly.

However, once one jettisons the assumption of a traditional narrative, progress can be made. The most common interpretation, outlined expertly by Alan Shaw,[181] is that the first three-quarters of the film are a dream that Diane has, not long after she has been informed that the murder of Camilla has been carried out. The remainder is composed of the rest of her story leading up to her suicide, intermingled with memories and hallucinations. The dream is an attempt by her subconscious to construct a different version of events, thereby allowing her to deal with the sadness and guilt that plagues her. As a dream it is a mixture of order and chaos, because it is her mind trying, not completely successfully, to conquer the latter with the former; the primary source of chaos that she wishes to put right is her failed relationship with the dark-haired and beautiful Camilla. It ended badly, with Camilla two-timing her with an unnamed man, and jealousy felt by Diane at the difference between the progress of their acting careers; hence the depiction of her ex-lover as the amnesiac who adopts the name Rita. The identity which causes so much pain to Diane is swept away and replaced with a blank canvas, one that she can reconstruct in a more pleasant style. Their relationship can begin again, but hints of the past remain, such as the ominous music that scores the scene when Betty and Rita make love for the first time and the former declares her love for the latter. Earlier Betty says to Rita: 'it'll be just like in the movies. We'll pretend to be someone else'; this is a clue both to the identity of the two of them, and much of what purports to be reality in the film.

In Winkie's, the diner where various scenes take place, the deal between Diane and the hitman is struck. She gives him cash, and he tells her that when it is done he will leave a blue key in a place they discussed before; it is not explicitly identified, but

---

[181] 'A Multi-Layered Analysis of Mulholland Drive'.

the evidence strongly suggests that it is behind the diner. There is something there that haunts a man in her dream who appears to be having a therapy session in Winkie's, and, when he and his companion decide to face his fear, the appearance of a witch-like homeless woman causes him to collapse. After the conversation between Diane and the hitman ends, there is a nightmarish sequence in which the woman is there again, holding a blue box. In reality, there is no blue box, as is evidenced by the laughter of the hitman when Diane asks what the blue key unlocks. It is a symbol for the terrible thing that she has done, and when Rita opens it towards the end of the dream there is black nothingness inside. In Diane's last few moments of life, the face of the woman from behind Winkie's merges into her own, making it clear that she is a dream representation of herself and her horrible crime.

Many of the ingredients out of which Diane constructs her dream are provided by her memory of an evening she spends with Camilla and Adam Kesher, the man she left Diane for. It is very possibly the last time she sees her alive, providing the trigger for her decision to have her killed. She receives a call from Camilla, reminding her to attend a party being held somewhere on Mulholland Drive; she is taken in a limousine, just like the one that Rita is in at the start of the dream, and Diane speaks her words: 'what are you doing? We don't stop here.' Whereas Rita has a gun pointed at her, Diane is surprised by Camilla who escorts her to the party, but her joy at this does not survive the evening. She watches as an unnamed woman, who appears as Camilla in the dream, kisses the real one seductively, and then hears that she and Adam are to be married. Other faces from her dream are sourced here: Coco, the friend of her aunt who shows her to the apartment, is Adam's mother; one of the mobsters threatening Adam is an unnamed man who looks at her; and the cowboy who delivers a message for the mobsters is someone who walks by in the background briefly.[182]

Amongst everything else that vies for the attention of the viewer are hints about the trajectory of Diane's life before she arrived in Hollywood. The elderly couple, who Betty stands in the spotlight with during the jitterbug scene and later walks out of the airport with, seem pleasant enough, but as they are being driven away they have odd expressions, like fixed smiles. They are not seen again in the dream, but towards the end of the film they behave as if they are monsters, cackling maniacally and terrorising Diane to such a degree that she runs to her bedroom screaming, finds her gun and kills herself. In her dying vision she is again in the spotlight, but this time only with Rita in her blonde wig.

A clue as to why this elderly couple should cause such a reaction from Diane comes in the audition scene in the dream. Betty is paired with a smooth-talking older actor named Woody, who takes the opportunity to stand with her in an intimate pose. The characters they are rehearsing are a young female and a man called Chuck, of at least similar age to her father and who is his 'best friend'. He asks her to do something which she is so opposed to that she threatens to tell her father and for which Chuck would go to prison, but she has done it before and not completely against her will: 'I hate you... I hate us both!' Considering also their embracing and kissing each other while she holds an imaginary knife, the most logical interpretation is

---

[182]In what is probably a nod to this character, there is one in *The Many Saints of Newark* credited as The Man in the Cowboy Hat; he has no impact on the plot and has no obvious reason to be dressed in that way.

that they are in a sexual relationship, even though she is under the legal age.

These two elements taken together suggest that Diane was abused by her paternal grandfather, her father's 'best friend', and that her grandmother did nothing about it, pretending with him that everything was fine. The elderly couple with the fixed smiles who later drive Diane to suicide are those grandparents. When Adam discovers Gene in bed with his wife, the latter says: 'just forget you ever saw it. It's better that way.' This is a strange comment, sounding more like what Diane's abuser would say to his wife discovering him in bed with her. There is a definite resemblance between Gene and the magician on the stage at Club Silencio;[183] the latter develops a particularly demonic expression and his act, when he strains and then relaxes in a manner reminiscent of a man ejaculating, causes Betty to cry and shake in fear. As this is a dream there is no reason, in line with the phenomenon of disjunctive cognition, why Gene, the magician and the old man accompanying Irene cannot be representations of the same individual, who has had such a powerful impact on the life of the dreamer.

Further evidence that Diane is a victim of familial abuse is the famous portrait of the young woman that hangs in Aunt Ruth's apartment. The subject is believed by some to be Beatrice Cenci, a Roman noblewoman who in 1598 murdered her father, Count Francesco Cenci, after years of sexual abuse by him; she was consequently beheaded on the orders of Pope Clemente VIII in

---

[183] It is this character who utters the phrase 'no hay banda', used as the title of this chapter. It means 'there is no band' in Spanish, and implies that much of what Diane is experiencing, including the music in the performance on stage, is an illusion.

1599. The portrait is attributed to either Guido Reni (1575-1642) or Elisabetta Sirani (1638-1665), and, as corroboration of both the subject and artist is lacking, it is 'an image whose own dubious identity corresponds to the multiple and shifting identities in the film.'[184] The same point can be made about the fact that the original hangs in the Galleria Nazionale d'Arte Antica in Rome, so, at best, what is hanging on the wall in Aunt Ruth's apartment is a reproduction in a dream.

Much of the detail in *Mulholland Drive* therefore lies half-hidden, only to be deciphered either by bringing together disparate elements that initially appear to have no connection, or interpreting something in an unconventional fashion. With the simple moving of the space 'Aunt Ruth' becomes 'a untruth', and points to the many falsities and deceptions the viewer must beware of. Diane suffering sexual abuse as a child is alluded to by both the name of the diner and the actor she auditions with: 'winkie' and 'woody' are both names used by children for the penis. A poster of Rita Hayworth is a suitable source for a name for the amnesiac woman, as the famous actress was born Margarita Carmen Cansino to a Spanish father, but boosted her career by taking the maiden name of her American mother of Irish and English ancestry, and dying her black hair red.[185] There are many more examples like these scattered throughout the film.

Colours are also utilised as a narrative device, in that they are given associations which hold true in certain circumstances.

---

[184]Susan Felleman 'Source Hunting in a Dreamscape', *Lola*.
[185]Kat Eschner 'How Margarita Cansino Became Rita Hayworth', *www. smithsonianmag.com*.

Green usually has pleasant connotations to environmental phenomena, but in *Mulholland Drive* a vivid green connotes for Diane the loss of the woman she loved. As the man in Winkie's talks with his therapist, there are bright green posters on the windows, and as they walk outside to face whatever lies behind the diner, they walk on a path and pass two poles, a section of the roof, something like a bollard and the handrails of the steps that are all of this colour too. It is later learned from another part of the dream that the gardens around the apartments where Diane lived with Camilla are full of greenery, and from a flashback that she finally realised that the relationship was going to end when the two of them were lying together on their vivid green sofa. It should be noted that these and others like them are not blanket associations: sometimes a colour is just a colour with no additional meaning.

There is much to recommend this interpretation of *Mulholland Drive*, but there are other points to take into account. Most importantly, the film does not contain as much reliable material with which to judge the dream as many assume. Diane is clearly a deeply troubled and unhappy person, who may have been a victim of child sexual abuse, and this is sufficient to explain why she is prone to visions and waking nightmares. It would not be a surprise if she uses illegal drugs, although if this is so, it is not made obvious. Nothing precedes the jitterbug scene, but after it there is what sounds like a long inhale, before the breathing returns to a normal rate and the face of the subject buries itself in the pillow and the dream begins. The long inhale could be evidence of the use of a drug like cocaine, which would explain the vividness of the dream, but no paraphernalia associated with drug use is visible.

There are moments of cold, hard reality, such as when Diane is alone in her kitchen making coffee, but they do not last. She is psychologically unable to remain calmly in the present moment for long. The nominally waking segment, as well as the appearances to her of those who are not really there, such as Camilla and the elderly couple, also contains what appear to be memories. Recall of past experiences by even the most emotionally secure people is prone to inaccuracy,[186] but this is even more so for someone like Diane;[187] a question-mark therefore hangs over everything presented in the film. At the very least, there is a decent probability that everything that happens after Diane appears to wake up at the sound of the door knocking could take place in a very small area, between the bedroom, front door, kitchen and lounge in her apartment, with everything else constituted of periodic trips into her consciousness. It could, however, also be a dream from start to finish, as just because a subject appears to wake up it does not necessarily mean that the dream is over, as can be seen from The Test Dream, Join the Club and, according to the thesis of this book, Made in America. Another, less radical, possibility is that what are commonly taken to be her memories of events, such as the party at Adam's house and the meeting at Winkies to arrange the murder of Camilla, are in fact fantasies, fuelled by her resentment and desire for vengeance.

Is Adam truly a film director who stole Diane's lover? At the very least, there is reason to suspect that Kesher is not his real name. Kesher is the Hebrew word for 'connection', raising the

---

[186] Jason Arunn Murugesu 'Your short-term memory can be unreliable after just a few seconds', *New Scientist*.
[187] Deryn Strange and Melanie Takarangi 'Memory Distortion for Traumatic Events: The Role of Mental Imagery', *Front Psychiatry*.

possibility that it is an all too familiar antisemitic slur on the part of Diane's subconscious: Adam is 'connected' to the Jews who are secretly running everything, including pulling the strings in Hollywood. His surname is not heard or seen after Diane wakes from the dream. It may be that his true surname is Gonzalez. On the list of residents at the Sierra Bonita Apartments, Number 16 is listed as being occupied by A. Gonzalez; in the seedy hotel in the dream that Adam takes refuge in, his room is also Number 16. When Diane and Camilla argue on the couch in Apartment Number 17, the former asks 'it's him, isn't it?', gesturing with her head in a way that can be taken as indicating someone in a nearby apartment. Adam and his mother converse in Spanish briefly at the party, Coco is commonly a Spanish name, and she dresses in a style reminiscent of the country. Adam could, of course, still be Jewish if he is of Spanish heritage. Perhaps his first name is not Adam, either? This is a name with a strong Hebrew heritage, and it would make sense, in the context of the perception by Diane of his role in her life and Hollywood, if she were to think of him as the 'first man'.

The film company Metro-Goldwyn Mayer (MGM) was formed in 1924, partly out of Goldwyn Pictures Corporation. Goldwyn is an amalgamation of the names of Samuel Goldfish, who was Jewish, and the brothers Edgar and Archibald Selwyn. In *Mulholland Drive* similarly, a young woman called Selwyn wishes to achieve Hollywood success by uniting with a director with a Jewish name. Is Selwyn really the name of the central character of this movie? Perhaps it is a stage-name, if not completely fabricated by the dream.

One should also consider whether Camilla is quite as real as she appears. There is reason to believe that she could be an idealised version of the woman who visits the apartment to collect her belongings. There is tension between Diane and this woman, which suggests that she was more than just a roommate. Camilla's beauty sits uncomfortably alongside the reality of Diane's sad life;[188] is Camilla to this woman what Betty is to Diane? The woman's name, according to the list of residents of the Sierra Bonita Apartments in the dream, is W. DeRosa. Her surname is Spanish and can be translated as 'of rose'; 'rose' sounds like 'Rhodes', but also 'DeRosa' is an anagram of 'Roades', a variant spelling of Camilla's surname. The Spanish origin of her name is another potential link to Adam. The number of Aunt Ruth's apartment in the dream, 1612 Havenhurst, points to a link between the numbers 16 and 12 in Diane's mind, which on this reading would be how she has been hurt by the occupants of those two apartments.

Diane, like Tony with respect to Made in America, is an unreliable narrator, as we all are when dreaming. The unreliable narrator is an artistic device with a long history, and there is value in comparing its use by Lynch and Chase to that by Vladimir Nabokov, a skilled exponent of it. *Mulholland Drive* in this sense is similar to *Lolita*, his most famous and notorious work from 1955. The vast majority of *Lolita* is a confession or memoir by a man who hides behind the pseudonym 'Humbert Humbert', prefaced by a foreword by an author called John Ray, Jr. It does not take long before suspicions arise about the reliability of Humbert as a witness to the events he recounts, and herein lies the value of Ray, Jr.'s foreword, in that it is a source

---

[188]Steven Dillon concurs with this; see *The Solaris Effect: Art and Artifice in Contemporary American Film*, p. 94.

from a different author, which helps the reader to read between the lines of what Humbert writes.[189] For example, a distressingly common misinterpretation of *Lolita* is to report that, according to Ray, Jr., Humbert had been in jail awaiting trial for murder[190], whereas he in fact only refers to a trial for an unnamed crime.[191] This opens up the possibility that Humbert lied about being a murderer and, indeed, there is reason to believe that his purported victim, fellow hebephile Clare Quilty, is a figment of his imagination, created so that he can project what he admits of his own worst qualities on to someone else, and give them the punishment 'they' deserve. The home that Humbert finally tracks Quilty down to, Pavor Manor, is a contradiction: in a state of disrepair when viewed from outside, yet inside 'a library full of flowers' and a room 'with ample and deep mirrors and a polar bear skin'.[192] The theme of the double or doppelgänger is a persistent one throughout the writings of Nabokov, another example of which is his 1934 novel *Despair*.

Made in America, on the other hand, is a different kettle of fish. It is enclosed and unitary, a dream from beginning to end, containing nothing from other sources along the lines of Ray, Jr.'s foreword. There are aspects of it, such as the explosion of Phil's head, which suggest that it is not a regular narrative, but,

---

[189]There is, however, at least one reason to doubt the independence of the foreword from the confession of someone with an unhealthy interest in the young. John Ray's initials are 'JR', an abbreviation of 'junior', and his name is therefore 'Junior, Junior'.
[190]Frohock, Christina M. 'Legal fiction: reading *Lolita* as a sentencing memorandum', p. 7.
[191]Vladimir Nabokov *Lolita*, p. 1.
[192]*Ibid.*, p. 335.

by and large, to understand it one must look beyond it, primarily to previous episodes and the prequel movie. Only in this way can one learn the key to unlocking its mysterious grammar.

Only a surface summary of the structure and meaning of *Mulholland Drive* has been presented thus far; it is an incredibly complex and detailed work, rewarding repeated watching and ongoing study. What this allows, though, is the recognition of it as something which stands in an artistic and conceptual connection to the dreams and other hidden stories in *The Sopranos*. It was released in America in October 2001, five months after the broadcast of the finale of the third season, and eleven before the opener of the fourth, so roughly halfway through the initial broadcast of the show. Over the next almost six years viewers were regaled with a number of extended dream sequences, culminating in Made in America. This is not a coincidence.

It is highly unlikely that there is no link between, on the one hand, Diane and Betty in *Mulholland Drive* and, on the other, Tony and his alternate self in Join the Club and Mayham. Both pairs consist of a character and an idealised version of themselves. Betty is the version of Diane who appears in her dream; she is confident, popular, successful in her acting career, emotionally secure and positive about the future, whereas, in reality, Diane is deeply unhappy, lonely, a drug-user, mentally unstable and going nowhere with whatever acting skills she has. In his coma dream, Tony imagines himself as if he had taken a different path in life: he is a precision optics salesman with a more well-spoken accent, is married to a woman who is not Carmela, and their children sound different on a phone call to Meadow and AJ. Finnerty is a man he is searching for because he believes that he has his briefcase, a metaphor for his life as a whole; he is only seen in a photograph on a driving licence. He is not the ideal version of Tony in the way that Betty is for Diane, but in the metaphysical sense that he represents his soul and essential self, that which every fallen human, according to Catholicism, strives to remain in contact with.

Mulholland Drive is a film about identity and, partly as a consequence, reality also. Identity is an aspect of objective reality, what someone is, but in that it is also who someone considers themselves to be, it relates to subjective reality too. This is the reality that is not given to a person, but which they construct for themselves. Made in America is a record of subjective reality as a dream of Tony, as are the other dreams and deceptive states of consciousness in the show. In that both *Mulholland Drive* and Made in America are concerned with reality, they relate to the structure of their respective narratives, from the three-fold distinction outlined at the start of this book. They also relate to authorial intention, what Lynch and Chase are aiming to achieve in designing their works as they did. Meaning to an extent is also relevant, as how a viewer interprets either of these partly depends on whether they are subjective or objective realities and, of course, whether the viewer spots this.

There is every reason to believe that *Mulholland Drive* inspired Chase, as it did so many other writers, and in his particular case, to go further down the path of using dreams to tell his stories. Those in the later seasons of the show are more intricate, of greater length, and more embedded in the overall narrative, than their earlier counterparts. Part of the fuel for this development is his love of cinema and desire to make films: 'there's the viewing experience in a movie theatre of a large screen…where the vistas are really large, where the sound is really nuanced. Where you can hear every line of dialogue and every sound effect works... and the close-ups are 20 feet high. That's an overwhelming, magical experience, and you don't get that on television.'[193] It is well-known that Chase originally planned *The Sopranos* as a film, and this 'cinematic approach to TV storytelling'[194] created something that HBO advertised as 'not TV'.[195]

Made in America is the final dream of a mobster on the losing end of a vicious war and a life he has not navigated wisely. Like the dream, hallucinations and flashbacks of Diane, it is not explicitly acknowledged as such. One must stand back from our perception of both to reflect upon what exactly is being presented, as opposed to what we assume or are being led to believe is. Doing this allows for the recognition of strong similarities between them. Both the finale of *The Sopranos* and *Mulholland Drive* are either completely or mostly representations of the subconscious mind of their subject, grappling with what concerns them in their waking life. As both subjects are asleep, the tools are more emotional than rational; events happen and people behave in line with the dictates of emotions such as desire and fear. *Mulholland Drive* may be seen as riddled with anxiety in the specific sense of 'entrapment in illusion and deceit that must be uncovered in the hope of an ever more complete liberation'.[196] Diane demonstrates at least

---

[193] In Lawson, *op.cit.*, p. 219.
[194] Gary Edgerton *The Sopranos*, p. 3.
[195] David Lavery 'Read any good television lately? Television companion books and quality TV' in McCabe and Akass *op. cit.*, p. 232.
[196] Daniel Bradley 'Brokenness and Hope: David Lynch's Contribution to a Phenomenology of Anxiety in *Mulholland Drive*', *The Journal of Speculative Philosophy*, p. 182.

some grip on reality in that she is awake as she takes her life, but Tony dies whilst dreaming.

At the audition Betty is treated like royalty even before it begins, more like an Oscar winner than an unknown actress. They are all very impressed and it is obvious that 'this is the girl'. This is how Diane wanted her audition with Bob Booker to have gone, but she tells Adam's mother at the party that 'he didn't think so much of me'. That is why Bob is presented in her dream as only able to offer garbled and meaningless advice to actors, and command no respect from his colleagues; her biases have a similar impact to the way black people end up through the lens of Tony's.

This is not the only time that inconsistency is observable: it is particularly so between Diane and her idealised version of herself. Betty has the world at her feet, she is a talented actress in demand from those in the industry, and men want her: Woody cannot keep his hands off her, and she has barely stepped on to the set where Adam is working before he is entranced by her. It is as if she has stepped straight out of a film from the golden era of Hollywood. Despite all this, though, she is kind and self-effacing, always willing to put the needs of others before herself. Unfortunately, the reality of Betty is Diane. A film career is out of her reach and she has been rejected by the woman she loves. She is bitter and depressed, forced to make ends meet as a prostitute, and spirals down even further after her plan to have Camilla executed is carried out. Her attempt to outrun her despair and pain, caused by the sexual abuse she received at the hands of her grandfather, is a failure. This is a clear demonstration of how the manifest content of a dream, what is experienced on the surface, can be very different to the latent, the emotions which feed it.

As in Made in America, the phenomenon of disjunctive cognition that is common in dreams is also found here. There is no evidence that any of the characters look physically different between dream and the waking world (although this will be the case if the old man, Gene and the magician are representations of the same person) because most of the film takes place in a sleeping mind, and much of the rest is composed of memories, which are not completely trustworthy as records of the past, and hallucinations. Diane is an unreliable narrator, and therefore it is impossible to say with complete certainty what characters really look like or how they behave. The vast majority of the film, possibly all, is told from her point of view. Still, she responds to characters in ways which are not appropriate to what can be guessed of their true identity and behaviour. At the airport, Betty is open and relaxed with the elderly couple who performed and did nothing to prevent her childhood sexual abuse, and in her hallucinations later, Diane acts as if they are monsters rather than people. Betty welcomes the amnesiac woman she finds in her aunt's apartment, provides her with material and emotional support and begins a relationship with her, even though in reality she despised her enough to have her killed.

Another facet of disjunctive cognition is the unrealistic functioning of time. A good example of skipping occurs during the scene when Adam returns home, after the meeting in which he is ordered to cast the dream version of Camilla in his film. He finds his wife in bed with the pool cleaner, and in revenge takes her box of jewellery to the kitchen and pours pink paint into it. In the brief amount of time it takes him to do this, his wife is able to put on an elegant dress and confront him, to which one asks why as well as how. This sartorial matter is not the only case of the absurd that shows up, as one would expect from Lynch. Camilla staggers out of the wreckage of a serious car crash and explosion, that kills the two men who are about to execute her, with only a mild case of concussion and a head wound, and then manages a long walk. After Betty arrives at Aunt Ruth's apartment, Coco tells her that a man who used to live in one of the others kept a prize-fighting kangaroo: 'you just wouldn't believe what that kangaroo did to this courtyard!'.

There is a farcical scene which begins with two men laughing hysterically in an office at a story about a car accident, then one, a dream version of the hitman employed by Diane, kills the other. In cleaning the gun it goes off, and shoots through a wall an obese woman in the buttocks; they fight, and the result is that both she and a janitor are also killed by him. The latter inconsiderately left his vacuum-cleaner on, and rather than turning it off the killer shoots it, which causes it to fuse and set off an alarm. There is another sequence of a similarly preposterous nature when Adam's wife and the pool cleaner fight with one of the mobsters looking for her husband.

As with the numerous occurrences of the word 'dream' in Made in America, some of the clues that most of *Mulholland Drive* is a dream are delivered through dialogue that has a double meaning and does not properly fit the context. When Louise Bonner knocks on the door of the apartment, Betty gives her name, and receives the reply 'no, it's not'. There are also visitations from the deceased in the dream, memories and hallucinations, two of which we can be fairly certain of. The first is Camilla, because the blue key is now in the possession of Diane, and she is wracked by guilt. There is also Aunt Ruth, who is seen leaving her apartment by Rita, and briefly appears again at the end of the dream, once the opening of the blue box has caused the two lovers to disappear; at the party Diane says that she died. It is possible that her grandparents could be added to this list given their age, but there is no way of confirming this, as they only appear in the dream and hallucination.

Associations of a greater or lesser degree of randomness are also a feature common to both stories. The man in the dream, who is terrified by whatever lurks behind Winkie's, is a random stranger Diane glimpses at the counter when the hitman tells her about the blue key; an attractive waitress, whose name-tag identifies her as Betty, serves them during their conversation. When Diane is thinking back to when she finally realised that Camilla was going to end their relationship, she recalls saying to her 'it's him, isn't it?', and this brings up the memory of her having to watch Adam and Camilla becoming overly passionate during the rehearsal of a kissing scene; this then leads her by association to the memory of Camilla moving out. Colours are associated with emotional responses, actions, particular people, and so on, such as pink with innocence: it is a colour that Betty wears but not Diane, and it is pink paint, poured on the jewellery by Adam, that is how her subconscious expresses the sexual abuse she received as a child. Other things act in a similar way as symbols, like the blue box, which is only seen in the dream and hallucinations, and stands for what in reality is paired with the blue key: the execution of Camilla.

The artistic output of Lynch has been hugely influential. He is regarded almost universally as one of the most significant filmmakers of the last fifty years. *Mulholland Drive* is his most successful film: in 2001 it won him a share of the Best Director Award at the Cannes Film Festival, and an Academy Award nomination in the same category. It would therefore be a surprise if Chase, as a long-time fan of his work, were not influenced by it. One might even go so far as to say that Made in America is Chase's response to Lynch's *Mulholland Drive*, an answer developed over almost six years to the aesthetic questions it poses.

Interestingly, there is no record of Chase saying anything publicly about *Mulholland Drive*. Given his admiration for Lynch, the success of this film and the time it was released, this is surprising. In the final *Talking Sopranos* podcast, when discussing the directing of Made in America, he responds to Imperioli's comment about the influence of Kubrick, but does not mention Lynch.[197] Chase has been interviewed numerous times since the release of the film, so this sort of thing could be another example of his evasiveness when answering questions that was remarked upon earlier; but there is also no evidence of him being asked directly about it either, so interviewers may have made it easy for him to avoid the topic.

Something that has eluded previous commentators is the likelihood that the influence of Lynch on Chase would show itself most vividly in special or milestone episodes, such as those in which major plot points occur, or season finales. Those wishing to understand the finale of *The Sopranos* properly should particularly note the amount of detail and level of precision, and the understanding of the dynamics of the dreaming mind, that went into Lynch's film, and expect the same from Chase.

---

[197] 91, 9.14.

Conclusion
Everything Comes to an End

What has been presented in this book is a detailed analysis of two key storytelling techniques utilised in *The Sopranos*, one of which has largely escaped the attention of commentators. Although the role of dreams has been discussed at length, the hidden stories outlined here have not; this is to the detriment of the understanding of the show and needed to be put right.

One should be grateful that Made in America is a dream because otherwise it is, in technical terms, by far the worst episode of the show, and possibly of any Chase has worked on. It looks inconsistent, jumpy and poorly edited; in short, full of the type of mistakes that those planning a career in the television industry hope to leave behind in film school. But, as we all know, this is not *The Sopranos*. As stated previously, those who have worked with Chase repeatedly comment on his attention to detail. Even by the standards of other highly successful shows it is extremely carefully planned, sometimes with a narrative detail paying off that was set up a season or more before.

I did not expect to write this book, particularly the material relating to Made in America. I assumed the fact that it is a dream would become common knowledge long before now and remain astounded that it has not. As Chase remarks in the much-quoted interview with The Star-Ledger, two days after the broadcast: 'anybody who wants to watch it, it's all there'. All of the information necessary to properly understand Made in America is provided, although it does presume familiarity with the form and content of previous episodes. Much of the success of *The Sopranos* is due to it asking a lot of the audience, and the finale is no different. It was never going to be a spectacle that could be fully grasped on first viewing, or even second or third, but that it has been watched repeatedly over the last seventeen years, and no published commentators have considered the possibility that the mysterious finale of a program that has made great use of dreams might be one itself, is astounding.

When exactly the penny dropped for me is lost in the fog of memory, but it was no more than two or three years after the broadcast in 2007. Surely it would not be long before others figured it out? Years later I was still waiting, so I decided to put together a YouTube video in PowerPoint format, entitled 'The Sopranos "Made in America": Tony's Final Dream', and uploaded it on September 11th 2018. It offers a basic summary of what has been presented here, but despite the reference by Bernard on Sopranos Autopsy, it has not exactly set the internet on fire, and neither have those that followed it.

Since 2007, there have been more people open to the possibility that there could be a hidden story, in the form of a drug trip, three episodes earlier in Kennedy and Heidi. Although there are not many compared to the myriad other theories that interest fans, on various forums one finds threads and comments discussing the extent of the effect that peyote has on Tony's consciousness in the last segment. After he takes it, in the apartment of Chris' ex-mistress Sonya Aragon, he rushes to the bathroom and vomits. He then stares up at the light on the ceiling as if in a trance, which makes some wonder whether what follows is not a standard narrative, but a sequence of fantasies as he sits on the bathroom floor, not dissimilar to the events of Isabella, both the obvious ones and the phantom therapy session with Jennifer that was examined in Chapter Four.

The greater interest in this as a potential hidden story is ironic because it is a false positive. Tony does not remain on the bathroom floor, but accompanies Sonya to the casino and then the desert. In the language of dreams in *The Sopranos* that the reader will now be very familiar with, there is nothing of any substance to suggest that it is an altered state of consciousness, rather than a standard narrative. This point is all the more cogent because the episode was co-written by Chase himself, the lexicographer supreme of the language of devices, signs and symbols in the show, so a consistency of expression can be expected.

As we have come to see, a recurrent feature of dreams in *The Sopranos*, as in reality, is the presence of absurd and impossible events. There is, however, nothing of the sort in this segment. The winning streak that Tony enjoys in the casino is unusual, but does happen; if it did not, then gamblers would not be willing to risk their money in the hope of huge and life-changing returns. Tony is actually the type of person who is more likely to experience such a win, given the historical connections between casinos, such as Caesars Palace where this takes place, and the Mafia.[198]

---

[198] This is the subject of *Casino*, the 1995 film by Scorsese, and *Casino: Love and Honor in Las Vegas* by Nicholas Pileggi, on which it is based.

A gangster being given a helping hand in a casino at the expense of the other gamblers is a metaphor for their impact on society more widely.

The narrative lacks other signs that it should be taken as a drug trip. There are no unrealistic time skips, no explicit references to false realities in dialogue or songs, nor any inconsistencies with other events or behaviours in the show. If it were to be a dream, it would have to use a different language to all those presented before, something that is not productive for artists. If Chase had intended to surreptitiously fit a drug trip in here, then the parallel between Tony staring at the bathroom light and later at the sun, the occasion for his epiphany, would be the best opportunity.

It does not need to be a false reality to achieve what it sets out to. It is a very successful depiction of the moral depravity of Tony, fitting snugly with the overall theme of irresponsible behaviour that runs through the episode, including the dispute between he and Phil over the disposal of asbestos-riddled waste. Tony rids himself of his ongoing annoyance and disappointment in Chris by murdering him, and this ultimate sanction, applied to someone who was a member of both his families, appears to bring him nothing but reward: he flies in luxury to Las Vegas, has sex with Chris' ex-mistress, and wins big in the casino at Caesars Palace. Tony collapses in a fit of hilarity at his perception that there is a causal connection between his murder of Chris and his good luck. The circular patterns on the carpet which become visible at this point are undoubtedly a reminder of the nihilistic conviction of Livia, the woman who raised him and conspired to have him killed, that life is 'all a big nothing' (from D-Girl), and a suggestion that he has embraced it. This is further emphasised later in the desert, when he experiences an epiphany and shouts joyfully 'I get it!'.

Tony feels that he can do what he wants, no matter how unpopular or despicable the behaviour in the eyes of others, but in the remaining three episodes he is disabused of this by the consequences of his beating of Coco, ongoing lack of proper input to his therapy with Jennifer, and unhealthy lifestyle. Two episodes earlier, in Chasing It, Carlo mentions in a discussion with Tony the episode of *The Twilight Zone* titled A Nice Place to Visit, from 1960.[199] It tells the story of Henry Valentine, a deceased man who cannot tell the difference between Heaven, where he thinks he is because of the ready availability of pleasurable experiences, and Hell, where he truly is. This is a deliberate parallel, as throughout the show, and in Season Six in particular, Tony is unable to see that he is in a similar position to Henry. One of his concerns during Made in America is what will happen to Junior's money, and although he tells him during their final meeting that it should go to Bobby's children, even the most charitable of viewers would not trust him to look after it for them, on the basis, in Chasing It, of his treatment of Marie and her children after the murder of Vito. Even as Tony is on the verge of death and dreaming about a conversation between himself and Paulie in front of Satriales, he still says of Chris: 'I tell you this, since his death my gambling luck's done a one eighty', i.e., improved dramatically; at this point he is unredeemable.

Why, on the contrary, are people uninterested in, or even opposed to, the idea that Made in America might be a dream? Aside from understandable but unjustifiable motivations, such as

---

[199] Written by Charles Beaumont.

being unwilling to admit that they missed something substantial, and the devaluing of their own accepted interpretation, in discussing it over the years there are two other reactions and perspectives I have encountered repeatedly that deserve comment.

The first is the belief that Chase hoodwinked them, that he wrote Made in America, and readied it for broadcast with the production team and actors, in order to play a trick on those who had watched *The Sopranos* from the beginning and waited patiently during long hiatuses between seasons. This is a most peculiar reaction from fans of a show, as they are its lifeblood, without which it will not survive beyond a few episodes. Perhaps when this devotion is no longer necessary, when a show is coming to an end, a writer, free from any sense of responsibility or gratitude, will take the opportunity to have a joke to celebrate the occasion; there are fans of *The Sopranos* who have drawn this conclusion from Made in America. Chase addressed this interpretation in the 2007 interview in *The Star-Ledger*: 'no one was trying to blow people's minds, or thinking, "Wow, this'll p*** them off." People get the impression that you're trying to f*** with them and it's not true. You're trying to entertain them.'[200] In another interview, a few months later: 'we don't have contempt for the audience. In fact, I think *The Sopranos* is the only show that actually gave the audience credit for having some intelligence and attention span. We always operated as though people don't need to be spoon-fed every single thing.'[201]

---

[200] Seitz and Sepinwall, *op. cit.*, p. 457.
[201] Martin, *op. cit.*

This does not mean that Made in America is not a layered and complex episode, the substance of which will not be easily grasped; it is, but in this it is no different from all of the others. If it is a 'screw you' to the audience then it is the eighty-sixth, and if anyone believes that Chase has been doing this nonstop since the Pilot, it is hard to fathom why they carried on watching for so long. The finale is in fact a compliment to those watching, along the lines of: 'you have consistently demonstrated the ability and willingness to get your teeth into the complexities of what we have produced so far, so here is one final opportunity.'

There is a long tradition of hiding details in great works of art that will only be discovered with ongoing study and attention, examples of which from Bergman, Kafka, Garland, Lynch and Nabokov have already been provided. Some of these are necessary for a full understanding of the work in question, while others are simply interesting flourishes. In *Blade Runner* from 1982, there is a suggestion that Rick Deckard, who spends the movie hunting artificial humans known as replicants, may be one himself. He has a dream of a unicorn, and at the end picks up from the floor an origami unicorn which has been left by Officer Gaff; Deckard studies it, nodding as if he has realised something. A more definite hidden detail has been discovered in the 1533 painting *The Ambassadors* by Hans Holbein the Younger. In front of the two men and a variety of recognisable objects is a strangely elongated shape, which looks very out of place. When viewed from a different angle it is revealed as a human skull, believed to have been included by Holbein as a reminder that our mortality is never far away.

In *Psycho* from 1960, Norman Bates watches Marion Crane through a hole in the wall that is hidden by a painting. It is from 1731 by Willem van Mieris, although some attribute it instead to his father, Frans van Mieris the Elder. It depicts the story of Susanna and the Elders, from Chapter Thirteen of Daniel in the Old Testament, in which two old men serving as judges spy on a woman as she bathes. As a precursor of the distasteful practice seen on screen it makes a suitable addition to the Bates Motel art collection. Finally, there is the plausible suggestion that Jar Jar Binks, the annoying and buffoonish character from the *Star Wars* prequel trilogy, is, despite appearances to the contrary, an agent of the evil Sith. Evidence offered for this conclusion includes his habit of surviving highly dangerous situations, possession of abilities unusual for his species, and having yellow eyes, a characteristic observable in other Sith.[202]

The second reaction I have noticed is fuelled by negative connotations of the story of Bobby Ewing in the American soap-opera *Dallas*. In 1985, the actor who played him, Patrick Duffy, decided to leave, so in the final episode of the eighth season Bobby dies, after being run down deliberately by a car driven by his sister-in-law Katherine, who has been in love with him for a while but did not see it requited. However, a year later, neither Duffy's career nor *Dallas* were in good shape, so it was decided that he would return. Instead of opting for something more plausible, like writing in a long-lost twin of Bobby, the ninth season ended with the character who had supposedly died a year before being found in the shower by

---

[202]See the users Lumparoo on Reddit, Vincent Vendetta on YouTube and Arnav Gander on Quora. I am unsure which of these, if any, is the originator of the idea.

his widow Pam. When the show returned for the tenth season, it was explained that his death and the entirety of the ninth had been a dream by her.

Although *Dallas* continued for another five seasons after the resurrection of Bobby, and returned for three more from 2012, the use of a dream to allow Duffy to return is not looked back on positively. The revelation that all or some of the prior events in a story have taken place within the sleeping mind of a particular character does not always fail as a storytelling device, as the success of *The Wizard of Oz* proves, but this one stands as a notable and infamous example of shoddy and lazy writing out of sync with the rest of the narrative.

This device has a much greater chance of being successful if the dream is used as a window into the soul of a character. *A Christmas Carol* achieves this perfectly: whether the dreams are really visitations from Scrooge's deceased former business partner Jacob Marley, and the spirits of Christmas Past, Present and Yet to Come, or products of his conscience and imagination, is open for debate, but they allow the reader to understand the psychology and life of the old miser much better. This is how all of the dreams in *The Sopranos*, including Made in America, are used, reflecting the interests of Chase, and it is all the better for their inclusion. Not a single one of them is a last resort, rewriting parts of the story that have gone before in order to allow the writers to get themselves out of a creative hole; rather than saving a failing story, they add further to the quality of a first-rate one.

One other point needs to be considered in the light of these two reactions, and that is that, as has been intimated a number of times, there is a disconnect between Chase and the tastes of the general viewing public. He is a highly intelligent and precise writer, whose output is characterized by a subtlety and depth that does not appeal to many, perhaps most, people. This includes more fans of *The Sopranos* than one might think: evidence for this includes the number who dislike the dream sequences, and those who overlook the presence, or even the possibility, of the hidden stories. The filmmakers that Chase adores and emulates, the likes of Bergman and Lynch, will never achieve mass appeal. On this basis, it may be that, even if many fans become aware of the argument of this book and the huge amount of evidence provided in support of its thesis, they will struggle to see its value.

There is, in a very important sense, nothing new about Made in America: it is the type of story that viewers have been presented with a number of times before, using techniques which should also be familiar. The only difference is that this is the first time that an episode is composed entirely of a dream, and only the third where there is no explicit acknowledgement of an altered state of consciousness – a fourth would be added in *The Many Saints of Newark*. To be fair to the vast majority of viewers who have failed to spot this, Chase did a sterling job of hiding the fact that it is a dream; many of the clues are incredibly subtle, secreted in the episode in such a way that they can easily be missed.

There is another sense in which the revelation about Made in America offered in this book should not be a surprise. As a young man participating in the Graduate Film Program at the Stanford School of Communication, Chase made three films, one of which he later described thus: 'it was sort of an existential sort of thing...about a guy who, as he was being killed, he was imagining his escape on a jetliner.'²⁰³ A film about the dream of a man on the verge of death, in which his mind desperately conjures up images of salvation? This cannot be a coincidence. The interview from which this comment is taken occurred in 2000, seven years before the broadcast of the finale, at which point Chase may well not have decided the fate of Tony, but the similarity between the student film and how he completed the story of his most famous creation is undeniable. He recycled an idea that he had been carrying around in his head for over three decades, in so doing adding the finale to the list of narratives which utilise the trope of the dying dream, such as the films *Taxi Driver* (1976), *Jacob's Ladder* (1990) and *Carlito's Way* (1993).

There is a level of detail in Made in America more extreme than any of the other episodes. It is a homage to the work of Lynch, in particular *Mulholland Drive*, and other filmmakers admired by Chase, such as Buñuel, Kubrick and Bergman; each demonstrates the sheer conceptual and narrative complexity that he was aiming for. If it is not obvious by now, one should beware simplistic theories about Made in America which are prevalent, particularly on the internet. These tend to place their emphasis on one aspect of it, such as the execution via the bathroom scene in *The Godfather*, or Bobby's 'you probably don't even hear it...' quote from Soprano Home Movies. Crammed full of all sorts of details and allusions, Chase put at least as much thought into the final chapter of his magnum opus as he did each of the previous eighty-five and the prequel movie. A comprehensive analysis

---

[203] Interview on 5ᵗʰ May 2000, published in Allen Rucker *The Sopranos: A Family History*, page number not provided.

which takes the complete run of the show into account is required to understand it, something which will be of substantially greater length than that of a tweet or even a news article.

Made in America is a remix of The Blue Comet. Recent experiences, emotional responses and discoveries are mixed up with issues that have bothered Tony for a long time, and the current condition of his body and mind; but there is little rationality to the process, as the narrative is the product of his sleeping mind. In this way, the final two episodes fit in with those of most of the previous seasons: in what other shows would consider an anti-climax, more of the dynamic events happen in the penultimate episode. In the second season, the main antagonist, Richie, is taken out of the equation in The Knight in White Satin Armor, and Tony spends most of Funhouse ill and having strange dreams, although time is found to dispose of an old friend who is betraying him to the FBI. In The Blue Comet, the Lupertazzis have already effectively won the war, Tony's brother-in-law is dead and his consigliere is critically injured, and Jennifer ends their therapeutic relationship. Apart from the trivial matter of the central character of the show dying, nothing really happens in the finale.

None of the clues discussed in this book in themselves prove that Made in America is a dream; a handful of them make an interesting case that warrants further investigation; but their vast number, taken together with precursors in previous episodes, leads to only one conclusion. No other theory about the nature of the narrative has been supported with anywhere near this amount of evidence, despite the volume of material that has been published over the years about the show. This is because there has been virtually no theorising at all about the nature of the narrative: viewers and commentators en masse have fallen into the trap of assuming that a standard episode is being presented. It has not even occurred to them to verify it or to investigate other possibilities. For the purposes of rigour and balance, if my research had produced any evidence, or uncovered any suggested by others, that contradicts the conclusion that Made in America is a dream, it would have been presented. There is none: no dissenting voice has to this point done anything more than simply state, in one way or another, that `it is not a dream.'

It does not take the closest of watchings of *The Sopranos* to spot the fascination of Chase with dreams, nor that the focus of the show is the mental and emotional turmoil of Tony. What more appropriate way, therefore, to bring down the curtain on it than spending an entire episode in his sleeping mind?

Acknowledgements

I am very grateful to the following for their interest in and support of my research: Ron Bernard, Conor McAteer, Rachelle Kaufmann, Alan Stevens, Charlie Jamison, Leigh Simpson, Stephen Brammer, Marc Dyen, Chuck Scarpello, Scott from The Sopranos Club on Twitter, Stephanie Rosendorf-Diaz, and Paolo Sottile.

To them, and any others I have thoughtlessly overlooked: salute!

Bibliography

Books

Barthes, Roland (1978). *Image, Music, Text*. Translated by Stephen Heath. Hill and Wang.

Benatar, David (2008). *Better Never to Have Been: The Harm of Coming into Existence*. Oxford University Press.

Darwin, Charles (2017). *On the Origin of Species by Means of Natural Selection, or the Preservation of Favoured Races in the Struggle for Life*. Macmillan.

De Laclos, Pierre Choderlos (2007). *Dangerous Liaisons*. Translated by Helen Constantine. Penguin.

Dillon, Steven (2006). *The Solaris Effect: Art and Artifice in Contemporary American Film*. University of Texas.

Edgerton, Gary (2013). *The Sopranos*. Wayne State University.

Freud, Sigmund (1991). *The Interpretation of Dreams*. Translated by James Strachey. Penguin.

Imperioli, Michael; Schirripa, Steven and Lerman, Philip (2022). *Woke Up This Morning: The Definitive Oral History of the Sopranos*. Fourth Estate.

Kafka, Franz (1999). *The Complete Short Stories*. Vintage.

Mann, Thomas (1999). *Doctor Faustus: The Life of the German Composer Adrian Leverkuhn as Told by a Friend*. Translated by John E. Woods. KNOPF.

McCabe, Janet and Akass, Kim (2007). *Quality TV: Contemporary American Television and Beyond*. I.B. Tauris.

Nabokov, Vladimir (2001). *Despair*. Penguin.

Nabokov, Vladimir (2008). *Lolita*. Penguin.

Nagarjuna (2013). *The Middle Way: Mulamadhyamakakarika (Classics of Indian Buddhism)*. Translated by Mark Siderits and Shoryu Katsura. Wisdom Publications.

Pileggi, Nicholas (1995). *Casino: Love and Honour in Las Vegas*. Simon and Schuster.

Poe, Edgar Allan (2008). *The Complete Poetry*. Signet.

Rucker, Allen (2003). *The Sopranos: A Family History, Updated for the Fourth Season*. New American Library.

Sanders, Steven and Skoble, Aeon (2008). *The Philosophy of TV Noir*. University Press of Kentucky.

Schopenhauer, Arthur (2014 and 2020). *The World as Will and Representation* (Volumes One and Two), translated by Judith Norman. Cambridge University Press.

Seitz, Matt Zoller and Sepinwall, Alan (2019). *The Sopranos Sessions*. Abrams.

Sepinwall, Alan (2013). *The Revolution Was Televised: From Buffy to Breaking Bad - the People and the Shows That Changed TV Drama Forever*. Schwartz.

Shakespeare, William (2017). *Macbeth*. (Alpha).

Sorensen, Charles E. (1956). *My Forty Years with Ford*. W. W. Norton.

Yochelson, Samuel and Samenow, Stanton (1976-86). *The Criminal Personality, Volumes I-III*. Rowman and Littlefield.

Articles and Websites

Bernard, Ron. *Sopranos Autopsy: Examining TV's Greatest Series*. (https://sopranosautopsy.com/)

Boseley, Sarah. 'Happy drug Prozac can bring on impulse to suicide, study says'. *The Guardian*. 22/5/2000.

Bradley, Daniel 'Brokenness and Hope: David Lynch's Contribution to a Phenomenology of Anxiety in *Mulholland Drive*'. *The Journal of Speculative Philosophy* 2015 Vol. 29 (2):180-193.

Brown, Charles H. 'Drug-induced serotonin syndrome'. *U.S. Pharmacist*. 17/11/2010.

(https://www.uspharmacist.com/article/drug-induced-serotonin-syndrome)

Canadian Cancer Society. 'Does stress cause cancer?', retrieved 16/1/2024.

(https://cancer.ca/en/cancer-information/reduce-your-risk/myths-and-controversies/does-stress-cause-cancer)

Cancer Research UK. 'Causes of cancer and reducing your risk', retrieved 16/1/2024.

(https://www.cancerresearchuk.org/about-cancer/causes-of-cancer)

Chase, David. '"*The Sopranos*" Creator David Chase on "*The Twilight Zone*": "It Made a Mammoth Impression".' *Variety*. 20/12/2023.

(https://variety.com/2023/tv/columns/david-chase-the-twilight-zone-favorite-tv-show-1235833208/)

Cipolletta, Edoardo; Tata, Laila J.; Nakafero, Georgina; Avery, Anthony J.; Mamas, Mamas A.; Abhishek, Abhishek. 'Association Between Gout Flare and Subsequent Cardiovascular Events Among Patients with Gout'. *Journal of the American Medical Association*. 2022; 328(5):440-450. doi:10.1001/jama.2022.11390

Civil Aviation Authority (UK) 'Aviation noise and health: the effects of aviation noise', retrieved 27/3/2024.

(https://www.caa.co.uk/consumers/environment/noise/aviation-noise-and-health/)

Clemson University 'Tigers United University Consortium', retrieved 19/01/24.

(https://www.clemson.edu/tigers-united/consortium/index.html)

Cleveland Clinic. 'Hallucinations', retrieved 24/1/2024.

(https://my.clevelandclinic.org/health/symptoms/23350-hallucinations)

Cleveland Clinic. 'Vena Cava', retrieved 20/1/2024.

(https://my.clevelandclinic.org/health/body/22619-vena-cava#conditions-and-disorders)

Cruz, Gilbert. 'The Anniversary You Can't Refuse: 40 Things You Didn't Know About The Godfather: What's with All the Oranges?'. *Time*. 14/3/2012.

(https://entertainment.time.com/2012/03/15/the-anniversary-you-cant-refuse-40-things-you-didnt-know-about-the-godfather/slide/whats-with-all-the-oranges/)

de Semlyen, Phil and Singer, Matthew. 'The 100 best TV shows of all time you have to watch.' *Time Out* 2023 Oct 13.

(https://www.timeout.com/film/best-tv-shows-of-all-time)

Dockterman, Eliana. 'Creators of *Lost, Fargo, The Sopranos* and Other Shows on How *Twin Peaks* Influenced Them'. *Time*. 11/5/2017.

(https://time.com/4769270/twin-peaks-lost-fargo-sopranos/)

Eschner, Kat. 'How Margarita Cansino Became Rita Hayworth'. *Smithsonian Magazine*. 17/10/2017.

(https://www.smithsonianmag.com/smart-news/how-margarita-cansino-became-rita-hayworth-180965275/)

Feinberg, Scott. '"Sopranos" Creator David Chase Finally Reveals What Happened to Tony'. *The Hollywood Reporter*. 2/11/2021.

(https://www.hollywoodreporter.com/feature/the-sopranos-david-chase-tony-ending-the-many-saints-of-newark-1235040185/)

Felleman, Susan. 'Source Hunting in a Dreamscape'. *Lola* 2016 Nov; Issue 7 *Ages*.

(http://www.lolajournal.com/7/lynch.html.)

FireRescue1.com. 'SUV bursts into flames after driver parks it on pile of leaves', 25/11/2023.

(https://www.firerescue1.com/vehicle-fire/suv-bursts-into-flames-after-driver-parks-it-on-pile-of-leaves)

Forebears.io. 'Fegoli surname', retrieved 12/1/2024.

(https://forebears.io/surnames/fegoli)

Frohock, Christina M. 'Legal fiction: reading *Lolita* as a sentencing memorandum'. *Albany Law Review* 2022 Vol.86 (1):1-21.

Greeley, Andrew. 'An Ending with No Meaning'. *Chicago Sun Times*. 15/6/2007.

Greenberg, James. 'This Magic Moment'. *Directors Guild of America Quarterly Magazine*. 2015 Spring.

(https://www.dga.org/Craft/DGAQ/All-Articles/1502-Spring-2015/Shot-to-Remember-The-Sopranos.aspx)

Hammadah, Muhammad; Kindya, Bryan R.; Allard-Ratick, Marc P.; Jazbeh, Sammer; Eapen, Danny; Wilson Tang, WH and Sperling, Laurence. 'Navigating air travel and cardiovascular concerns: is the sky the limit?' *Clinical Cardiology* 2017 Sep; 40(9):660-666. doi: 10.1002/clc.22741. Epub 2017 Jun 8.

Heart UK. 'High cholesterol food', retrieved 20/1/2024.

(https://www.heartuk.org.uk/low-cholesterol-foods/foods-that-contain-cholesterol)

Henry Ford Health. 'Cardiology', retrieved 22/1/2024.

(https://www.henryford.com/services/cardiology)

Hobart Cardiology and Medical Specialists. 'Bundle branches', retrieved 26/1/2024.

(https://hobartcardiology.com.au/the-normal-heart/bundle-branches/)

Hooper, Rowan. 'Dreams decoded: 6 answers to the mysteries of the sleeping mind'. *New Scientist*. 22/3/2018.

(https://www.newscientist.com/article/2164099-dreams-decoded-6-answers-to-the-mysteries-of-the-sleeping-mind/)

Koteska, Katerina. 'Is Smelling Toast A Sign of A Heart Attack?'. *Brussels Morning*. 3/3/2023.

(https://brusselsmorning.com/is-smelling-toast-a-sign-of-a-heart-attack/31163/)

Marc Lallanilla. ' JFK "Magic Bullet Theory" In Spotlight On Anniversary Of President Kennedy's Assassination'. *Huffington Post*. 21/11/2013.

(https://www.huffpost.com/entry/jfk-magic-bullet-president-kennedy-assassination_n_4317369)

Lusher, Tim. 'The Guardian's top 50 television dramas of all time.' *The Guardian*. 12/1/2010.

(https://www.theguardian.com/tv-and-radio/tvandradioblog/2010/jan/12/guardian-50-television-dramas)

Marcos, Natalia. '"The Sopranos" creator David Chase: "I've never watched the series. I've watched a couple of episodes."' *El Pais*. 10/1/2024.

(https://english.elpais.com/culture/2024-01-10/the-sopranos-creator-david-chase-ive-never-watched-the-series-ive-watched-a-couple-of-episodes)

Martin, Brett. '"Sopranos" creator on "pissed" fans.' *Entertainment Weekly*. 18/10/2007.

(https://ew.com/article/2007/10/18/sopranos-creator-pissed-fans/)

MasterofSopranos. 'The Sopranos: Definitive Explanation of "The END".

(https://masterofsopranos.wordpress.com/the-sopranos-definitive-explanation-of-the-end/)

Murugesu, Jason Arunn. 'Your short-term memory can be unreliable after just a few seconds'. *New Scientist*. 5/4/2023.

(https://www.newscientist.com/article/2367992-your-short-term-memory-can-be-unreliable-after-just-a-few-seconds/)

National Health Service (UK). 'Psychotic depression', 13/11/2023.

(https://www.nhs.uk/mental-health/conditions/psychotic-depression/#:~:text=The%20delusions%20and%20hallucinations%20almost,sit%20still%2C%20and%20constantly%20fidgeting)

National Institute for Occupational Safety and Health (USA). 'Aircrew Safety & Health – Noise/Hearing Loss', retrieved 27/12/2023. (https://www.cdc.gov/niosh/topics/aircrew/noise.html)

Nochimson, Martha 'Did Tony die at the end of The Sopranos?'. *Vox*. 27/8/2014.

(https://www.vox.com/2014/8/27/6006139/did-tony-die-at-the-end-of-the-sopranos)

North Bristol National Health Service Trust (UK). 'Spinal Fractures', retrieved 11/1/2024.

(https://www.nbt.nhs.uk/sites/default/files/attachments/Spinal%20fractures_NBT03193.pdf)

Prostate Cancer Foundation of Australia. 'The Genetics of Prostate Cancer', retrieved 12/1/2024.

(https://www.pcfa.org.au/awareness/pcfa-tv/the-genetics-of-prostate-cancer/)

Salem, Rob. 'There is no answer - deal with it. Tony Soprano is dead. Long live Tony Soprano.' *Toronto Star*. 17/6/2007. Entertainment, p. 4.

(https://www.thestar.com/entertainment/there-is-no-answer-deal-with-it/article_6f900bb8-6e61-5030-93b2-eec763398f0c.html)

Sepinwall, Alan. 'The 100 Greatest TV Shows of All Time'. *Rolling Stone*. 26/9/2022.

(https://www.rollingstone.com/tv-movies/tv-movie-lists/best-tv-shows-of-all-time-1234598313/)

Schredl, Michael. 'Characteristics and Contents Of Dreams'. *International Review of Neurobiology*. Volume 92, 2010, pp. 135-154, ISSN 0074-7742, ISBN 9780123813220, https://doi.org/10.1016/S0074-7742(10)92007-2.

(https://www.sciencedirect.com/science/article/pii/S0074774210920072)

Shanahan, Ed. 'Louis Eppolito, Police Officer Turned Mob Hit Man, Dies at 71'. *New York Times*. 7/11/2019.

(https://www.nytimes.com/2019/11/07/nyregion/louis-eppolito-dead.html)

Shaw, Alan. 'A Multi-Layered Analysis of Mulholland Drive'.

(https://www.mulholland-drive.net/analysis/analysis01.htm)

Singh, Jasvinder. 'Gout Attacks Strike Mostly at Night'. *Arthritis Health*. 5/1/2021.

(https://www.arthritis-health.com/blog/gout-attacks-strike-mostly-night)

Sopranos Club, The. 'CONFIRMED...Ralph DID kill the Horse'. Twitter / X. 22/12/2021.

St. James, Emily. 'The Sopranos: "Made in America"'. *AV Club*. 19/12/2012.

(https://www.avclub.com/the-sopranos-made-in-america-1798175338)

Strange, Deryn and Takarangi, Melanie. 'Memory Distortion for Traumatic Events: The Role of Mental Imagery'. *Front Psychiatry*. 23/2/2015; 6:27. doi: 10.3389/fpsyt.2015.00027. PMID: 25755646; PMCID: PMC4337233.

Suskind, Alex. 'David Chase can't escape "The Sopranos" finale: seven years after The Sopranos ended, creator David Chase is still being asked to explain its infamous cut-to-black moment. (And no, there's no movie in the works.)' *The Daily Beast*. Updated 12/7/2017.

(https://www.thedailybeast.com/david-chase-cant-escape-the-sopranos-finale)

Turing, Alan. 'Computing Machinery and Intelligence'. *Mind*. October 1950. LIX (236): 433–460.

Videos and DVDs

Bergman, Ingmar (director). *Persona*. 1966. Sweden; AB Svensk Filmindustri.

Brahm, John (director) and Beaumont, Charles (writer). 'A Nice Place to Visit', *The Twilight Zone*, series 1, episode 28. Broadcast 15/4/1960, CBS.

Butler, David (director) and Serling, Rod (writer). 'The Bard', *The Twilight Zone*, series 4, episode 18. Broadcast 23/5/1963, CBS.

Chase, David (creator). *The Sopranos*. 1999. USA; Chase Films, Brad Grey Entertainment and HBO Entertainment.

Else, Steve. 'The Sopranos "Made in America": Tony's Final Dream'. YouTube, 11/9/2018.

Garland, Alex (director). *Ex Machina*. 2014. UK and USA; Film4 and DNA Films.

Imperioli, Michael and Schirripa, Steven. *Talking Sopranos*. YouTube, 2020-2021.

https://www.youtube.com/@TalkingSopranos:

- #12: '*Isabella*'. 15/6/20.
- #24: '*House Arrest*', interview with Louis Lombardi. 7/9/20.
- #89: '*The Blue Comet*', interview with Steven Van Zandt. 6/12/21.

- #90: 'Superfan Episode'. 13/12/2021.
- #91: '*Made in America*', interview with David Chase. 20/12/21.

Lynch, David (director). *Mulholland Drive*. 2001. USA and France; Les Films Alain Sarde and Le Studio Canal+.

Taylor, Alan (director). *The Many Saints of Newark*. 2021. USA; New Line Cinema, Home Box Office and Chase Films.

Wild, Sophie and Naikoi, Josie. 'The Scandalous Life of Pastor Ted Haggard…And His Dark Return'. YouTube, uploaded by Not The Good Girl, 30/11/2022.

Correspondence

Stevens, Alan. Email to author, 13/3/2023.

Cover Images

Béclu, René. 1913 sculpture *Le Secret*, in the Parc de la Tête d'Or in Lyon, France. Photographed by William Crochot and made available on Wikimedia Commons (license CC-BY-SA 4.0).

Dou, Gerrit or van Rijn, Rembrandt Harmenszoon. Circa 1635 painting *Man Hiding Treasure*. Museum of Fine Arts, Budapest.

EULOGY
Jerusalem 70 A.D.

EULOGY: JERUSALEM 70 A.D.

Copyright © 2024 Redmond Holt

Paperback ISBN: 978-1-915223-39-5

All rights reserved.

No part of this publication may be reproduced, stored in a retrieval system, or transmitted in any form or by any means, electronic, mechanical, photocopying or otherwise, without prior written consent of the publisher except as provided under United Kingdom copyright law. Short extracts may be used for review purposes with credits given.

Except in the case of historical fact, any resemblance to actual persons living or dead is purely coincidental.

Published by

Maurice Wylie Media
Your Inspirational & Christian Book Publisher

For more information visit
www.MauriceWylieMedia.com

Dedication

For Blarkey, Squeaky and Buzz Bike.

Contents

Chapter 1   Dwellest we in the mist 9

Chapter 2   Shibboleth 29

Chapter 3   Upon this Hill 49

Chapter 4   Tale of olde and new 67

Chapter 5   Jerusalem; a cup that trembleth 89

Chapter 6   Dwellest we in the hope 117

Chapter 7   Epilogue 125

CHAPTER 1

Dwellest we in the mist...

Dwellest we in the mist
between the time of giants and the return of The King.
Those giants, mighty pretender ones of fallen earth,
titans of confusions far reach;
potentates of a twisted insidious creep.

Here death reigns,
it's companion time
breathing corruption upon youthful intent.
Contempt also spread upon cobwebbed men
who plot their last vain charge,
unless they earlier spent.

Apportioned to each a role
in the continued folly dance of earth bound men.
For I, to suffer and toil,
yet for mine son to play the fool;
his lessons nare learnt
for his time didst soon by flee.

Thus began the eulogy.

Selah.

I am numbered amongst the soil men of Jerusalem.
With this cart I have ploughed these paths some thirty winters.
Jerusalem;
this celestial citadel,
bruised cauldron of deceit and mocking holiness.
Plotters, deceivers,
religious factions of self intent.
With cruel smile these absorbed rulers
carriest with unbridled pomp
the intentions and fervent desire of Majesty on high,
yet alas,
they spiral downward in a heady mix
of politic, avarice and malicious intrigue.
It fair comment to remark
that I collect the ruminations and solid ponderings of wiser men than I.

Knowest I each street, thoroughfare, brick and darkened alley.
Traverse I daily with sound of clog weary mule
and squeak wood axel;
my wheel cart full and heavy with vigorous labours,
hazed with putrid stink.

They hide, these Jerusalemite men;
lofty noses held high,
talk always mute as I pass,
remaining silent as I shovel their groaning mumblings.
It must be someone else's excrement I perceive,
these goodly fair men far too righteous for mere defecation.

For you see
my roots are brushed with Samarian taint.
Assyrian blood,
mixed to defile.

Chapter 1. Dwellest we in the mist

My Mother's labours
deposited I in Bethal;
home of Jeroboam's calf of gold.
The tales of olde I heard as youth
would tell of those with obsequious bow to Kingly reign
and of those who failed to tribute pay.
The disobedient then would shed their bloodied crowns
by edge of sword to crimson stained soil.
Two hundred years of unrighteous rule
brought in judgement the haste of northern foe,
then leathward my people sank from saving grace,
traversing north in prisoner file,
while those left mixed seed and life,
birthing forth a new generation to hate
for those who in Judah's grail reside.

The Kings of Israel pillaged: killed.
By fear they ruled;
scribes capturing a history of rage and ruin.
Even the Lord's anointed they murdered,
despatching truth by bloodied spear.
Each blow
harkening God's vengeance upon blood lust minds.
Their baal sacrifices to idol stone
sent a reminding salve to angel's record.
False gods demanded complete abandon
breathing decay upon consciences searing.
The killing of sons.
The ravishing of daughters.
The failing of hearts;
finally the murder of innocents
bringing forth the prophecy of Assyrian slaughter.

It is to that history I was born.
Now the proud sanctuaries of Jerusalem's courts
declare me blemished,
speak of me as base and ignoble,
shamed, forever unwashed.
I am ere long despised,
lacking of welcome,
deemed too common for princely men.

Selah

My latter years have proved a curse,
the vacuous blessing of an earlier era lost.
Oft time the cavern of mine mind
journeys to what I deem more dangerous and prosperous days.

Tutelaged like now dead Saul under learned Gamaliel,
I to Pharisee ranks was promised.
With zealous intent
and fervent application to the law I didst my will surrender,
bending my ambition by strength of hand to satisfy Decalogue's demand.
If Saul were righteous I was twice so.
We took letter, jot and tittle,
stone and sword to punish,
to reign misery with violent intent.
Ere many we despatched to their God,
each blow a satisfying thud
pleasing master and
serving ambitions plot in equal measure.

We were heroes for that bloodied hour,
combating scorn, an ideology we reviled and abhorred,
but more so a threat to incumbent's power and wealth.
We were both to learn and pay the price for defection.

Whilst riding tide
we succumbed to a certain celebrity:
notoriety opened doors.
Honour and political manoeuvrings were advanced,
decanted vines furiously guzzled,
the delicate embrace of harlots vigorously enjoyed.
Our senses buoyed,
inextinguishable desire burned; we always craving more.
We killed for pleasure
and the approbation of Court.
Those younger sought our Seal,
many vicious joined our ranks,
yielding not;
seeking their own accolades:
the laurels and fog bound promises of worldly might.

We left many dead and many more to injury,
male, female, beast and child; it mattered not.
Houses and fortunes seized,
adding spoils to already abundant coffers.
Some tried flee,
some fought,
some silent stood,
others begged the Lord's mercy, nare for selves,
but for us in our maddened rage.
Many names and shadowed faces haunt my restless nights.

Selah

We left one morn under instruction,
one hundred miles plus north,
Damascus our final destination;
swords required again to hasten gore.
Those on the street bowed and waved,
outside city walls the celebration continued

with the broad salutes of country farmer;
our quest for peace from fiend always applauded.
We laughed and joked,
some fool the victim of our amuse and ceaseless jesting.
We would mock each one another playfully,
though at times it came to blows,
coins sometimes spent in comradeship wager.

The perfidious fable of a risen Christ
had to the cobbles of Damascus descended.
We Jerusalem's ten messiahs would root it out,
but for now we amiably travelled.

Without warning, suddenly Saul fell.
We thought his horse lost nerve,
it's neighing and nostril flare showing agitation;
but Saul bowed.
At first we laughed and mocked our friend
remarking he now aged and failing,
yet soon to our discomfort
he raised himself to knee and humbly begged.
He cried for mercy to One we could not see
his trembling voice becoming but a quiver.
Still he kneeled,
then slowly arose
saying he could go no further.

He said this Christ had just appeared
to Saul resounding words He had spoken,
The Messiah's life was proven quick,
by grace Saul a new creation.
Eight others ran and fled,
I to Saul,
him I aided.
We spoke at length,

Saul bid me leave the trappings of my engagement.
Yet I dared not.
To Jerusalem I didst return
bringing news of Saul's new direction.

They paid me quiet,
though from then my sword I could not handle.
I was accused of treason,
false witness sought,
my cherished robes and rank dishonoured and discarded;
rejected by the Court I had so gloriously served.

Selah

The heavenly realm
for Job did dice block roll.
Job lost all,
but was restoreth;
double blessing bestowed upon his tale of woe.
For me, no such comfort,
for all semblance of familiarity was targeted and shattered,
no double portion gained;
I fettered, racked, still broken.
Position spent, home asunder,
I like leper became,
yet unlike the diseased they spurned me not outside the city wall.
Some time then I chained to cart
becoming a proverb,
witnessed by the many I pass upon my daily chart.

I remained bitter for a time,
then awhile cared not
but remained rejected by men;
alone.
My wife, she didst depart with child in tow.

My son grew, his years I in secret sought.
The touch of his mother's love was attached to my ambition,
seeking arms then fled to stranger's embrace and richly pocket;
her days ere long gone.
She, I have long forgiven but alas is now confined to rotting clay,
awaiting judgement: that feared final day.

Mine blessing of yesteryear is long vanished,
mine manhood vanquished,
mine mind surrendered,
subjugated to numbed dull;
alas no longer thinking
and devoid of dream.

Unlike the banker who pegs his raiment at end of day,
my stink is permanent,
carried everywhere,
both near and wide.

Selah.

Despite myself and the circumstance that doth prevail
this city doth me charm.

Jerusalem.
Meleke limestone,
Herodian chiselled,
slabs of Judean hillside checked to height and weighted balance.
Ezra and Nehemiah's
Jerusalem stone,
white to yellow, hued in sunlight pink,
tracing season's shadow across forgotten time.
Soft, smooth burnished cobbles,
trod upon by God and devil's mercenary,
shining glint from cooling rains,

Chapter 1. Dwellest we in the mist

sounds; echoes and their burnt stone bounce.
Sinonian and Cenomanian layers of walled intrigue
celebrating the plotting of canny ancestor
and martyr's scorn.
Stones raised up to praise
fallen and again elevated,
Mason's carved signet denoting time.
Eras of sanctuary and rusted war
of joy and funeral passing.

Jerusalem;
the heaving orchestrations of commerce and trade.
Masters and slave,
attired in the busy manoeuvrings of gain and survival.
The shout and roar of barter;
hagglers grumbling seeking common ground afore exchange,
both sides leaving assured of profit's bargain,
verbal skills sheathed for another day.
Scents and allure of coloured spice,
fruits and produce packed tight,
salted meats seeking salivating mouths for savour.
Spending of silver and coin of mite,
clamour, tumult, babel yelling.
Industry;
honesty and vice mingled together,
a sweeping swearing sweltering storm.
Jerusalem;
priests and soldiers,
rich and poor.
Women veiled, dignity shielded from the gaze of common men,
the baying of unrighteous lusts tempered;
left to imaginations to plot and covet.
Playing, running children
midst the impatient waiting of working beasts.
Pilgrims seeking solace, nare oft found,

their heavy brows flint set,
laboured breath their travelling companion.
For them to smile as rare as summer snow;
perhaps God would to levity's mirth respond!

Jerusalem.
Tempestuous, tumultuous,
impassioned heat and midnight squall.
An agitated undercurrent
promising more than mere stone could ere deliver.
Siege promised, yae assured,
but still the city ignores:
denial obscures all discomfort.
Proud citizens dismiss the dust of approaching foe;
enemy soon expected.
Like times past pillared watchmen observe with languid sleep eye,
feigned vigilance to the fore, the threat still somewhat distant.

Jerusalem: history's fulcrum and melt pot.

Selah

Survival becomes the trudge of all the masses
while labour's tax
and penny pinching
affords the few grandeur's hall.
Jerusalem's court differs not
for pretence and fake majesty will always rule.
Those dressed in sartorial elegance
embrace their perch with plumaged squawk,
deference becoming their universal expectation.
Uprising changed not one jot.
The price soon by Roman sword we all shall pay.

Court separates men from clan and kin.
Violent intent and its play

birth forth the entry key;
there a royal nod for earthly title
or a priestly dispensation
flatters those who triumph plot,
grasping egos falling quick to pride.
Soon after, wealth will knock upon their door
secured but not by fruit of labour,
base mammon eradicating embarrassing roots
the domains of childhood despatched to past's confine.

Same world over,
by nation, by land.
Plotters rising
others falling,
fickle dance of scythe cut time.

Opulence grows a shrouded girth filled not by weight of purse,
those of Court will favour cully
selling soul for future glory.
The ground though doth oft times slip
hindsight required in head and sleight of hand,
entry ticket becoming satan's demand.
The doors to throne are locked and veiled
each room a grease pole ladder,
ostentation requires obsequious reach,
words backed by hidden dagger.
Nearer the throne
the higher the cliff
those who fail secure hard landing,
oft life cut short by sword or nail,
corpses naked to rot by knotted hanging.
For I this cart
and mire infused cough:
a walk from the Court that I can to this day still hear laughing.

Selah

This ego men must slay,
like Saul who later didst again appear.

A decade plus past that day we didst depart
my name I heard, he didst me call.
Now Paul, he seemed unashamed by my demeanour,
residing he a while with a man called Peter
whose wife Paul said would bid me too a homely cheer.
My shame I must confess made red bluster
but Paul he didst me fond embrace
and strengthened then by firm held clasp
I did so repair to their repast.
We spoke at length
he didst me tale tell of distant land,
his quest not death but rather gentile salvation.
Others met I too,
words we read which he composed on parchment paper,
my conscience sated by cerebral interrogation.
Paul of letters explained life new,
he bid me meet all sinning man's Saviour.
Days later I bent my frame to heaven's rule;
repented I of things long since done.
Confirming choice,
immersed then whole in baptism's waters.
Then warmed and burning from inside
I didst me rest with Lordship peace and long sought succour.
Paul explained my sins Christ Jesus, Messiah, He had taken,
forgiveness gifted by Blood soaked death and quickening resurrection.

Despised I not then my worldly role,
new life birthed solace in my degradation.
Learned I in years that then didst pass
it is better to experience this life's hate
than seek the useless bounty of pride and mocking favour.

Earthly power doth reside but just a day,
Christ's love however herald's forth an eternal bounty.

Selah

Paul didst succumb to Nero's harsh decree
but left in grace to sing in worship praise.
Nero died.
For him a quick descent,
to darkened pit;
anguish, terror, flame eternal,
grind and gnashing spit.
Not I a judge, yet Court must wary be,
for like Nero to pit they destined go
where oblivion's furnace
doth punch sore raw,
false righteousness brought to fear; rewards scream of unbelief.

Selah

Alas, arriveth the day
my son to Nero joined.

Selah

That morn was bent and shapen like most.
I awoke to face familiar routine;
struggle ahead for the day just broken,
though for springtime Nisan's sky promised dry but cold.

My faithful mule, he who has served so well,
readied I him for the day.
We departed afore first light
always to start furthest point away;
the day's physicality's walking us home for eventide.

Past sleepy neighbours we didst skulk,
streets still, silent,
but for the regular modulated rhythm of empty cart.

My mind didst wander I declare to earlier years
for I at this time wouldst home return
after a heady mix of wine and play.
I cast a wry smile
yet plunged it deep to memory reservoir;
it will alight another time.
I licked my lips and marched on.

Reaching far point we turned.
I said a silent prayer,
scanned the horizon
as I steadied shovel and nerve.
Our walk didst commence.
Shovel's scrape
resulted in the curses of hidden sleepers,
those clasping the last minutes rest
afore they too would rise for indentured toil.

By the fourth hour I was tired.
We rested but a while;
mule enjoying drawn waters
while he contemplated my bearded yawning.
I oft times wonder his thoughts,
whether he aware of my past and current situation.
I nodded, he again rose for shackles,
alas he forever associated with my demise;
mine chains while invisible draw the attention of all.
The odd apple for he does mine guilt assuage.
Hark.
A voice; wheezed and punished
with hollow racked breath.

A runner.
His face portrayed sweat brow and florid boil.

"Sire!" He called.
"Sire! Sire!
The world of men have perpetrated mayhem upon thine son."

Turned I to cast full consideration upon
this emissary's frame.

"Sire! Thine son!
The rebellion's Prince,
He ist dead."

This news the harried conveyed
with all the subtlety and nervousness of a drunken youth,
ere fore he fled.

Rooted I then to ground of worn stone
to digest this not unexpected disclosure.
Drawing forced breath
mine back didst stoop
and clasping mule's reins
I drew the beast's warmth closer.
Then fell I,
aided by black dog brain,
to mourn.

Sometime then I arose
but was set upon by thieves,
vagabonds of alley life disorder.
I, a poor man, was sacked slim of coin
taken by sly poachers.
I fumbled,
lifted hand to feel blood bruise,

mine memory did cascade
and I again didst slide.

None came to aid.
In my worst of days I never felt so alone,
even wished my mule could speak
but he was no Balaam's donkey.
He did though stand to side
taking sun's brunt,
shadowing me too from further nefarious intent.

Mine son.
Mine very blood.
I resolved I must he find.
Though I him from childhood knew
he spared me no quarter,
his eyes spent full on ambition's moving.

Selah

The emissary had made haste escape.
I arose a third time,
shook my length down
and drying eyes
contemplated a safe direction.
To watchman guard I bid my steps
slow at first,
then to gathered pace.
A guard I found, to me his back he turned,
while walking off, a laugh he didst me spurn.
I sought another,
he too didst me despise
but upon the third I didst some comfort find.
His voice kept low
mine ear to lips he did me beckon

informing me,
Court's fate upon my son.
I mumbled quavered appreciation,
pressed his elbow in thanksgiving
this man midst mice I willst long remember.
With mule we set our path,
toward city gate our compass us brought.

This solitary walk resembled mine own path to desecration,
tortured steps escorting me closer to slaughter.
Though no wood upon my back
I felt full stare and loathe of city dweller,
citizens turned full back,
recoiling at my step echo.

Observed I the curious and measured gaze of silent children,
peeping from shielding skirts
and broken pane less frames;
fear pronounced visibly,
mine meanderings to be etched on tiny minds,
wondered if this day would
nightmare visit upon these fragile strangers.

Mine pathway proved clear.
Stall holders closed shop
spitting at me their loss of coin
and mounting detestation.
Doors shut,
tight bolted till I passed
those inside afraid to help
least they too rewarded a share of my disfavour;
to be shamed by hoards of like minded.
Was this revulsion for me, though it I already bear
or for my son,
their nemesis who taxed their labours?

Some ventured forth,
to grab,
to pelt with cart's choicest flavours.
Mine cloak covered full mire,
even mule cast a wary eye;
threatening them his fair warning.

We slugged to city gate,
opened they quick to my satisfaction
and passing through to open sky
mine eye didst then perceive a crown of vulture prey
who winged quick down
to a heap of blood soaked armour.
I halted.
The noise of nature I tried scatter
with stones I flung to reach of cloud;
opportunists cleared swearing vengeance as they sought retreat.

Selah

My son.
Thine blood it fell,
but not by fault these hands,
to soak in soil midst armour and rough clay.
Mine tears released,
mine heart didst pumping heave,
his hand in mine,
with him alone I grieved.
I tried to rise
feet though found no strength,
I forced mine mind
alas my will was spent.
With eyes that ran with water I bent low,
a salted tear found a path to you.

Blood and water mixed in life and death.
Blood and water mixed in life and death.

All noise was silenced in that shard of time
eternity stopped, paused for just a while,
those from walls and gates pursuing eyes didst divert,
we were alone upon that hill of blood and dust.

Jehoiakim, son of Josiah, thought Court a guarantee,
secured himself a brutal crushing end,
akin the kings of northern tribe my son too enemy found,
consigned to him now the burial of forgotten donkey.

I sat tween city and approach of Roman imp,
the rocks and shale upon I sat I gathered round,
a sepulchre of stone shall mould to form,
forever marking testimony of the scorned.
I built his grave with sighing laboured graft,
stood beside,
composed an epitaph.
I didst that night sit beside my son,
to let mine memory wander afore fabled city I return.

Selah.

CHAPTER 2

Shibboleth...

Sat I that night neath stars and weak light moon,
aside a shroud of rough cut rock and stone,
drawn round and packed with pebble shale,
stick fire stealing warmth from end of day.
Crack glow snap and rise of dull grey smoke,
shadows stretching long,
heralding night's approach.

History toasts the victor, not the lost,
mine last night with son to mourn his loss,
half mile from tents of Roman sword,
half mile from gates that wall the doomed.
God held His peace, from retribution hid His face,
but then He drew his arrow, set His bow,
wrath released with sudden furious pace,
first my son,
tomorrow for His city no escape.

Mine mind began to wander of times past,
the story of our lives came quick and fast.

Selah

Mine father was called to city,
I but boy,
he a soldier, applied his course to rise,
ambition blinding, hardly ever failed,
secured commission,
under Rome's regal grace.
Then in battle south he took his legends stand,
one hundred men his charge,
their lives his proud command.
They fought fierce, all fell but few,
my father claimed by death,
yet tale returned of those he bravely slew.
I wallowed then for years
but gloried in his name,
taking mine own advantage,
serving self for gain.
I picked not sword,
my war I waged with brain,
acquiring authority by politic,
securing favour by strategic plan and trade.
A politician cuts and thrusts with cunning zeal,
double tongue doth mostly furnish prize,
words parried smart and forged to kill,
prestige is gained, for less practiced always pay games price.
Then asked to join the ranks of rising Saul,
I took the offer,
found the violence didst me enthral.
Returned to Court to inform of Saul's betrayal,
my Assyrian roots by wife had been discovered,
tyrants sentence passed,
one from which I nare recovered.

Afore this curse
I found a choicest bride,
lauded in company
I rejoiced at her aside.

Chapter 2. Shibboleth

Bathsheba's beauty, most succumbed her wonders bright,
in the hearts of men licentiousness flame she did excite.
The company of each I muse we didst full enjoy
but at Court she proved duplicitous and twice wise.
Our child, a boy
established succession's line,
alas our dynasty bride Jezebel didst destroy.
My boy then raised by wolves, a lamb to slaughter,
he hardened quick,
becoming a perspicacious plotter.

These thirty years I sought him out by stealth,
he first a child,
then esteemed; a man of substance wealth.
I watched,
observed,
drew back when nearly found.
My love for him didst grow,
birthed forth from broken hearts concern.

Selah

Thoughts my sons life I didst distil,
mourned I his loss it seems since he fair child,
he taken under cover darkness
upon my glory's demise.
Watched I he plot his path to Court,
brick by brick he built unsavoury course,
had I known then this gruesome end
perhaps we would have purposed
our very own abscond.

At sixteen he joined Rome's legion men
yet a hint of foreign nature most discerned,
shibboleth tongue attached itself mine son,
separating speech,

sounds of words from which he could not run.
At first enforcer was his licensed badge,
with intimidating stature he was framed,
disposition mean
so violent were his ways.
Becoming feared in barracks midst coarse men,
his character, later famed,
remained skin thin.
A perfect soldier for Judea's hot land,
shielding armour covered tempest's heart,
though it beat
pumping life through steel of vein and gut,
despatched he to hell those he killed in sovereign's campaign.
No hint of fear betrayed beguiling smile,
no trace of vulnerability
he expressed from conniving eyes,
his cloak more soaked in blood by passing time,
upon his mantle bloomed a stripe of pride.
Thou wouldst say he was neither prince nor king
yet the title "legend" attached to scheming brain.
He smote a graven image upon his heart,
a high place,
temple altar to he a god;
placed he there by subterfuge a diadem tower,
collected he the accoutrements of magnificence
and of power.

In growing authority he legitimised his lust,
fidelity to Emperor he shrewdly deftly feigned,
started then he a search
for a kingdom that he alone couldst reign.
By mid twenties more power he wielded by strongman's grasp
liquidating thousands by brute and blood forced hand,
leaving trails of innards and whitened hollow bones,
always gaining advantage

mine sycophantic son.
Acolytes, soldiers all,
attached themselves his sun,
then garrisoned north he forced mercurial rage,
acts hastened, so awful,
recorded not upon history's page.

He filled palaces and darkened halls
with devils and desperate men,
self-reliant,
boastful,
he a demon chief of hell.
Deranged, unhinged,
satan's perfect prize,
messages of his exploits I'd roundabouts hear.
Knew I then that death stalked mine son,
reaper grim plaguing sore my sin cursed one.
Perfected he the black art of Babylonian ways,
to Nero's games despatched he many captured slaves,
young and old,
weak and spent,
strong and near the grave,
they'd sate Rome's crowds,
the sacrifice blood required to satisfy their needs.
My son's strings Nero would purse with realm's coin,
at this the lad wouldst smile,
for he could save to build his path;
plus fortuitously a double blessing; fewer mouths required for he to feed.

Selah

Returned he Jerusalem,
a stranger I didst not know.
Procurator's Adjutant for the city,
continued he a while to rise.

Observed I from distance
his regal life's descent,
one never sees their own end,
until that coin is spent.

Cloven hearted goat,
devoid of love and all curious affection,
distrusting,
cruel,
impenetrable,
poisoned serpent's sting infection.
Enclosed his chest a black heart chasm,
cavern of dark depth deep,
withered , wretched, hardened, calloused,
chamber of death; malcontent's obsidian chalice.

For a wayward son a father hopes the best,
fatted calf always ready for the taste,
yet spurned he all kind friendship calling,
spiralling him further;
his path to damnation he continued falling.

First amongst unequals
Governor watches all,
Solomon's wisdom,
deliberation,
discovered Rome's chief a flaw.
Upon the air mine boy didst smell a change,
switched his side,
complicated he his game.
To a new leader he extended gracious bow,
time for Jerusalem the Romans they to overthrow.

Selah

I fear I nodded,
slumbered but a while,
warmth evaporated into encroaching circling mist.
Stirred I to kindle sticks,
while mule shifted from composed rest.
Thought I our working days perhaps over;
if with autarky blessed, promised him fresh pasture.
Foraged on cured scratching and sun burnt root,
listened to distant plea of Prophet's walled lament.
Spotted I a faint gate lamp,
those informed took flight to mountain sanctuary;
steadied pace, cut tight to dark tall walls,
each step confirming testimony of trusting faith.

Tensions built in this fractured cauldron,
a few hours to tumult roar and impending rout.
Thoughts returned mine son;
alas this boy knew not difference
tween statesman and base tyrant.

Mine only born,
despoiler of hamlet,
deflowerer of maiden fair.
Thou crimson fiend,
choicest of raging fearsome men,
walked he from his own bleak creation
into a darker, more terrifying black.
No merge tween dark and light,
no grey distillation,
found he no less guilt whilst playing either side.

Selah

Each Emperor rules with hierarchical fervour.
Emperor first,
then regional King who oversees a local Procurator.
All Rome's charlatans cut a political swagger;
quick with a smile,
twice as fast with a dagger.

Each Empire requires a gentleman to shine the throne,
to sway the power of senate
and control the aspirations of an oft baying crowd.
To him the subjugated tribute pays
designed to keep Caesar warm midst winter's cruel decay.
He lies neath robes of finest purple furs
while plebs outside consider how best betray.
An Emperor too an expert in the rites of Kings,
self-preservation,
terror,
fear,
hardly ever life's good things.
From steps so high, protecting gilded cage,
he waves his sceptre wand,
a piece of wooden stick,
made to glint in gold and gemstone charm.
Jerusalem has seen its share pretender men,
Alexander,
Nebuchadnezzar,
even Pharaoh for a time.
Most left a trail of innards in their wake;
conquests of respective visions
each tried to undertake.

Rome's man sits greedily in his tower,
licking lips from vittles
and sweet cakes of finest flour.
Robed in gowns

so opulent to amaze,
those who surround too frightened
their intentions and views to state.

At a whim these Nephelim
prosecute dissenting voice,
nare excuse required
for they love to execute.
Rome's glorious gift to this a dying world,
a cross of wood,
sequence of twisted hammered nails.
This gift they exported through their lands
to display empires warnings to troublesome rebellious minds;
Emperor so distant
he easily washes hands.
So brutal fear became Rome's fondest friend,
keeping Emperor safely tucked in bed
despoiling virgins on demand.

Agrippa, the last of Herodian line,
was himself a virtuous and brightly King,
orator's gift,
devised he verse and rhyme,
constructed he speeches,
so illustrious and sublime.
Using meaty words and flowery machinations,
persuaded listeners departed baffled by his intellectual orchestrations.
He spoke of Rome's triumphant history in near and distant lands,
of the Greek, Assyria, Britannia, the self obsessed Gaul,
of garrisons and legions of savage heathen men.
Bernice and he fled,
when in Jerusalem his troops could not he defend:
pomp and contrived circumstances brought to sudden end.

The Procurator is appointed by Roman foe,
to dispense conquering justice
by righteous rule of law.
Collect they too the tax of crop and coin,
ensuring none avoid
Emperor's weighty gain.

Believest I politicians begin with benevolent intent,
forward march they plot a guiding star,
but the road to accolade winds fair steep,
like water deep and dark most fall quick and far,
soon their feet get covered full with dirt,
the kind I oft collect with mule and cart.
Intentions soiled most choose a different path
for power corrupts like a corpse in heat of rust.

Such were Rome's men who came our way,
appointed for a time
to marshal looter's sway.
Procurators,
men of wisdom and of stealth,
each trying hard the Emperor to cunningly impress.

Selah

Felix spent a week of years,
from Caesarea he did rule,
set the seed for Jerusalem's ruin,
combating disturbances and internal feuds.
A descendant from old regal claim,
a freedman of the Greeks,
he bent under Claudius' fist,
bowed as low as his lard could scrape.

My son joined under Felix's decree,
in Caesarea's Legion cut his cloth,
caught the eye of Governors grace,
majesty's favour followed forth.
Arcadia's past riches and earthly might
tempted Felix toward unrighteous gain,
lover of mammon and engorged lust,
especially gold that doth not rust.
They drew allegiance
my son and fiend,
partnered cruelty knew no bound,
delivered malfeasant scheme and cheat,
Rome's auditors they didst so easily confound.

Paul appeared again
but chained,
used the opportunity to witness,
held in prison, again detained.
Methinks Felix formed lure to bride
but Paul remained punished,
under guard and threat of nail.
For two years Paul spoke true words,
of life and love,
of Saviour's blood
and Christ's resurrection triumph;
caught the attention of Felix's ear
but his heart remained unchallenged.
Paul met mine son
who passed me letter of greeting and salutation.
I oft times Paul visited
also tried find my boy
but my company he had again forbidden.
Pleased I was to see mine friend,
saddened too by mine own blood's exclusion.

Selah

Festus wore a cloven hoof of charm,
replaced he Felix for a time,
enflamed hostilities by acts deemed gross obscene,
used he my son for his wicked plots and not so innocent schemes.
Fortune appeared to follow my boy;
the question though could well be
how much he himself devised?

Festus' tongue was harsh,
like blasted brass he'd bray,
he well able compass brinkmanship ploy
and quietly let the priests and chiefs
their politics and ramblings play.
Watched he the plotting of Paul's death
with intrigue and detached remain,
and let Jerusalem their merry dance,
but at the end would not allow
destruction onto death.

Festus and Agrippa,
company of hungry thieves,
listened Paul again,
Agrippa near believed;
of dark and light,
eternal life
secured by sins forgiven,
by the Son of Man,
who lived to die,
then grace filled resurrection.
At night they sat, my son their aside,
debated how justice could be wrought,
but Paul appealed by Roman right
to Caesar for consort.
Goodfellow three agreed demand
for Paul to Nero devil,

they knew full well this be Paul's end,
his freedom never again envisioned.

Mine son handed Paul to Centurion Julius,
set him upon the seas,
we both stood upon harbour's edge,
saw Paul's last glimpse through sea crest breeze.

Selah

The hand of time contrives through generations to replace men,
the rules devised so we cannot win.
Smoke rises thin from funeral pyre
and while not quenched,
another arrives;
his time to light ambition's fire.

Festus died far from Nero's maddened rage,
Albinus transferred;
his time to escalate theft and gruesome dying,
new name pressed on Emperors stamped seal.
Afore his arrival he was petitioned for a kill,
The Lord's brother;
James,
toward whom the Pharisees wished ill.
High Priest was deposed by Rome
while Albinus set to plot new ruin.

Recommended by his predecessor
mine son was hastened quick,
he given free tenancy to crime;
Albinus extracting percentage each act my son did commit.
They devised inventions of evil
here to fore unheard,
they say the devil learnt new tricks

from the vice the city endured.
Promoted Adjutant,
mine son his funds didst waste as easily as he earned.

The city recoiled,
spawned a brute force,
Sicarii called to action
for Rome they wished to hurt.
Assassins and murderers
revenge they did plot,
my son constructed defences
the uprising to stop.
Striking force by terror fear
he planned unrivalled affliction
leading many corpses to terror and to rot.

After Jerusalem
to Africa Albinus sent.
In all Jerusalem's evil
Albinus had his say;
only those left in prison
were the captives his bribe they couldst not pay.

Selah

There is something sinister about a Roman Turk,
twice as wretched
with thrice the irk.
Florus entered with the speed of a wasp,
stung all around
afore he was squashed.
In that rogue
a brother my son found,
with style and aplomb
their crimes didst quick abound.

Chapter 2. Shibboleth

Mine son like a novice
aside this great man
who radiated brilliance,
thievery of such distinction,
a pageant of splendour
with practised deceit;
had his victims in laughter
searching out what else they for him could eak.

In terms of his elegance he never showed fluster,
the most debauched of offenders; indeed he a monster.
More mercenary than all others
made a choir boy of Albinus,
with a penchant for vanity
carried he an aura of majesty.

Florus filled Jerusalem with heartache and misery,
citizenry complained to the King,
to Caesar, Florus feared they'd turn.
Only one way Florus thought out,
excite Jerusalem to violence; incite rebellion.
From that time he tolerated all that was impure,
all forms of barbarous depravity,
all wickedness took shape,
no method of disorder he ever omitted.
He executed,
rampaged,
all laws he defied,
one day over three thousand
he unjustly crucified.
In the stead of legal reprimand
Rome came to assist,
the vilest of Procurator's continued to kill,
the people to trample,
he even entered the forbidden,
appropriating gold from the Temple.

Midst stench, sweet stink of clotting ulceration
the city sank to stark decay
and bloodied evisceration.
Leaders met,
Eleazer, Yosef ben Matityahu and Sicarii,
plotted how to end Florus' carnal devastation.
Florus enraged,
his hate turned blind,
sent troops to the city,
many leaders were whipped then crucified.

Twelfth year of Nero,
Emperor was advised of city's rebellious story,
a northern battle was waged
and at Beth Horon the Jews gained victory
with plans they had so well devised.
Florus was removed as quickly as he came,
Julianus appointed successor,
but for my son things would not remain
for Julianus would bring death not succour.

Mine son crossed words with Rome's new power,
gauged a change of climate air,
sought out Sicarii
offered services at a price felt fair.
Son changed faction
for Jerusalem he fought
with gusto and great zeal;
promised a role, his skills he put to play;
second in command if Jerusalem won the day.
Delusions of grandeur,
saw himself a Prince,
Sicarii knowing not his vivid imagination
took not long to convince.
Co-ordinator of rebels,
all groups he advised,

Zealots, Idumeans,
those of politic and those who would fight.
He soon headed provisional government,
knew all forms of attack,
punished the Romans,
from the city the foreigner drew back.
Nero commanded unrest brought to end,
sent Vespasian and son Titus
the empire to defend.
With legions a plenty, no shortage of men
the rebels confounded the generals again and again.

But undercover of dark
with shielding black cloak,
Titus sought out my boy,
entered Jerusalem's gates unchecked, unmarked.
They met midst halls, discussion the reason,
Titus offered mine boy elicit bribe of treason.
To change sides once more
but wear spy's disguise,
a Procurator's role for mine son
his loyalty wouldst him buy.
So mine son sold himself a pawn
to Rome's men again,
the result now lies at mine aside.

Tonight I'll rest here and ponder awhile
for tomorrow Titus asserts for victor's prize.

Mine charge has been left with nothing,
no love,
nay children or comely wife;
that's the price one pays
when one dies of living an exciting life.

Selah

O what secrets doest thine lips behold,
once alive, now cast down cold.
What ravaged sounds and dreams once spoke with pride,
lie dormant now behind quenched darkened eyes.
Un-quivered arrowed words and thoughts misspent,
mirrored meaning besieging hearts own quest.
O lips with honeyed sweetness taste,
never truth, its own yearning now manifest.

Thine lips that once flattered the majesty of Crowns and Kings,
whose deceitful plotting raged far from Emperor's gaze,
forged by tongue so smooth as bride's silver prize,
once quick to cut
offer now no silent praise.
Savage cauldron,
wicked heart's disguise,
once smiling proud with drunken reveller's pride,
carouser's blush now dead,
caused by sins own lies.

Destroyer's plot that thickened was not born to hurt
but lips deceived purchased a senseless thought,
his quickened heart completed deed in haste,
then peace not found,
brought Sicarii's spear to test.

Lips that plot a vanity cannot rest
for boasters tongue with ale doth rush to tell,
to courts once walked a tale will always flee,
swift justice brought to face I now do see.

O silent pride.
O silent mockers scornful stain.
In which home dost thine Spirit now reside?

What wish to call from where thou canst flee?
What silent tear is offered for a glimpse of liberty?

Time erodes this mortal earth,
consigns men's idols to dismal dust,
like Haman's conniving to kill The Lord's chosen,
shibboleth I commit now to dirt.

Selah

CHAPTER 3

Upon this hill...

He who holdeth the hill
winneth the battle
and the war entire.
Justice procured
nay by grasp of hand
nor chariot speed.
This world He won
at wooden stake,
pitched and held in force,
stones washed and held tight
by martyr's blood.
His expressed intent of Holy salvation
secured by outstretched limbs
and briar thorn of flesh cut crown.
This Mighty King,
Creator unfurled
in anguish and in hope.
He was raised to battle
and we must mourn,
then unashamedly rejoice
for our earthly sins
He put to paid.

Beauty stood midst death
but Beauty to death didst not succumb.
Death defaced eternal Beauty
with whip and nail and thorn,
beat Beauty on wood cut twice,
bruised Beauty with devil's bludgeoned zeal.
Beauty though dead didst by resurrection arise,
while death stepped back to bow with bended knee.

Beauty sits, surveys His realm for a time
for to this place He willst soon return,
heralding justice for the meek,
this world's Nimrods to overthrow.

Stand fast in saving grace.
Stand fast await His trumpet call.
Stand fast forevermore.
Let Beauty thou enthral.

Selah

This is no Eden
midst Jerusalem's walls
and Rome's death drum beat.
It is the hour of darkest dark,
it is the time of deepest deep,
it is a mind of ceaseless thought,
a time I couldst not sleep.

The third night watch struck its past,
a single drum announced the fourth.
The echo drew a solitary cleft rest raven,
its raucous call boomed against creviced wall,
stirring others with harbinger call.
Departed they then unobserved in pitch,

warned fore slaughter.
A timely return will herald bounty,
city corpse upon which to feast.
Shook I the cold from limb and thought,
this sad night drawing toward a close.
The silence returned,
still,
quiet.
It was the soft of night,
though unlike others this peace wouldst breathe an end,
to entice the temptation of encircling fiend.
The walls seemed all but black,
tall enceinte shadows,
devoid of hope's assurance and of life;
inhabitants comfortable in denial.
The surrounding tents appeared likewise indolent,
a behemoth of inertia,
languid, sluggish; rather otiose.
A faint lamp captured anticipation,
perhaps the tent of expectant Titus and gathered general's rage.
Mine eyes cast downward
toward coiffed rubble heap,
mine son now covered,
his face now forever hid
from the sun
and open tempt of sky blue reach.

Selah

No stranger I this recognised slope,
elevated hillock visible from any point one can see,
discerned from city,
adjoining field afar,
observed by noon scorch
and fading night star.

This place; Golgotha,
Calvary's place of skull,
close forty year past
mine memory drawn to another Son.
This hill of death aside the Potter's field
witness to massacre of authority's seal.
Observed I He from heaven sent,
life eternal who took on flesh,
He spoke in parables,
creations secret tales,
of heaven's Kingdom,
Majesty's reign.
He taught forgiveness,
through miracles blessed,
healed the multitudes,
put faith to test.
He came to save sinners
the self-righteous to expose,
to impart peace
for those who He they chose.

Then I was loyal, Pharisee sworn,
advancing occupations delusion,
full knowing His truth
we voted His death in considered collusion.
I was there, full witnessed His years,
laughed like a scoffer,
a fool midst my peers.
Treacherous, malicious
so violent and cruel,
what we know now as triumph
was used for crucifixion's fuel.
Those days now over became mine sin's curse;
I exchanged grace filled purpose
for furtherance of purse.

Selah.

Recollect I now the minutiae His days,
let the record be straight and true,
of us in counting room
midst splendours and riches not few.
Caiaphas arrived with father-in-law's command,
fevered, clapping, boisterous in demand,
sought us arise;
to the Jordan we didst sojourn.
John, called Baptiser, Zacharias' own son,
immersing citizens for the remission of sins;
visibly calculating Messiah's soon arrival.
Spied he us,
we he welcomed with a bellowed blast of scorn;
methinks "brood of vipers," he us addressed.
We readied swords,
alas reins held by Annas
who ordered observation and not cruel encroachment.
One by one neath waters they disappeared,
then arrived He and John didst fall to kneel.
He too submerged then upon return,
an assault of heavenly voice,
some said Yahweh Himself;
we blamed echo of some intruding distant blast.
Returned we to Temple ground;
quieter though than outward.

Scrolls of olde we hastened sought,
for of Bethlehem we Messiah knew.
Dusted the pages of census date,
escaped He Herod's extermination.
That wicked King,
but half a man,
for sent he troops,
who by their own hands perfected infanticide slaughter.
Yet later, out of Egypt God called His son;
His one and only begotten.

Our ranks didst soon dissention debate
for goodly men didst our order flee;
one either chose remain
or leave devoid of favour.

Jairus first,
he bid farewell,
for he to Saviour turned for help,
his daughter dead but by this Christ raised to life;
Jesus Himself becoming her sweet redeemer.
She died not, we convinced ourselves;
encouraged we one another.
Under cover darkness Nicodemus went,
by night he talked with the Teacher.
He stood there at the end,
acknowledged as friend,
mourning deep while searching for succour.
There were others too encountered God,
He not just a carpenter king,
He fulfilled prophecy by word of page
and with scripture you cannot argue.

I was thirty,
the influence of my tide rising.
Caiaphas encouraged me this man to follow,
under cover of poverty attired in cloak like now.
Amid the crowd I hid my face,
opened my ears taking record of note.
I watched this man in boldness grow,
singular in purpose,
dignified in principle.
Our law,
He met each points demand
by jot and even tittle;
no fault I found, nay not one.

Chapter 3. Upon this hill

Watched I His works,
signs we Pharisees wished silent.
This Jesus exercised compassion,
demonstrated authority over disease,
over all infirmity visible,
over principalities and powers; realms unseen.
Displayed He Lordship over Sabbath,
over death's grim shadow,
over life itself.

Feared I then the receipt of my finding,
I must admit,
I to Caiaphas lied.

Selah

Gethsemane,
the name,
the memory doth makest me shudder.
For at that garden
Judas we had paid,
he to place in our hands
his Master.
Silver his price to unleash blood,
to release our lust to murder.

Judas led us, villains all,
secreting us to spring egregious design,
delivered he us to hiding cover.
We He watched,
waiting;
waiting impatiently for weakness.
In the heart of garden keep
we watched His helpers sleep,
He laboured, vexed with sighs so deep

then to ground to moan and weep.
Rebuked He his men,
though they slept soon sound again;
we fraid, lest we perhaps mistaken.

Like tempest fire, Malchus roared
we then to Christ paraded,
observed a kiss to tear filled cheek;
we chained and beat this Jesus.
One indigent drew sword,
quick blade we heard,
frenzied brute decided draw nearer
and swinging weapon with angered rage
off came our tempest's ear hearer.
Memory serves to tell this tale,
no flourished embellished flavour,
this Jesus stooped down to bloodied ground
attached this ear His enslaver.
We quieted, then marched He back in file
to Annas and Caiaphas, for He too they must defile,
unlawful He to kill determined then;
sent Him to Pilate Procurator.

Rome's man had enraged us Pharisees twice afore,
knew we he keen to avoid much dispute,
explained our plight with rigorous aplomb,
our prisoner a flagrant breaker of our Holy Laws.
No fault Pilate found,
we unawares if bribe he didst that time seek,
sent he Jesus to Herod
but with that monster's lineage Christ remained silent;
He did not once word compose.
Pilate again no fault found
yet he savage,
this Jesus he near impaled;

said he would He scourge afore release.
Crucifixion we roared for we sought His demise,
Pilate, even fast warned by goodly wife,
decided to satisfy our ferocious demand,
released Barabbas
then of Christ he washed his bloodied paws.

There was no beauty that we ought to desire,
He despised,
He rejected by men,
including Peter at sound of crowing hen.
This silent sheep
we beat with stick and heft staff of bloodied nail,
a crown of thorn atop,
we hailed God's own sent King.
Battered,
bruised,
broken,
His frame we dragged by rope,
anointing His reign with royal purple shroud like robe.
No man afore was stricken such
a smile from Caiaphas I didst glean,
a nemesis of years he smote
perpetrated with viciousness obscene.
We prodded,
goaded,
drenched He in angered spit,
furious,
unrestrained,
we each a hell infused beast,
so aroused by blood we nare couldst speak.
Our leaders called a halt
we stopped our torture game,
what we thought could not get worse
the High Priest though desireth His public affront,

on wood cut twice,
by hand a tree bolt tight,
to display vague victory;
to restore position of heaven given power and might.

We washed He down by water pail,
reviving we His form,
His stripes then crude revealed,
we stood aghast our works wrought storm.
We laid His back,
tied on wood
and marched Him naked through the gate.

Selah

Nare fore in history had hardened enemies associated with agreed coalition,
subjugated and conqueror,
Jerusalem and Rome;
unified in the unholy conception of murder.
Two begat one flesh,
devils together,
confirmed in their infidelity;
seamless harmony,
perfected symmetry.
All that was unclean, together,
spawning a hideous tentacled hybrid,
they contorting all righteous and lawful into their grotesque image;
designed to leave no trace.

Jesus Christ's walk was slow,
each step painfully ponderous,
each heartbeat a lonely step of haggard humiliation;
a shuffle of anxious but committed thought.
He dropped to ground,

wood's weight added to by shouted ire
and taunting charge;
words and expressions nare oft heard.
Such hate was carefully nurtured,
reserved for only an occasional outing,
only for the foulest of fiends.
Knowest I now that this Man
was undeserving of prosecution's intimidation.
He fell again,
labouring under shackle of lumber.
Upon a third,
a man, innocent of all wrong endeavour,
was tasked upon by spear to aid.
Simon left two trembling children in his wake,
boys fearful that their own father was now
subject to authority's pleasure.
This world is cruel,
the young most vulnerable,
their requirement, love and secure footing
afore most turn themselves into brutish men.

Narrow cobbled streets claimed a bloody footprint trail,
earth's solitary witness,
for spitters, mockers,
chastisers of bile and brute
wouldst this day conscience flee.
Fools romanticise violence,
enthuse they the horrors of dysfunction.
Execution is traumatic:
slow ending, agonizing.
Carried He that day
our sin upon His back,
curse's fragrance of death,
sunburnt,
clawing sickly scent from already rotting flesh.

At the fore one hundred men.

One hundred men in tunic red.
One hundred men in armour shine.
One hundred men with scutum shield.
One hundred men in helmet bronze.
One hundred men with spear and sword.
One hundred footsteps of hardened lead.
One hundred hounds of raging hell.
One hundred men to marshal death.
Medals, badges, amulets of pride,
for the victor all the battle's spoils.
One hundred men again at rear.
One hundred purveyors of ruthless fear.

Midst protection,
Pharisee men,
marching silent in formal rank.
Full regalia of stunning robes,
bells and whistles,
shining gold.
Looks dispassionate as if this work despised,
hiding behind reprobate minds.
Observers at passing would divert their eyes,
Caiaphas clasping authority's prize,
assured his sanctuary again restored
drawing both Pilate and Rome to his accord.

Selah

My mind disturbed a time
by sound of drum beat four,
tried I concentrate again,
remembering that day's contentious roar.

The scene of Calvary opened

Chapter 3. Upon this hill

upon our venture outside the gate,
walls casting precipitous shadow
shielding gaze from sun blast heat.
The rugged pathway opened quickly,
full procession toward the hill.
Witnessed I the fragment remnants of previous occupiers,
criminals despatched with haste of speed,
the slightest of charge the guarantee of rewarding nail.
The odd witness hillside strewn,
a broken sharp of drinker's flask,
black sticks of kindle olde,
olde nails, tatters, segments wood, all type apparel,
eyes by path then drawn to hillock and surrounding bleak.

Rememberest I the buzz of corpse fed fly,
our arms quick to insect brush,
we fraid their bite
lest we too secure infection and too soon death.
Thousands those bugs,
in sky and on the floor,
seeking succulent chops upon which they would soar.
This Golgotha, hill of complete abandon and distain,
only those under order wouldst soon remain.

The death of three summoned that fateful day,
two companions securely installed,
growled they too in loathsome welcome;
such greeting for Israel's King.
Marauding troops of chosen and gentile army
stood to slow then thumping stop.

Tortured Christ surveyed His grim surround,
sacked full force then to ground,
for Him the executioner nails must pound.
Metal shards,

twisted to point of sharp
I held with tremble these mine hands,
passed I them for crushing blows;
hammered in with slow, not too delicate deliberation.
We raised then His mortal frame,
lifted to high,
physic dropped to slide
with sudden dreadful stop and shock.
Such tremor of shattering pain
midst laughter and cruellest taunt,
His cross base then packed tight
with stones, solid shale and rock.
High Priests doffed their scoff,
mocked, then hailed this dying King,
turned their backs and took to disappear;
Jerusalem's feasting table to glut,
wearied dusty bones to rest and wash.

I stood awhile to watch His gruesome end,
the calls for angels,
for Elijah,
for He to descend and come to save Himself.
Pointed words He spoke,
hope at the end He gave,
thief turned to Him,
pleading he to save.
Guarantee of paradise that night
though the other continued fight and spit,
we later witnessed the second's death;
destination hell with flame in gnashing pit.

Rejected He,
alone to die His end,
those who stayed watched now He afar,
His mother, sisters, brothers, friends, followers but few.

Event most strange occurred that day,
visiting of dark seemed like for hours,
as if Hades deep had come to stay.
Nestled crowds grew fearful,
many left,
beseeched to home;
their safeties keep.
Our sin blast mocking drew bit quieter,
our fears realised, perhaps indeed for Him a saviour,
a saving angel, perhaps even aforementioned Elijah.

Then as if a victory shout,
vociferate He loudly.
Eli, Eli, lama sabachthani?
My God, My God,
Why have You forsaken Me?

It can take a long time to crucify a man,
a lifetime to plot,
then hours to drain life's vitals,
little rest for blood to clot.
Christ denied our attempts at His resuscitation,
no to liquid,
no sour wine savour.
Jesus cried out again and with a loud voice
He yielded up His Spirit.

An earthquake rumbled ground,
tore the temple's veil in two,
access, I later realised granted,
to God Almighty for repentant sinners to be heard,
redemption paid nay by our toil,
our purse coin can buy no favour.
Salvation is by grace alone,
by faith in His blood shed by He who came to suffer.

A soldier later His corpse he struck by spear,
pierced skin allowing trail of water.

Blood and water mixed in life and death.
Blood and water mixed in life and death.

Selah

His body taken ground,
some tomb for His hereafter,
deed done,
we laughing drew our frames for supper.
We drank our mighty fill of vines that damning night,
rememberest I now two days of inordinate hangover.
Caiaphas with no shame,
comedic role he didst play,
relived all parts his nemesis' slaughter,
mocking, jesting,
different voices for he each character,
then took the part of Pilate's contribution
and washed his guilty hands with no contrition.
Encouraged he that grim eventide our amuse
midst fornication, loudness and much booze.

The son of perdition knocked upon the door,
entered,
cast his treasure wildly upon the floor,
inflicted self-end that very night,
we guessed he shamed by blinding betrayer's plight.

Selah

Upon the third,
all quiet in hedonistic stupor,
a charge of noise we congregated heard;
hearty roar of soldier greet with resounding echo.

Chapter 3. Upon this hill

This Jesus' body gone,
the stone rolled by strong celestial angel;
His followers calling it His Holy resurrection.
Sadducees took upon visage of heartfelt shock,
bare couldst contain contempt and outraged fervour.
Annas forever clever,
talked this soldier
then paid his quiet with coin and favour;
organised with Pilate a transfer to some distant war flung border.

Ventured we devise sagacious scheme,
Christ's corpse we said
taken under cover dark by some pugnacious robber.
We all took this part,
sweeping truth from mind and heart.

Ten more years ambition I employed
until that time I brought already mentioned news
of Saul's defection upon hot sweat Damascus trail.
Cast they then I out, attaching cart,
life's course drastically changed for me and for mine charge.

Thinkest I now,
through all time that passed,
we had a choice,
all us at that time.
A day to choose a path,
choice to Saviour follow
or continue enjoy Court;
narrow gate to sanctuary,
broad way to demise.
Sit I here with wet companion tear,
wishing now I had earlier
overcome my ego and my fear.

Selah

CHAPTER 4

Take of olde and new...

The generations fearful, stood silent midst the dock,
each individual questioned by creations ruling Judge,
steadied He their nerves, focused thoughts upon His law,
confirmed each their guilt from life's actions
for from memories secret and unhidden He didst draw.

Thou hast worshipped falsehood; other gods over Me.
Thou hast stooped their images and didst not flee.
Thou hast cursed my name in open and in heart.
Thou hast spurned my Sabbath, hast thou not?
Thou hast scorned at parent times seven yet again.
Thou hast killed in mind; shed blood of kin and friend.
Thou hast lusted to adultery's sinful gaze.
Thou hast stolen from others, even trampled upon their dreams.
Thou hast falsely lied to seek thine own advantage end.
Thou hast coveted even when thou had riches own to spend.

The law is perfect,
it is God's Holy brand,
yet it we canst nare keep
for only Christ's Blood satisfies it rigorous demand.

Widow stood with mite's bit two,
demonstrated mercy over sacrifice as she should,

her salvation secured by grace alone,
for from her heart she sought mercy through His Blood.

Justice by person, nations too he arranged,
separated He the wheat from chaff that day the court arraigned.

Like each dreadful shepherding day fair justice He displayed.
But by fault their continued disobedience,
His sanctions carried swiftly out by those He Himself didst raise.

Selah

A short slight soak rain fell
perhaps to defy the approach of new born sun.
Huddled I to contemplate judgement and grace
though some questions we mortals canst ere answer.
It as if mine son's fate fore sealed
and he didst merry dance
head first quick toward his murders end;
I same deserving but somehow found release.

What separates one from one other?
What step in heart is quickened toward peace?
A choice of self or nudge from He on high eternal?

This quest doth busy the might of theologian brain,
my only answer is to He thank;
to worship and praise His Holy Name.

Trampled my boy this Jerusalem ground
though neither peace nor contentment o'er time he found,
his corpse to lie forever after in shadowed wall surround.
I he now soon must leave,
dirt and worm to rot his bones
cast down in dormant heap.

We shall not meet in heavens hereafter,
sand and grime will pass these stones by dust;
morning will demand I leave him here at light first.

Life didst flower her summer leaf
to grow and rise by sun drench bright,
to sing and toil neath shelter's branch,
yet perish by mid autumn night.
We enjoy earth's verdant green
our play to love or rage,
for each must soon their petals pass
leaving history to assault each mortal page.

Selah

Mine own fate now unknown
for this ground I must vacate,
boisterous men will stake their games
then Jerusalem soon to storm and take.
Clung I one last time my son's eternal tomb,
mine mule didst rise his labour's day,
bid I he rest again
securing smile discerned from welcome bray.

Goest I back to city?
Deny they me sure my entry:
I as welcome as a dead Son.
Goest I toward Rome's waking camp?
They wouldst me shoot with place of practiced arrow hate.

It is a time to trust
to ready for mine own demise;
by grace my peace I found.
If I die this day...
I full assured of rest and peace eternal.

Shouldst I live...
it will be to herald His Majesty's glory.
Not with ease I forge and charge these words,
mine own frame took a lifetime to surrender.
Remember Gethsemane,
how mine Lord didst weep,
He wast sore tired tested
for He could have run afore Judas' death creep.
Bathed He though in knowledge of what He already knew,
steadied He Himself in prayer,
affirmed His choice to Father's will,
standing His ground,
resolute,
confirming stance
to participate in our sins purge.
Faith at times nay an easy walk,
we too like Jacob wrestle,
to subjugate our own devices,
to He we do by His mercy follow.
These victories not without test be won,
we stumble, rise then wallow,
then lift our cross to path again,
our pride and self serve to swallow.

Selah

Disobedience is the currency of fate already sealed
for He Almighty canst against His own Word lie,
His rule sovereign,
for history reveals His heart's desire.
Jerusalem,
no stranger to foreign foe,
no stranger to destruction gore,
for what is about to occur
has occasioned oft afore.

Selah

We eulogise those we love,
mostly upon their scythe,
by their actions alive too
we contemplate fair tear.
Lament I this city cauldron,
self assured Judah Keep,
midst promise eternal fury,
bricks beckon not
no Lazarus resurrection
but alas destructions sleep.

Of olde we know of records page,
displayed roots of promise and God's own favour,
centuries of history linked,
in this bounty of milk and honey.
Land and people.
People and land,
inseparable;
each generation teaching,
a remnant left each age
to live out God's covenantal calling.

Faithful Abraham
righteousness salted to faith's gathering,
struggle of his hand laid down,
subdued o'er time to God's promise.
Isaac taking then full his root
and though he oft deceived Jacob too learnt
to plough God's Holy trail.
Yahweh was patient,
demonstrated His love was true,
orchestrated His instruments
conducting all history
toward that day His only Son
drank bitterest of dregs;
for from the broken chalice of earth He drew.

We are but small with tendency to err
yet God's breath held not by fugit's time,
neither by mountain range
or man's ceaseless moving borders:
tidal waters eroding not God's eternal rhyme.

Jacob's son was sold by brothers feuding,
to Egypt he was cast in prison cell,
yet Pharaoh's call commissioned Israel's salvation,
Joseph through famine didst life to seventy extend.

Four hundred years His people lived affliction
promise of home when Amorite's wickedness complete,
for this, God raised palace grown Moses,
this humble stutterer Pharaoh crude despised with mocked deceit.
Yahweh executed justice o'er Egyptian gods of idol,
His instruction of Passover Moses supervised,
Israel then fleeing after first born slaughter
celebrated baptism's water through Red Sea divide.
The chosen enjoyed manna and much favour
their path displayed by cloud then fire by night,
God shielding, shepherding His people,
each Holy miracle wrought alone by His power and might.
Forty days Moses to mountain ascended,
returned cut stone of law,
with contempt to ground he threw
for calf of golden idol drew entire attention,
mark of Cain attached to camp of which God already knew.
The law teaches guilt to fallen sinners,
constructed by ten which we canst safe keep,
for us our righteousness secured by faith like Abraham,
God cut His covenant afore law when Abraham didst sleep.
God displayed His faithfulness,
like in Noah's day of olde,
chastising in His disappointment,

His children He didst scold.
Confined to roam the desert,
like in the flood all betrayers died,
God dispensing justice,
forty years of sand swept tide.

A battle soon will pillage
Jerusalem's narrow sacred streets,
nothing new for miscreants
God's tale of justice He willst complete.
We mourn not these people
but join in disowning these events,
it seems however we canst nare learn
for each generation mistakes and war repeat;
the march of conquering army repeat, repeat, repeat.

Selah

Joshua and Caleb,
only two of spies company to enter the land,
ten giant fearers left lying neath judgement's sand.
By city waged they victory campaign,
circling by seven
to trumpet tumble walls.
God Himself remained faithful His Word and scarlet thread
securing twelve tribes their pledged abode.
Time evaded that Holy dedication,
man's disposition crumbling like trodden stones,
ingredient of exasperation deposited upon Yahweh's calling;
His wrath their sins exposed.
Judges to judge,
they too fell,
a king the crowd demanded,
handsome Saul enthroned
but a manifestation of unrighteousness

he likewise regimented.
David the hero of ten thousand ten thousand,
Goliath of giants he subdued,
he too fell to flesh temptation and Uriah murder,
upon repentance had grace renewed.
Restored to throne but trouble didst follow,
Absalom confusion entered his home.

We canst to mirror our holiness hold,
within sin blots our breathing cadaver,
millennia will pass and prove quick fair point
each person will need a Just Saviour.

Reflected I upon God's prophets,
those He sent to anchor unyielding foals,
desireth He to signal His heart's intentions
to draw His people toward eternal hope.
Explain Samuel.
Explain Elijah.
Explain Isaiah and Jeremiah,
Ezekiel in keeping.
Zechariah's future caution,
Micah, Jonah, Hosea...
Explain God's penchant for exhortation,
for kindly Kingly counsel,
His voice over time giving warning.

Methinks only Love can explain
His faithfulness to His calling.

Division split God's Kingdom.

Jeroboam was raised to lord ten tribes of north,
he who by hand constructed his gods of gold.
The baals stole ground,
not only dirt but of beating heart;

other kings raised o'er time to murder.
God promised vengeance
and to His people explained His wrath
by voice of lonely prophet.
His people grew dull, ignoring prophetic yearnings,
northern tribes falling to captivity
and blows of Assyrian murder.

Good king,
bad king,
bad, good, bad,
observed in Judah too,
high places built and knocked again
cold hearts growing black to blue.
Ahaz walked in the way of the north,
sacrificed he his son,
his own family blood to idol baal.
Wickedness didst abound,
constructed they altars to foreign fiend,
committed they their own abomination of desolation.
Respite time grew thin;
Manasseh too his own son's blood he shed.
God turned His back
yet not afore a righteous plea,
a return to holiness His prophets didst implore,
but black blue hearts focused on self gain,
His people His voice didst sinfully ignore.
Wrath kindled its end,
the sword of battle warmed,
chariots roared,
descended to inflict Yahweh's ire,
raised He a name of dread:
Nebuchadnezzar.

Selah

Gallant voices of lonesome holy warriors,
the motivations of prophet's pleas ignored,
their might weighed not by blade of iron
but by plead of earnest prayer and heart seared tear.
Alas no fear of God fore Judah's eyes,
the righteous path each convicted sinner didst surely despise,
giants of men killed by hearts deranged,
Isaiah, Jeremiah warned forthcoming of Babylonian flame.

Yahweh's hand took axe of history olde,
the grind of stone He didst so kiln sharp,
tested strength Himself to nick thumb raw,
satisfied,
stood back to contemplate His end of full versed seethe.
Yahweh placed His axe to tempest root,
nipped His cherished fig tree bough,
crafted the branches clearing for exact assault,
then wielding fury cut He thin to quick,
with vengeance power He didst smite to dust.
The defilers stood proud in pride of breast,
suddenly tumbled slain to battle floor,
ambitions extinguished, flattened by expose,
chains and death marked Babylon's oppose.
Jacob stood desolate by mile marker,
borders quiet, prepared for Sabbath rest,
all trade ceased, Jerusalem now eerie silent,
no merchant call midst street burnt quick by heat;
children's voice of play and cry complete.
Widows veiled in black with pain and horror,
men of strength dashed,
crushed midst wealth and forbidden fruit carnal.
Alas Jerusalem found now silent,
Yahweh's axe bloodied,
fully sated,
cleansed and greased then stored for some future blight,

justice procured for this tempus satisfied
for sin cannot approach pure heaven's light.

Selah

Babylon,
result of disobedience forewarned,
bastion of Nimrod's first labours,
mud brick hewn.

Babylon,
announcing the servitude of the nation,
seventy year judgement for Sabbath rest foregone.

Babylon,
like servitude of Sinai wilderness,
only a future remnant would make it home.

Babylon,
Nebuchadnezzar's toil reward,
ruled he harshly,
this mighty head of gold.

Babylon.

Selah

One thousand six hundred miles of hard crust heat,
Daniel walked for sight a promised prison home.
Immersed they he in Babylon's royal courts
held he faithful tight all Jewish roots
defiantly respectful of Babylon's politic and charms.
Meagre rations and water the trodden consumed,
many fell
exertions claiming by death, lives unregistered, unknown.

This Fertile Crescent stretch
paved with harvest of lush cultivations,
its famed beauty ruled by base men,
those who common threat,
tried they eradicate all Jewish rite and heritage civilization.

Daniel be told held breath,
gasped this Polis surround,
pride he thought marketh this behemoth's boundary.
Fifteen miles square,
walls and towers held ground,
three hundred plus feet of tall surveyed this fortification,
entry granted by one hundred gates of sculpted bronze.
Double walled,
races held atop by chariot four.
Watchtowers, not few, over two hundred,
higher than walls;
approach of enemy they designed to expose.
A gigantic square of heathen mix,
Ziggurat stones contemplated statues of like composed gods,
nature by rain wouldst by clock reveal,
all this of grime and decaying mud.
The Euphrates of Genesis flowed through,
a straight line this river swell didst heave,
dividing Babylon in equal parts two,
providing water for life in this empire's soil baked streets;
current in spate neath city walls didst not slow.
Mightiest of cities,
thought they impregnable,
but akin all nations
time itself didst Babylon's bell sound toll.

Cometh the battle, arriveth the man,
One to wield weight sword,
at Carchemish Nebuchadnezzar's tale began unfold;
against Egypt, Chaldean might didst Necho he expose.

Upon sojourn, Jehoiakim of Judah,
for the sins of Manasseh,
to Babylon's reign vassal became.
Servitude of the nation had begun,
Chronicles, the book second, the Jew's sin unfurled.
Nineteen years later a further Jerusalem siege,
Nebuchadnezzar's third.
Those imprisoned upon the first visit blessed to live
as God's fury poured out onto siege the third.
Nineteen years of God's respite.
Nineteen years after Daniel's flight.
Nineteen years, Jerusalem the Chaldeans didst surround.
Nineteen years, Solomon's Temple scattered to bloody ground.

Nineteen years after servitude
The desolation of Jerusalem, Nebuchadnezzar didst pound.
Yahweh's promised wrath,
advised by prophet Jeremiah,
Jerusalem and His own people He didst wound.
I eulogise the passing these people.
I eulogise the passing of that time.
Lament I again our fallen nature.
Lament I the repeat of history chime.

Daniel and companions three served before the king,
stood ground midst examination,
Nebuchadnezzar realised they more knowledgeable by ten.
Magicians, Astrologers couldst not fair answer Nebuchadnezzar's dream,
Daniel pointed earth's passing king to heaven.
Enquired Daniel of Israel's Lord
who explained parameters of vision dream
and truthful explanation.
Imagine...
six hundred years afore Christ's crucifixion
Daniel minutely told prophetic revelation.

Nebuchadnezzar beheld an image great,
splendid and excellent in stature form,
head of gold,
with chest and arms of silver,
mid and thighs cast in bronze.
Muscled legs of iron,
feet shod in iron with mix of partly clay.
You the head of gold, Daniel pointed Nebuchadnezzar,
empire unlike any of future or of olde,
given him by God of heaven to sit on passing throne.
Silver to announce kingdom inferior,
for no mortal man will this world forever sway,
then bronze for a king
a time thereafter,
interestingly his reign would by four dissipate in disarray.
Another will arrive by strength of iron,
to crush and clash with cymbal violent force,
then at last a stone flung to chaos mingle,
iron and clay mix not,
but crumble all beneath.

The future God had revealed His servant
proven true by century time.
Babylon,
then Media Persia,
Greece by Alexander,
who at thirty two bored,
no further worlds to conquer fore he died;
generals four divided his endeavours accumulation.
Then Rome afforded this world
for its share of time.

At the end God will wrap up this decay of pages
and commence again His eternity to reign.

Selah

As it explained
is how it played,
though through generations grumblers didst try reason,
history revealed so precise,
they didst feel no earthly explanation.
Of this Daniel, Christ didst speak,
dispelling dissention and world's dishonour,
rememberest thou all detail recorded in Greek,
three hundred years afore Christ,
Daniel's words captured in Septuagint translation.

Daniel served his King, this imprisoning emperor.
Gabriel, Yahweh to Daniel despatched
to announce prophetic stirrings so fragrant and so very deep.

Seventy weeks of years of time
to detail this fleeting age,
for Daniel's people and God's Holy city,
to finish transgression and rout of sin,
to announce reconciliation and righteousness everlasting,
to seal up visions and prophecy
and to anoint The Most High.
The first sixty nine weeks of years,
The Messiah didst Himself revealed,
do the arithmetic,
for from Artaxerses' decree
173,880 days later
Jesus Christ made His triumphal Jerusalem entry.
Again one canst dispute,
Septuagint captured all detail,
Yahweh's glorious reveal,
for the earth a Saviour.
Isaiah's suffering servant by colt He exact day arrived,
for mine sins He alone didst die,
then resurrection prior His Holy ascent to Throne on High.

One week of seven years left,
to herald judgement's trial,
time our sins for us repent
and turn from crimes most vile.

Selah

Desolate she lay,
seventy years,
seventy summers and winters cold.
Her Sabbath she didst keep,
the law she didst fulfil and every Word uphold.
Nebuchadnezzar was humbled but fore he died
bid he the God of Israel his own pure delight.
Reported then entry of Persia's Cyrus,
met by Daniel upon his Babylon's arrive,
elderly now, Daniel didst bow
to grace his majesty with scroll Isaiah wrote,
one hundred and fifty years of faded olde.
Isaiah's hand constructed Yahweh's message,
Cyrus now God's instrument
for His Holy and righteous pleasure.
Make straight the crooked Yahweh decreed,
His wrath complete,
His people to plot a course home: freed.
Zerubbabel, Nehemiah, Ezra,
recorded in perpetuity their exploits brave.

Jesus Christ upon colt He sat,
fulfilled He His own Word.
One week of seven remains,
future days still unheard.

If each day left of the last week is a year like first sixty nine weeks of olde
and each of calendar's three sixty days is itself an individual year,
one calculation is to 2520 years.

From the servitude of the nations,
dare I say, if this world still exists, it be 1948.

If each day left of the last week is a year like first sixty nine weeks of olde
and each of calendar's three sixty days is itself an individual year,
one calculation is to 2520 years.
From the desolation of Jerusalem,
dare I say, if this world still exists, it be 1967.

This a timeframe I canst nare comprehend,
perhaps some events of consequence for my people shalt occur,
a gap unexplainable,
a gap again of nineteen years.

Yahweh, Eternal God, Almighty Father to carry His people
through more dissolutions years.
Daniel for his time faithful and true,
strength and reliance provided by the God he chose to serve.

Selah

Paul didst me talk fore voyage Rome,
at much length we future time surveyed,
perhaps Yahweh's people will reside back this land.
Made no sense till now
but soon Titus will rage his legacy demand.
Expect I more full destruction,
Paul's future hope I willst continue pray.
Titus appears to hold the reins,
but it is Yahweh's score to play.

Selah

There ist a fraud that stalks all lands
to scourge and suck all life,
a dark asp spewing poisonous froth,

a devil real who will raise his crop,
he'll plant his vines of tares for blight
whilst denying The Lord and eternal light.
Becometh this earth an ugly place,
forgiven sinners much warned,
love not this world we must be told,
words to heed from God's own voice.
Persecution and tribulation a guarantee,
for they willst beat with stick and hunt by nail,
like Nero who searched for them to flay,
then burnt their screams with embers bright.
Sinners hate committing to God's Holy rule,
it is a sign of weakness in their eyes,
yet God doth stretch His love's embrace,
while they turn their backs and He despise.
Satan has always had his man,
a fiend to run his tasks;
beguiling demons
sporting deceptions enticing mask.
Aforesaid Nero of satan's hall of fame,
acted he a starring role,
Herod too and Pilate Rome,
sought paths to extend evil's campaign.
Pharaoh of olde and pagan kings
Jerusalem experienced its sinister share,
those taking all possible means
to eradicate Yahweh's saving care.
Antiochus Epipfanses the very worst,
a flagrant two fingered affront,
desacralized he the Holy of Holies with idol Zeus,
altar sacrifice of pig sealed his eternal route.
This what Daniel for earth's future warned,
watch close a time some future,
aforementioned perhaps my investigations with Paul
next time this how the final antichrist willst he himself reveal.

Jesus pointed that future slaughter,
a time to make personal choice;
choose ye the devil's eternal damnation or bow by mercy,
repent to God's forgiveness and His saving grace.

Selah

Jesus said not one stone be left atop another
perhaps I here now at this junctures arise,
for there must be hereafter a regather,
for Zechariah stated in future two thirds will die.
What a frightening anticipation,
what devastation be wrought our nation fair,
regathering for some future covenantal annihilation.
Fathers, mothers, children be found at remnant's calling,
all others alas…beware.

Selah

This day draweth forth for promised murder,
close now to ear I listen drum beat five,
knowest this hillside I must abandon
but for me each option warrants destructions prize.
I tried deny all pressing circumstance,
my conscience rambling,
a decision to be made,
I admit much stress didst me trouble,
closed mine eye to rest but little while.
Soon after felt prod my slumber body,
mine eyes opened,
Josephus my front in raiment dark he arranged,
provided he some measure consolation,
he returning Rome's camp
for his city bound family he couldst not find.
He a scribe now for Titus' pageant,

employed to record scroll of battles wage,
vowed he nought but death I linger longer,
bid me safety passage at his aside.
He warned impending violent bloodletting,
Titus' desire to spare none of any age,
said Rome's leader akin Nebuchadnezzar
for upon siege third the city he didst raze.
Josephus knew mine son, this place his graveside setting,
recognised he mine frame from pavement's mire dressing.

Shackled my mule I left this outcrop,
prepared we the hillside to leave,
we stood erect to leave my youngster
his past and city standing we didst contemplate,
sang together a psalm and prayer for blessing,
then with my mule took first steps this place to leave.

Selah

A psalm of Israel to the glory of God.

Let all Israel sing praise to Almighty God,
all tribes play instruments for the King
all people in harmony for Israel's Saviour.
As the wise abhor foolishness and folly
let the wicked understand Yahweh's loving kindness.
Let Israel sing praise for God's protection and favour.

O Lord! Judge the sin of our enemies,
our foes defeat with righteous verdict.
Their murderous intent is like a raging famine,
their violent desire is the promise of death.
Let Jacob sing praise for God's protection and favour.

O Lord! Break those who hold you in derision,
the contempt of fools shatter for all eternity.
Those who scoff are like a passing storm,
their mouth is forever a decaying tomb.
Let Jacob sing praise for God's protection and favour.

Let all Israel sing praise to Almighty God,
let the children play at their Father's feet,
all adults rest under their Saviour's wings.
The future of Jerusalem is safe in the Lord,
the salvation of our nation secure in Yahweh.
Let Israel sing praise for God's protection and favour.

Selah

Reliance is nare upon myself, nor son,
but upon He, mine Saviour Christ alone.

We took a steady pace.
I dared look back,
just once like wife of Lot of olde.
Mine son's grave vanished by step from sight,
his mound of moulded rock and clay.
Secured I his memory midst saddened heart,
held it tight with tears to overflow of grief.

Selah

CHAPTER 5

Jerusalem; a cup that trembleth…

Stand we at the brink of eternity,
upon the edge of time,
the obliteration of covenant,
annihilation of the mind.
Are there no more tomorrows,
this the end of sage's play?
Is this the end of forever,
the end of saving grace?
Will blue skies keep rolling,
green mountains fade away,
stars collapse one minute past
the end this promised day?
Judgement,
He is calling,
claiming His demand,
blood drench,
staining,
drying neath the sands.
Love,
stopped nay by nature
but by the wicked heart of man.

Selah

Mine tears I dried.
His grave we soon out stepped,
harkened into view an enemy nest.
Jerusalem,
surrounded by camp of Legions four: V, X, XII, XV.
North we walked,
but short,
waking noise and clamour hitting senses fore arrive.
The camp mixed much bluster,
sound of beast and man;
scarce tell difference this rousing when day began.
Josephus bid me halt,
took shoulder grasp to instruct advisors warn.
I, he said, Titus wouldst meet
for the Commander had I upon hillock observed,
thinkest perhaps me a watchman spy;
assured Josephus I couldst this charge deny.
Then with hardened grip,
Josephus pleaded me a serious comport;
if Titus nodded any disagree
his confidantes wouldst me execute.
Upon my life he sounded
the dreadful harshness of this mine new surround.

At sentry gate we didst halt,
surveyed they me with close attent,
my companions receipt; recognitions nod.
Crude men handled harshly my aging frame,
mine raiment shook down,
quick,
they holding breath,
nare sword nor secreted dagger fell.
The guards bent to cleanse foul hands on wet,
the dirt mine clothes had left.
Closed I ears to grumbled curse,

their spewed dissatisfaction moaned,
with casual indifference
we pointed forward into Legion's fold.

Twenty four hours earlier I was yesterday rising.
Twenty four hours before Court extracted my son's slay.
Twenty four hours later to sanctuary of enemy camp.
Twenty four hours from now; I be either alive or stone cold dead.

Mine pace didst instinctive slow
to sluggard snail my step employed,
to enable me these things new observe,
this erected city that somehow sprang to life.
Tents in line by order,
a number larger than I know,
each pegged by side another,
little room to crouch or snore.
Beastly men,
thousands,
animals too;
many horses for cavalry charge,
cattle at rear for milk and food.
Life, this prophesised morning, well underway.
Those breaking fast held in Centurion's line,
warmed oats and breads
to encourage the blood fore angers fight.
Others too, arranging battle arms and dress,
shields and breastplates polished to impress,
to strike fear in their enemies chests.
Swords, spears and lances sharpened to perfect,
long queues formed,
each angling for blacksmiths best grindstone refining.
The sound of sparking fire branded blade
on stone revolving,
apprentices already busy,

ignoring threats of soldier taunt,
each Legionnaire desiring best sharp for mornings cut and thrust.
Experienced men and many new,
visible by outward compose.
Those older sat,
talked,
joked midst one another.
The younger forever fearing,
depositing many anxious ruminations
throughout their morning ablutions.
The smell of camp made even me near faint,
putrid stink of unwashed sweat,
wind carrying onslaught offence from cess pit crater.
Josephus pointed at one such hole,
told of tale of cowards drowned,
pushed in for punishment and harbingers warning.
Poor wretches left to disappear
in comrades waste and water.

The noise,
it made mine head throb.
Utter madness it seemed
this tumult of Empire resolve.
Brigades of pandemonium and commotion,
loud babbled responses to shouted orders.
To a stranger it seemed chaotic
but upon closer observe
noticed I a practiced adherence to instruction cadenced.
The camp now full awake,
bristling for action,
suspense building toward an expectancy of adventure.
I walked full assured of Titus' grilling;
strength of city,
her defending walls.
Perhaps my son had he already told…

Rome's banners blew gently,
slight crisp breeze identified insignia,
Legion arrangements tapered by lines dividing.
To each, drummers and flagmen,
each sound and flight of coloured material
would direct step and pulse of death flung arrow.
These holders, just mere lads,
learning the rope of military ways
for some future times engage.

Then at quick a solitary tent,
shielded by few.
A battle home for Titus Vespasian;
Commander of Rome.

Selah

The Roman Empire,
progeny of Caesar's clasp,
founded nay by fond embrace
but siege of earthly grasp.
All consuming stretch,
border's land to island sea,
captives a wild rag tag dishevelled bunch,
nare each other ere meet.
All languages, cultures of known world,
at first all proud, defiant,
then broken like a steed to Rome's fist encroachment.

Selah

Admit I, with nare degree embarrassment,
feral fear I felt inside,
answered I Josephus with panic tremor,
convinced knock of knee be heard by all my side;
head, heart and bowel to alert my vain disguise.

Titus.
Titus Vespasian.
Kind hearted to friend,
lethal adversary to enemy wild.
Loved and feared in equal measure.
Feared;
he loved to execute.
Loved;
many enjoyed his profligate favour.
In battle;
venomously loathed by foe.
In Court;
famously loyal to citizenry Rome.
Jerusalem for him mere stumble,
trusted by Emperor the city to sack,
coming war to improve his authority claim.
Constructed he his plans ambitiously
toward his strategic intent:
Rome and Empires purple robe
and ruling crown to own.

Titus.
A Goliath in short stature,
murdered to gain advantage,
toppling any usurper,
yet knew most his men by name,
prodigious memory famed,
recounted he facts
those displaying bravery in Empire's name.
Not yet thirty,
he a battle veteran,
accustomed the laurels of victory prize.
Son of an Emperor,
trusted he his father with fidelity and pride,
his hope a return to Rome
to sit as guardian at his father's side.

Chapter 5. Jerusalem; a cup that trembleth...

My breath stood thin,
Josephus, his hand, my elbow to steady
warning in no uncertain term
only if I received Titus' assenting nod
I then couldst reply.
If without nod I answered aught
Titus' guards their swords wouldst me acquaint.

Selah

Breath short,
sharp,
blood like ice
from head to temple,
mind and gut akemble.
Sweat mine brow didst weep,
alone,
desolate,
like those afore a judgement seat.

Entereth he of history page,
stooped I to gracely bow.
Bid he me stand affront,
then steely look,
eyes cut black,
they ablaze:
intense.
He squat,
broad as full,
shoulders cut,
carriest they a weight of mighty expectation.

Josephus introduced,
I soil man of city;
full knowledge he already knew.

Silent he stood,
I under close observe.
Then sudden showing not demeanour,
gently,
softly he spoke.

"Mine sword I sharpen when the tongue of others runneth blunt.
Friend or foe?" he of me enquired;
but stood no head with nod.

"Olde man,
thine daily work describeth how I feel...
Thou from hill I didst spy."
He circled mine space,
I like sheep to games slaughter.

"Didst thou me spy?" continued he.
I now pulled asunder internally.
"Friend or foe?" harsher with stately nod.

Almost imperceptive this nod,
Josephus gave me sign to speak.

"Neither yet Sire, but inconsequential as both," I heavily laboured.

Silence...

Then like many a month that passed by slow,
Titus laughed.
"Ah! An honest man;
first truth I've heard this year."
He nodded guardian withdrawal,
extended me a while his signet approval.

"Knew I thine son
for whom I hearest thou mourn.
A brave man methinks,
though also perhaps he was't also avarice's fool."

"Josephus I see,
he hast thou warned.
It is true,
I like, nay love, execution;
a penchant I possess for cruel crucifixion.
Afore mine mind thine fate decide
worketh thou at Josephus' side.
Show him thine city's secrets,
help paint his words,
when this cauldron of deceit be razed
then thine fate be heard."

Turned he with alacrity from tent
this day his war to rage,
though the battle we didst record
took him longer than desire to wage.

Selah

Mine breath I didst with sigh relief exhale
with hand clasp of table strong,
mine nerve like thunder frayed
with shoulders bent mine eyes didst almost tear burn.
Josephus too tried to merry cheer,
to release the room from angst and worry fear,
admit I, we both didst strike to laugh,
exited we, mine walk to chase the scribe.

Selah

The end of night watch four,
solitary drum beat to announce new day hour.
I stood, observed the city walls,
confusion ruled mine heart.
For the city leaders, I yearned for them a Judge
but reprieve for the citizens; they the city lifeblood.
To Temple they tithe in duty pay,
to Caesar his claim tax,
with what left their children's raise to strive,
daily labours to eak out morsel to prolong such misery life.
The greater many innocent;
wished for them life and not reprove.
This heart a loyalty divided,
one arm clothed in vengeance,
the other wishing flight.
Jerusalem to be pulled asunder,
yet these walls enclose mine home;
reality of judgement soon afoot to doom.

Mine only son singled out first to be a reproach,
to bear testimony to their own demise.
The battlefield his heart from youth to grave,
he assaulted each side
fore he gave himself whole to dark and evil tide.
Like Nebuchadnezzar who built a siege wall around Jerusalem,
mine son, mine only son,
built one surrounding his unrepentant heart.
This city too,
her sins will usher cleansing burn;
the hand of time and death to play their game of turn.

Selah

The camp split out near all surround,
Titus XII, XV north,

Chapter 5. Jerusalem; a cup that trembleth...

Fretensis X yonder Kidron to Olive Mount,
Macedonica V to valley west by Gihon.
The columns beat trail of sound and dust,
the air thick like blast volcanic ash,
feet shod in boots of lead the ground to shake.
No ships of war visible in Rome's red sea,
just a tide of readied men to beckon Titus' please.
Lines of supply held tight in positions rear,
stores of salted meats and fruits under Quartermaster's glare.

Titus stood ground,
bid his generals to close surround,
his mind in busy occupation,
opinions sought for his consideration.
His signals given,
the generals then despatched,
their Legionnaires to steady guide.
Titus' final instruction:
no surprise!

There is a rest of seconds fore a charge,
a perfect union of time and silent peace,
time suspended midst tempest of swarming beasts,
a moment each their eternity contemplate
but fear doth try to brush that silence past,
that sacred time, first slow then gallops fast,
a slice of brevity to engage each tempered mind,
full life of action fleet fore each one's eyes.
Each that searches will slow upon their chore,
some bow, their wooden idols to adore,
others stop all talk amongst their friends,
some stoop with hands to pray for the battle soon begins.
Many think of family and distant life,
engage thoughts of children and of wives,
these memories pure, to utopia their thoughts return,

in unison then rise for battle war;
they lift their swords, the archers string their bows,
embarrassed red for their humanity they didst expose.

Selah

Jerusalem loomed large and strong,
walls and towers replete with rebel men,
city armed to teeth,
cache of Roman weapons plundered at battle Beth Heron.
The sound of pounded foot brought intimidation near,
city commanders encouraged shouts to combat fear;
internal factions set aside for time,
leaders convincing comrades they could win.
The rebels had fought embittered split,
had killed many one another fore siege didst eve begin,
Titus had laughed, receipt his ears this news
for Jerusalem's own rebels were doing Rome's gruesome chore.
Simon bar Giora and John of Giscala had settled scores,
knew that respectful union was required,
arranged together defences,
walls topped stout and raised by further meters,
secured they underwater and sewer passage
from which defenders could emerge;
God's own city they to guard.
Lament and warn of prophets long ignored,
the battle already over fore a sword was even drawn;
Yahweh's vengeance on disobedience wouldst He Himself take charge.

Selah

A siege is a war of attrition,
it necessitates wise form of planned attack,
battlefield engines stationed ready by Legion,
rams, trebuchet catapults and tall siege towers,

mechanised stockpiles for use by hardened men
crafted to make walls difficult to defend.
Designs beyond the foulest of vain man's imagination
lay ready the weapons of the Lord's indignation.
Rome was ready,
preparations complete,
a fearful expectation
ran rampant in Jerusalem's maze of narrowed stone streets.

For an intelligent man, brave in brain and brawn
Titus made at first a stutter,
near resulted in his quick murder.
All his Legions he wished observe
so took his trusted steed and saddled sword
but no helmet or breastplate protection wore.
His small group the city to encircle
but on approach east
toward Mount of Olives, city rebels via Kidron didst emerge.
With gusto force and keen deliberation
speared Legionnaires down,
Titus, a fast retreat didst somehow beat.
The walled on watch took morale's encourage
and with adrenaline shouted their hoarse bluster's scorn.
The first blood to Jerusalem and not to Rome.
Titus' temper raged,
his face aflare in blaze,
regrouped to counter charge.
Held he no fondness for dying
his life too short for death flung rhyme
and with sword and many reinforcements
fought like a lion.
Rome's men attached selves not to shame,
gave death no favour or regard
and in sight of their Commander
took courage,

propelled themselves toward valour
and turned their enemy to flight.

That night Commander held his Court
made astute adjudication.
The city population at a swell,
pilgrims by thousands times ten had travelled there for Passover.
Lack of water not yet a threat
but if Rome could encircle the walls
Jerusalem's food provision wouldst suffer.
If the city walls could not be breached
the inhabitants would die of hunger.

Selah

Slept I that night warm with full food savour,
mine neck by blade was spared.
By Legionnaire's morn time rise
Josephus and I had our observers point secured;
both ready to record all labours.

Titus ordered full clearing round entire city wall,
this task the men were set.
Every tree,
all natural debris,
all detestable obstruction of nature's imagination
of hedge and bush
by space of many yard
was moved in concert union.
This was no task of ease
for each man a work of hard sore labour
especially on the east
for there the Kidron ravines are steep.
They filled ditches with salvaged rock,
laid cedar boughs to move siege engines

workers having to dodge,
from walled inhabitants
flagrant abuse of arrow and of dart.
Many fell to injury and even death,
some stoned by slabs of turmoil disorder.

For four days Rome swept its bounty clean,
Titus examined walls north and east,
instructed men toward siege ramp building,
signalling his orders;
a search for places weak.
Satisfied with impassioned zeal
ordered he in Rome's cruel inventions,
rams for battering, commissioned to iron topped length
held and force marched by men of tens.
Catapults of swinging orchestration,
mechanised twist with flame and fire of boil,
filled also with rocks and iron balls of spiked ornamentation;
no more space for verbal arbitration
but a planned onslaught of weaponised manipulation.
Wooden towers of strength and height on wheels to roll
with iron shields bolted front and side,
ladders inserted for scramble wall ascending.
To assist dart and sword
and the speed of arrow flight:
siege engine and brutal man would herald utter devastation.

Selah

Rome built siege ramps to chiselled rock,
Legionnaires beat and forged a murderous path,
at weakened point they struck their battle rams
with rage and incessant grunt of toil;
savage blows a breach didst eventually impale,
crews by ten this onerous task,

under cover shield
they subjected to provoke of boil and nail.
Jerusalem ached with bellowed moan,
defenders emerged again to battle roam,
archers arrows with finely tips of steel,
sharpened sure, unleashed to kill.
A frantic swarm the walls unfurled
through gate and also by descent of rope,
Titus led again a cavalry charge
to slaughter and scythe all rebel hope.
City warriors all fought brave,
targeted each their parry to kill,
we watched and wrote this tale to tell
that battle of third wall hill.

Flagman's ensign was held aloft
the siege towers shepherded in,
against the walls then to fight nonstop,
ladder climbers unleashed more blood to spill.
It rained that night midst mud and ground flow blood,
each one pursued their quarry,
maimed and killed by sword and dart
yet victory didst long tarry.
Zealots raged out with lantern fire,
siege engines desired they burn,
set alight that darkened night
but Rome's agitation they couldst not turn.
They stood on bones.
They sank in gut rot chowder.
Quenched life, each side, in flame hell slaughter.

For fifteen days the battle raged
Rome's lust proved then a winner,
the third wall broke, crushed, fell to dust,
giving the outer city to legion's banner.

One poor wretch,
prisoner name unknown
was walked to wall by Titus,
then hammered with nail
to crucifixions impale.
Titus' hope; the city unnerve to unravel.

Four days from breach Rome's infidels advanced,
all quiet,
then full quarter attacked,
missiles and barrage of Hades unleashed
by Jerusalem's hit and run sorties.
By place of arrow many foreigners died
but sheer numbers outweighed city fortune.

Then awhile peace
to regroup strength for later.

Selah

Half a city of stolen ground,
Titus boasted a hard fought month,
strengthened flanks both east and west
vigilance unsheathed against surprise rebuff.
Simon's sorties enthused to distract
but poverty was beginning to bite,
the numbers dying didst steady increase
from necessity bare and lack.

Infighting too gifted thousands death,
those refused to fight each faction slew,
my people stood this juncture point,
remedy required the leaders knew;
Simon given authority's rank
John the Temple Mount to secure.

Regrouped and rearmed a wild intensity I surveilled;
Titus to plot how best Jerusalem's narrow streets assail.
First though to broker peace,
sent Josephus to negotiate Empire's terms,
the scribe spoke in native tongue
to encourage surrender to oppressor's charms,
Spoke he of Jerusalem, a history proud,
Yahweh's faithfulness His Word,
but Josephus they too rejected,
all pleas for peace ignored.
Josephus returned in saddened contemplation,
the impiety of Jerusalem's inhabitants securing fate;
their soon complete annihilation.

Selah

The troops moved by flank each side,
the end Iyyar birthed forth a hotter sun,
city crave of eat of food, reservoirs running down,
heat sapping efforts, evaporating strength of arm.
Antonia fortress became Rome's next quest,
battering rams put Jerusalem's defence to test,
arrows, darts, bolts and plain olde stone
showered from height to renew the plight of Rome.
Siege engines fired Titus' pointed aim,
cutting enemy flesh bringing carnage, death and shame.
Fire erupted, the inferno didst take hold
then Antonia collapsed, more bloodshed didst unfold.
Simon set his sorties, engaged they in waves
but Titus made a number ready
to assault with cavalry charge.
He at head this Legion upon his steed,
sword in hand to cut and blind wild wield,
Legionnaires applauded with mighty cheer,

their leader encouraging morale,
next the Temple to secure.

Selah

To secure the Temple
Titus first looked beyond the city walls.
No stranger he the blunt weapon of hunger,
lack's wrath he keenly understood,
all this knowledge stored in mind
from campaigns fought in Empire's western fronts.
Instructed he a wall of total circumvallation,
five miles of wall Jerusalem to surround.
This wall Legionnaires wouldst close assemble,
to stop those fleeing and those in search of victuals sustaining.

Generals said this wall would take months to build,
albeit Titus was much smarter.
Turned he this task into strident competition,
promised laurels and payments
to Legions that fast constructed.

Three days it took to build death's prison cell.
Three days to cut escape and hope.
Three days to assure inhabitants their hell.
Three days to fashion hangman's noose.

Peace he roared,
no need for further slaughter;
carnage fray has swept enough away.

Josephus he again didst summon,
Josephus, Titus' yearning to relay.
A second time the city offered sanctuary,
after the third offer

Titus planned his Legion's last foray.
Like the cock that crowed at Peter,
the city leaders Josephus too denied.

First light came like any morning,
but this day
full assault of archer's bow,
artillery, siege engines without warning
distilled their mayhem's reach designed to blow.
Crowbars engaged at blocks to release mortar,
furious attempts to pound battle's charge,
many died both sides midst blood lust racing,
breach secured,
at last a grim reward.

Selah

There is no such thing as friendship in hunger,
you become only one...
you alone to survive...

Walked I the city of the living and the dead,
streets hardly longer visible,
brick by brick,
broken,
in two cityscape Rome didst rend.
Deuteronomy's curse;
Jerusalem in full receipt her plague.
All exceedingly dreadful,
wholly consumed by wrath through heaven flung rage.

I looked.
Behold a pale horse
and the name of him who sat on it was Death
and Hades followed him.

Mine eyes couldst scarce look,
I shielded nose and with Josephus set feet forth.

The innocent lay perished with the guilty,
many killed by their own;
those in search of meagre sustenance warming.
The moribund,
those lacking vitality
lay in terminal decline,
each bidding blade for suffers ending.
The moaning,
mine ears couldst nay relinquish
those sounds of dry bone throat.
Men, women
darkened corpses,
rotting,
bruised to sickening hue and clot.
Children too,
small limbs cast broken,
some intentionally speared.
Rebels stalked the city,
killing,
looking for the least bite;
anything,
something to chew.
We formed close guard and stumbled on,
glad mule secured in camp
for here he'd succulently ease funeral's wailed lament.

Despite circumvallation
many in last gasp attempted escape.
They skulked low but straight Legionnaire arms,
five hundred a day crucified;
they plied, full display, this barbaric ground.

Bodies banished their pestilential stink,
feasted on by bloated fly and vermin,
venomous foraging creatures fully brave,
no longer retributions strike fearing.

Gold and jewels,
intestine found,
many were killed for sport,
healthier eager to see what bounty cadaver's sprung forth.
Nothing is as venturesome as covetousness,
with gold fever John of Giscala became consumed,
he in Temple contemplated treasure stealing,
booty spoil he undertook to plunder.
Others scoured sewers,
for something sweet to savour,
the bowels of the city were cleanly licked with haste.
Once hallowed,
once blessed,
Jerusalem lay now condemned
by He who sits on High.

One lady,
Mary by name they say,
roasted a new born child.
Half he then eaten
afore rebels entered her abode to seek scents treat.
Recoiled they in horror this fevered desecration,
left this poor maddened lady
and bolted her inside.

Unfortunates screamed from walls,
some jumped their death from towers,
Legionnaires added to the vice,
taunted the hungry by eating fore their eyes.
These Roman beasts Titus didst reprimand;

executed a number,
sent remaining the frontlines to die.

I shook and trembled,
full awake that night.
Know not else to say,
this pollution and misery grim,
there are some memories one canst banish,
seared forever it seems, fastened onto brain.

Selah

Men suspended reason,
experted themselves in the heavy pursuit of murder,
blood became their currency,
exchanged with spear and torture.
The second battle for the Temple commenced;
seven thousand Legionnaires shuffled through Antonia's ruin.
Chaos ensued,
pitch battles in Women's Temple Court and Sanctuary
fore Rome didst beat a hasty retreat.

In the northwest corner
Titus plotted siege ramps four
but rebels assaulted the circumvallation;
strong attempt to deflect Rome's Temple quest.
The third attack,
city walls near Temple by rebels set alight,
to dry wood and bitumen ignite.
Many men of Rome burnt bright,
corpses blacked and charred,
others purposed jumps of flight,
streaks of flashing flame.
Perished they;
each Icarus dance to escape in vain.

Summer months grew darker
with sky plumes, smoke and fire.
The beginning of Av,
announced battle month four.
Titus planned last ditch attack,
archers and artillery tasked
while Legions marched against plaza,
against flanks.
The Temple bastion exposed,
the Legions held their ground,
Commander exhorted a push
with use of cavalry charge.
A pair of Legionnaires
grasped a debris flame,
with arched approach
threw their incendiary
the sanctuary chambers caught full blaze.
The summer heat purchased fortune's flame,
fire didst spiral and lost all control.

God gave His house over to destruction,
Yahweh condemned His whole nation.
He took every course that was for preservation taken
and turned it quick toward destruction.

The city leaders were paralysed
while Rome plunged further forward,
repressed rage was quick released
Titus himself couldst not regain disciplined order.
Young and olde put to sword,
grounds ransacked for choicest gold,
delirious swings of blade and axe,
flesh cut with battle sabre,
aim of dart and arrow point,
deranged with merciless fury.

Blood and water mixed in life and death.
Blood and water mixed in life and death.

This Holy place of Solomon olde
didst succumb to smoke's abound,
no pillar by night of guiding fire,
no day sweep directing cloud;
for the city a death,
for Jerusalem a shroud.

Selah

So it is with wicked men
a sudden ignominious death.
Titus again offered surrender
yet the furious few abased him to his face.
Herod's Palace their last refuge,
yae by calamity
this ground too Rome wouldst soon erase.

The depths of hate are deeper than any blade can plunge,
twisted gut,
cold steel lunge.
Dying eyes and broken limbs
bring now this battle's end,
savage blows of hands with swords
encircled those few brave,
with batter of rams
the last walls began their fall to ruin.

Selah

Jerusalem was judged,
akin a clap of lightening in wilderness sands
she rewarded with physical and spiritual death.

Jerusalem became a stark branch,
no tender root planted,
she laid low,
devoid of nourishment and life;
complete absence of succour and suckling breast.
Jerusalem,
for a time cut off,
twice dead by foe of Empire grand.
Jerusalem, Jerusalem, Jerusalem,
a witness to divine faithfulness
and Sovereign's righteous demand.

Rising smoke of the city
nay a sacrifice to Yahweh
but His communication
of its desolate abandonment.

Selah

As fast as it commenced
thus endeth the war;
no anticipation of further expectation.
Addressed Titus his fighting men,
they he humbly thanked,
promised home return,
fore depart instructed them to final tasks.

Legionnaires ranked Jerusalem's remain
then walked Titus each group,
his consideration their determined adjudication.
For Simon: Rome.
Triumph parade humiliation then ritual strangulation.
John to prison: thereafter eternity.
All males were shackled,

death in Egyptian mines or gladiatorial rages.
Women and children to slavery.

A Centurion turned,
to me he pointed.
Titus looked,
pondered;
to his tent pointed.
To it I didst walk,
one last dance,
wondering death or emancipation...

Selah

CHAPTER 6

Dwellest we in the hope…

Dwellest we in the hope
in this the era of grace fore King's return.
His mighty work on fallen earth
from resurrection's victory blast,
enabling sinner's reach to Throne ever last.

Now Christ reigns
in compassion and love,
breathing regeneration by His Holy Spirit on those who repent.
This love offered freely to corrupt men
who plot a last vain charge
until to their knees they fall.

Apportioned to each a time
to understand grace with peace and joy.
For I to share and teach
for mine sons to join in praise;
our lessons at last learnt
for in eternity we willst soon reside.

Soon endeth the eulogy.

Selah

Surrounded they I
with a ring of force marched intimidation.
Six strong Legionnaires,
six the number of man,
weapons of iron their protecting companion.
Titus' tent I arrived,
toward me they grunted,
ushered inside.
Stood they ready to guard,
two each front,
one each side,
battle hardened and weary.
Knew I if Titus ordered mine execute
comply they blindly,
then disappear
with no second thought.

Stood I to await,
to endure Titus' deliberate discombobulation,
suspended tween two horizons;
thin line separating life and death.
Afore wilderness the Jews saw tribulation,
fore their eyes the false gods of Egypt were judged,
escaped they though Yahweh's final wrath desolation;
ought this fate be mine determination?

Selah

Surveyed I quick Commander's tent,
simple needs this Legion's keep,
kit chest, chairs, bed to side,
battle plan table,
with scrolls piled steep.
Compassed directions, charted maps,
notes,

Chapter 6. Dwellest we in the hope...

handwritten deliberations by candle dark of night.
Numbers dead in column wrote,
progression dates circled for Rome's report.
Vague numbers canst the toll display,
the stink, the death, all extinguished hope,
destruction sounds, the things I've seen
written down in parchment clean.
One canst write silence and death moan loud,
scorching heat, passing cloud,
these last months resided I this prison cell,
this carnage recording in slaughter's hell.
Stood I there in trembling fear,
whatever his decision I near not cared.
Rememberest I rich man and Lazarus,
One for heaven; other gifted torment's chalice.
Soon here just two; empire and prisoner,
God's image us men,
craved I Abraham's Bosom to end all war's malice.

Selah

Josephus entered to bid farewell,
despatched Titus he to Rome,
an Ambassador, emissary of letters,
to carry news of victory found;
to make ready for Emperor's son return.
We clasped each the other,
gratitude expressed for we survived the fight,
survived we both all war's displeasures,
thanketh I full this man for he saved mine life.

One hundred men his royal protection,
watched him leave till out of sight.

Selah

As I stood, to God mine thoughts didst turn
for I may soon to Him be joined.
Deception's earth promises vague paradise shadow
but tremendous calamity doth oft arrive,
lusts and ego must be tempered,
vain glory and riches which I learnt despise.

Vanity I turned to probe, explore,
disciplined thinking to Solomon's words;
we grasp, we covet,
to gain we kill,
yet at the end what is if for?

Jerusalem enjoyed her share of spoil,
rank and honour and power and wealth,
plotted and schemed all people this city,
all burnt, demolished at battles end.
I watched the poor, observed the rich
now cast dead together in circumvallation grave ditch.

Selah

Why suffer?
An honest question, eternal through time,
seems to me two paths be taken,
considered musing helped me its fruit recognise.

Free will encourages boldly to venture,
leads many to participate in self serve life,
danger occurs when such men plot together,
universal reward;
death, famine and contentions strife.
God will not interfere with free will choices
but will judge all actions at end this life.

Why do people insist on blaming God when most problems the fault
of men?
Rememberest thou, it is easier to get into hell
than seek escape route out!

Secondly,
we each have but small time in a world that is broken,
good things will happen and so too will the bad,
its difficult to remember love when one experiences slaughter,
unfortunately we canst personally control all offered by life.
Be assured, sometime all be visited by affliction,
remember Job; eventually God answered with sound of advice.
Likewise Joseph; what the world meant for evil,
God brought to good but over long time.

Suffering is dreadful,
we encourage its quick depart,
in the cauldron her lessons we begin our learn,
and turn from self to bless another's heart.

Selah

Forgiveness is vital for both rich and poor.
Murdered the leaders mine son, mine only son,
but simply put,
mine own sin murdered the Son of God,
His only begotten.
Christ Jesus died,
not some imposter,
not as some already decree; satan's brother.
Vengeance is of The Lord,
He Himself will payment extract,
though none required
if we can one another forgive.

Learnt I to them extend forgive.
Easy?
Nay...I need it do each day,
for thoughts propel me to inward hate
and sin's momentum is difficult to dissipate.
If I be forgiven, I too must likewise it give.

Peter, by Holy Spirit emboldened spoke in holy truth,
said the very murderers of Jesus Christ could be forgiven
if they repented through The Messiah's blood.

Selah

Our God is a consuming fire.
Holiness and justice a two sided coin reveal.
Provoked to justice after severe warning,
Yahweh, with rigorous scalding, burnt sin clean.
It is a frightening thing to fall into the hands of an angry God.
Please take under considered advisement,
justice willst not forever be concealed.

Selah

Grace canst be by law
for the law we canst soon keep,
even the rich young ruler,
fell like Paul to covets reach.
Deuteronomy, Leviticus outline sin's curse
and death its price be paid,
we must weep fore heaven's Judge,
penalty not forever delayed.
But undeserved,
unmerited,

Yahweh bestows ransom favour,
by grace,
His choicest gift,
mercy offered to earth stretched bounds,
through Christ's Blood alone by faith.

Selah

What I ask you consider,
what I can scarce believe
is that while I trod on God
He took that punishment for me,
to die in my place,
to shed full His blood,
to forgive each mine sins,
by His grace in His love.

I can scarce understand
find it difficult to believe
that God The Holy Spirit
would come live in me.
Sealed for redemption,
clothed in His peace,
once convicted of sin
gifted by grace His release.

I fall on my knees
to God I do bow,
I can scarce understand,
find it hard to know how.
Quickened in body,
in spirit, in mind,
once I was lost,
once I was blind.

Yet we are His people,
peculiar and strange,
His name we count Holy,
Him alone we adore,
we His people rejoice evermore.

If all you have is this world you are the most sad of men.
If all you have is the hope of this world you are the most lost of men.
So afraid to die,
yet all the more fearful to live.

Hark a steed and roar of boisterous cheer.
Titus,
the victor,
draweth full near.

Selah

CHAPTER 7

Epilogue

In this world there are masters and men.
Both, masters and men, begin life as mere boy.

To discern the measure of a man make him a master.

Elevate a master too high,
he willst quick forget that he is but a man.

Masters oft tire of men
for they soon desireth to become gods.

Most masters forget that their Master is God,
the living God;
the God of Abraham, Isaac and Jacob.

Selah

Titus entered his tent
arrayed like an ordinary man,
fraid lest some rebel straggler
foul and commit him to hell.

He stared me down,
his eyes obsidian dark,

tired he seemed,
tried search out mine soul
not for comradeship sake,
nay,
rather to purchase slightest clue mine dissention:
any look portraying
hint of earned condition or favour.
He distrusting of all,
knowledge forewarned that even in sanctuary,
in Rome's own Court,
scoundrels, betrayers, murderers plot.
"Et tu olde man?"
He walked my round then to front.

"Jerusalem is now mine sacrifice.
You see olde man,
I know about thine God.
Pilate told mine father he but younger.

Yes I know about Christ Jesus,
dying to save sinners,
rising it be told to give new life.
Whilst I know,
I canst this man reign o'er me;
for olde man
only a few are a friend to a man on a cross.
Sacrifice I can understand;
for this battle cost mine finest men.
Both sides I'm sure,
brave men;
courageous.

I, olde man...
I happily exchange eternity for the temporal.
I canst comprehend eternity;

it eludes mine mind.
But I can understand today
and I can already taste tomorrow.

Rome awaits.
Mine own triumph march;
crowds of cheer and fluster.

I,
Titus Vespasian,
I shall be a god for a day
and that accolade I shall carry forth into eternity.
As for you olde man,
thou I covet,
bringeth thou me to envy.
Thou shalt live with God;
forever."

I perceived no silent nod,
composed mine heart and held ground.

"Thine execute wouldst end thine toil,
erase thine ceaseless pain.
Wish I for you to remember this anguish,
to live its continuance forbear.
All that is man is black heart and rage,
deserveth thou not death's emancipation.
For sake thine mule I set thee free;
find him rest in some green pasture."

He caught mine eye;
I feared portrayal to his dissatisfaction.
Caught I a slight wry grin.

"Go olde man,
witnessed thou ten life times grim.
Go olde man."

I to he nodded appreciation;
he both fair master and fair man.

In all those months,
near half year,
only seven words I spoke to Titus.
Seven the complete number of Yahweh.
Decided then I walk to sea,
to live and to fish,
to tell people of Christ Jesus' resurrection love
and judgement soon to come.

Selah

We two left the city,
stood observes hill on solid ground,
cast faint eyes all around.
Observed I fallen walls,
huge dislodge of campaign's rock,
then rested eye on mine son's mound.

Bid I he my love's farewell.

All empires fall to decay,
Rome too will have her day.
Some future time nations here shall regather,
assemble together,
encircle again this Jerusalem ground:
this cup that doth tremble.

Amen

ACKNOWLEDGEMENTS

This project would not have been completed without the assistance of many.

Firstly, I would like to acknowledge the ancient writings of the aforementioned Yosef ben Matityahu, known to the world as Josephus. Additionally, the histories of Suetonius and Herodotus provided insight into the time of Rome and Babylon.

To the many family and friends who came alongside to assist and encourage over many years. Finally, a call to Andrew Rowen and Derek Cooney for their kind assists with editing.

Let the final thanks be to Jesus Christ. He picked me up when all I possessed was but a weak pulse. He, who is alive, dusted me down and opened up a whole new life. I thank Him for Grace.

Let us hear the conclusion of the whole matter: Fear God and keep His commandments. For this is man's all. For God will bring every work into judgement, including every secret thing, whether good or evil. (Eccl. 12:13-14.)

Other books by Redmond Holt

Testimony: Onward toward salvation.

Mammon

dystHOPEia

Amercia

Are you inspired to write a book?

Contact

Maurice Wylie Media
Your Inspirational & Christian Book Publisher
Based in Northern Ireland, serving readers worldwide

www.MauriceWylieMedia.com

www.ingramcontent.com/pod-product-compliance
Lightning Source LLC
Chambersburg PA
CBHW041145110526
44590CB00027B/4128